Kn
The Purāṇas

Ramanuj Prasad

PUSTAK MAHAL®
Delhi • Bengaluru • Mumbai • Patna • Hyderabad

Publishers
Pustak Mahal®, Delhi
J-3/16 , Daryaganj, New Delhi-110002
☎ 23276539, 23272783, 23272784 • *Fax:* 011-23260518
E-mail: info@pustakmahal.com • *Website:* www.pustakmahal.com

Sales Centre
• 10-B, Netaji Subhash Marg, Daryaganj, New Delhi-110002
☎23268292, 23268293, 23279900 • *Fax:* 011-23280567
E-mail: rapidexdelhi@indiatimes.com
• Hind Pustak Bhawan
6686, Khari Baoli, Delhi-110006, ☎23944314, 23911979

Branch Offices
Bengaluru: ☎ 22234025
E-mail: pustak@airtelmail.in • pustak@sancharnet.in
Mumbai: ☎ 22010941
E-mail: rapidex@bom5.vsnl.net.in
Patna: ☎ 3294193 • *Telefax:* 0612-2302719
E-mail: rapidexptn@rediffmail.com
Hyderabad: *Telefax:* 040-24737290
E-mail: pustakmahalhyd@yahoo.co.in

ISBN 978-81-223-0912-6

Edition : 2009

Printed at : Param Offsetters, Okhla, New Delhi-110020

To
the Sages and Seers

responsible for

this wisdom

Acknowledgement

The author is indebted to Mr. G. Ramamurthy [vedantin], by profession an Industrial Engineer for his hard, sincere and selfless assistance with this work.

Thanks is too small, commensurate to his dedication.

Invocation

कराग्रे वसति लक्ष्मीः करमूले सरस्वती ।
करमध्ये तु गोविन्दः प्रभाते करदर्शनम् ।।

"On the tips of fingers is Goddess Lakṣmī, on the base of fingers is Goddess Sarasvatī and in the middle of fingers is Lord Govinda – look at the palm in the morning."

Transliteration of Devanāgarī

अ	a	क	k	ट	ṭ	प	p	ष	ṣ
आ	ā	ख	kh	ठ	ṭh	फ	ph	स	s
इ	i	ग	g	ड	ḍ	ब	b	ह	ḥ
ई	ī	घ	gh	ढ	ḍh	भ	bh	क्ष	ksha
उ	u	ङ	ń	ण	ṇ	म	m	त्र	tra
ऊ	ū	च	c	त	t	य	y	ज्ञ	jna
ऋ	ṛ	छ	ch	थ	th	र	r		
ए	e	ज	j	द	d	ल	l		
ऐ	ai	झ	jh	ध	dh	व	v		
ओ	o	ञ	ñ	न	n	श	ś		
औ	au								

Preface

The philanthropic children of the Mother India have commitment to the cultural heritage, the Scriptures of the yore to safeguard them. Messrs **Pustak Mahal**, the publisher of the book, is one such organization active in activating the values amidst the changing society and priorities.

The present work goes to mark the visionary's vision. The *Purāṇas* written by *Maharṣi Veda Vyāsa,* had certain purpose. He wrote them after consolidating the *Śruti* into homogeneous groups of *Vedas, Ṛg, Yajus, Sāma* and *Atharvaṇa,* as the essence remained dormant thereon, not explicit and adept to be adopted by the common masses. There also remains some sort of twist to the import of the substance by different schools. *Purāṇas,* as it stands, is the moral code of conduct of *Śruti,* extended and cast into the practical example to reflect and follow on plenary levels.

The *Purāṇas* inspire the aspirants to live a life of 'good deeds and virtues', a moral code of conduct towards fellow beings, faith in God and Scriptures. It constantly reminds that individuals are judged by one's intention and action and there is someone above to reward one accordingly. Sometimes one may find extravagance, but it does happen in glorification of anything: situation, place and individual. The benefit of meditation upon the legend of *Purāṇas* is the stimulated emerged fame, vitality, the power of the organs, energy and the essence of food. The suggested manner of meditation is, the northern rays of the sun are the northern honey cells [the beehive], the legends are the bees and its contents such as *'soma* juice' and the other thing is the nectar [of the flower].

All this [fame etc.] spread out to the sun and took shelter there to give rise to the deep black spots in the sun [this is a meditation upon sun], which is the sum total of good work done by human beings and thus imagined as honey of God. Heaven the cross bar, the sun rays attract water and the water drops in sun rays, the egg of the bees – [a highly imaginative *upāsanā.*] *Madhu vidyā* – From the galaxy of *Purāṇas*, here we intend to focus only on those, that have been inked by Vyāsācārya and one Śiva Purāṇa has been included as representative sample of *Upa Purāṇas,* which are Sanatkumāra, Narasimha, Nāradīya, Śiva, Durvāsas, Kapila, Mānava, Uśanas, Varuṇa, Kālikā, Sāmba, Saura, Āditya, Māheśvara, Devībhāgavata, Vasiṣṭha, .Visṇudharmottara and Nīlamata. The short account of Mahāpurāṇas may adore about 2000 pages, whereas this volume is devoted to rapid and affirmative study.

Purāṇas enjoy repeating the accounts again and again. For example, the stories of Yayāti Pṛthu are repeated in *Brahmā, Padma, Viṣṇu, Bhāgavata, Mārkaṇḍeya* and *Matsya Purāṇas, Ḍakṣa* eight times and seven times respectively. But here we have taken the chapters together and skipped over those which are same and similar, without any loss of material and substance to our readers.

The topics that occur in *Purāṇas* are: Creation of Lokas, Dynasties, genealogy of kings, incarnations, obsequies rites, duties of *Varṇas and āśrama dharma,* places of pilgrimage, prognostication through omens and astrology, science such as *Āyurveda,* health care, town planning etc.

The Presentation Spectrum

- Relativity.
- Intention and issuance of values.
- Isometric projection of *Purāṇas.*
- Background structure and extent.

To be blessed, the *Purāṇas* should be studied with devotion and faith. *Purāṇas* are not a routine news item but a philosophy of life, to infuse life, in our relation, action and the very way of thinking as it were and are.

–Author

Foreword

The sages of yore had been transmitting a unitive philosophy of life from generation to generation. Well before the Aristotlian division of knowledge, later taught through the discipline of science, descended upon the subcontinent of India through modern educational practices. Their words resonated with truth as they taught from their direct realization of the Absolute and the consequent deep understanding of life and the cosmos. They did not have access to libraries or reference books but relied on their prodigious memories to weave a rich tapestry of legends that blended fact and fiction, romance and realism into a sustaining saga that both inspired and instructed those who listened with rapt attention.

This spiritual culture that evolved on the subcontinent of India later came to be identified as Hinduism. It is futile to search for the origins of the Puranic legends in a culture rooted in perennial truth (*sanātana dharma*) with no recognizable human originator (apauriseyā). It was during the relative stability of the Gupta period (320-500 CE) that the compilation of the Purāṇas in their present form took place and through the development of temple cities along with *bhakti* to particular deities became the mainstay of popular Hinduism.

The Purāṇas are defined as:

sargasca pratisargasca vamso manvantarāni ca.
vamsānucaritam caiva puṛāṇam pancalakshanam.

Traditionally they cover five topics: the creation or manifestation of the universe; destruction and recreation of the universe; the genealogies of gods and sages; the reigns of the fourteen Manus or mythological progenitors of humanity; the history of the solar (surya) and lunar (candra) dynasties of kings, from which all kings trace their descent.

Mythology may be considered as the earliest attempt by thinking human beings to organize the three major realms of their existence: the cosmos (brahmānda), the politicos (samsāra) and the psychos (ahamkāra). Puranic descriptions are poetical with Mount Meru, the axis mundi, or center of the earth around which is Jambudvipa, within which is Bhārat, surrounded by oceans of sugar-cane juice, wine, ghee, buttermilk, milk and sweet water. Every major civilization and even native cultures around the world used myths and legends to express their religious beliefs and to describe their worlds and the powers that shaped them. Mythology can show much about ancient worship, history, philosophy, science, morality and even geography. A psychological study can decipher Puranic symbolism into a classification of human archetypes and personality types which transcend time and space. While a keen student must give due recognition to the heritage of Egyptian, Greek, Roman, Celtic, Norse, Native American and Aborigine myths, one has to acknowledge the depth, scope and vast dimensions of Puranic literature. Myths and legends from different parts of the world share many motifs and symbols and a comparative study can yield rich dividends by touching the common essence that unites humanity. While the myths of other cultures are now relegated to academic study and find little meaning in everyday life, the Purāṇas are living scriptures, continuously recited and heeded on important occasions, not only in India, but all over the world wherever the great Indian Diaspora has spread.

It is from the Purāṇas that the *pancayatna pūjā,* the domestic worship of five shrines and their deities began: Visnu, Śiva, Ganeśa, Surya and Devī. The Purāṇas established the mainstream Smarta worship of Viṣṇu and Śiva, which absorbs into it external, non-brahamnical and sometimes non-vedic or *tāntric* material. The importance of the Purāṇas is underscored by the fact that Śankarācārya, the great bhāysakāra and Vedantin, utilized Puranic divinities to elucidate some of his compositions. 18 major Purāṇas are recognized and classified as Sāttvik, Rājasic and Tāmasic. There are also 18 Upapurāṇas.

Humanity today is for time and increasingly under siege from both favourable and unfavourable socio-economic and political forces that sometimes seem beyond control. The world is getting polarized along religious and cultural parameters. Sometimes innocent people are marginalized. As the number of choices increases, so does the difficulty in making the right decisions. Under these circumstances, Sri Ramānuj Prasād's book is a welcome addition to contemporary spiritual literature. Few people have the time or opportunity to study the vast body of Puranic litrature, and therefore this concise book offers an essential guide to the teaching of the major Purāṇas. It may be studied with benefit by all people aspiring to lead a virtuous life.

Vyasa Prasad
Narayana Gurukula,
Fernhill-643004, Tamil Nadu

Contents

CHAPTER

CHAPTER I

Section I

Purview & Review

What It Is

The *Purāṇas* are the picturesque narration of the glorious episodes pertaining to the Hindu mythology. The very intention of these incidents are to bring forth certain points of view with regards to the moral values, that the *Purāṇas* wish to teach the humanity through examples of the characters, time and place in question – the customs and practice. There are ways to teach a particular religion and practice, what the people of the time believe and profess. The philosophy and practices are the theoretical presumptions and assumptions in real and relative life or we can say a life style of the general and particular society.

Each episode has been carefully planned and executed in normal sequence, but however there are many climaxes that climate does not endorse fully, if there is absence of faith. Mortar is the bond without which no two bricks will stick together. Now the question may arise whether the *Purāṇas* have come into being themselves? Our answer to this point is that 'no'. It is designed for a particular group of people from the substance that the *Śruti* bears in subtle form. The form that is not comprehensible to the masses is due to absence of the preparedness that it demands. The essence of *Śruti and Smṛti* is not in tangible state of condition, to be taken as such, for want of perceptional base.

Even now we see that after years of propitiating with the help of the teacher, we come to doubt whether such things are there at all, due to habitual trait. Therefore these values can not be owned up. *Purāṇas* bring a tangible, convincing climate that makes in-road into our personality, similar to the play on screen where the witness becomes a part of it, weeps laughs and experiences the situation which the characters go through. In other words, one becomes the dream individual of the world. Many times we have seen that dream tiger continues to haunt even after one comes out of the dream.

To demonstrate, we come to the Gīta teaching of 700 verses out of about one lakh verses of Mahābhārata. The war was between the two forces, depicting the embodiment of virtues and vices respectively. One followed the path of righteousness in speech and deeds and stuck to rightful assertion, whereas the second one was not only deceitful in nature but also claimed what was not justifiable on any count. This contrast between the two cousins was depicted through wrongful means that was employed to win the game, humiliation to the Pāṇḍavas and daughter-in-law Draupadī and attempt to burn all the Pāṇḍavas with their mother in the *Lākṣā gṛha* etc are the narrations and exhibition of *Purāṇas.*

The words uttered by Dhṛtarāṣṭra "*dharmakśetre Kurukśetre*" is also an indication that this war field of Kurkśetra was pregnant to the victory of *dharma*, though he was opposed to it and also knew that what was being done on his behalf was also not right. The culmination of the war was a natural phenomenon that *adharma* was bound to face opposition in the race and the right of righteousness was to defeat the evils and vice acts and its propagators. Virtue demands that it must oppose the vice. Virtue can not be complacent and can not just watch but it must free the society from the clutches of vices at any cost.

The above are the moral and ethical aspects of the ruler that have been taught through the episodes up to culmination of war. Lord Kṛṣṇa opens his mouth in the eleventh verse of second chapter "you grieve for those who should not be grieved for, yet you spell words of wisdom. The wise grieve neither for the living nor for the dead". [The Lord indicates that Arjuna is not wise with reference to his mental condition though it is covered with the talks that ought to have been of the wise and learned persons]. Before this point all had been the stage work. Arjuna wished to see the warriors with whom he had to fight and succumbing to the delusion, resulted in the change of place between Arjuna and Lord Kṛṣṇa The charioteer Lord, childhood friend of Arjuna became *guru*, the teacher, when the deluded Arjuna surrendered to the Lord as a disciple and requested in no uncertain terms to guide him in the situation, where his intellect had failed. In substance, eligible disciple and able teacher are brought together so that teaching can take place. This relation is important where there is faith, respect and understanding between the two.

These types of situations are seen throughout in *Purāṇa,* where a significant lesson is being the medium to teach the individual and society targeted as the audience. Nārada approaches Sanatkumāra expressing his discontent, though he was well versed in all the knowledges of the relative world such as Vedas, grammar, knowledge about snakes, wealth discovery and so many of them, which itself is a big list. Even then he was desirous of *Brahmā Vidyā,* which alone brings contentment in life.

In order to conclude that *prāṇa* energy is glorious, there was a dispute among the organs of knowledge, such as eye, ear etc. To show its importance, each organ went out of function for a period of time but this did not lead to the collapse of the entire system, whereas, when the *prāṇa* prepared to move out, the whole system was on the brink of collapse. Thus *prāṇa* was declared as the king, the eldest one, and sustainer of the other systems and pure, as in other story, evil forces were not able to corrupt *prāṇa* like the rest. The hand does good and bad deeds, so also the eyes and ears etc but *prāṇa* remains pure, it is the same in good people as well as in bad people. There is nothing like evil *prāṇa* as life energy is common in each and every one and the same.

The above intervening part of short narrations, even in *vedāntic* philosophy is also known as the *purāṇa,* though they do not subscribe to main eighteen, the exclusive in the subject. Thus the *purāṇa* is that part of the religious literature through which, a situation is brought into the play to exhibit a specific character of an individual / group of people like war and celebrations etc, cause and effect of natural blessing and curse, leading to lesson to be learnt, understand and practice.

Merits

The value justification of *Purāṇas* as means of religious perception, preparation and practice stands on better footing. In fact the *Purāṇas* came into being in pursuance to overcome certain difficulties, when it came for common application and it is heartening to observe that it has fulfilled the expectation. *Purāṇas* are more popular over other means of religious teachings as unlike in *Vedic* rituals it does not require any expenditure over the materials that go into the performance of the fire rituals, such as material for oblations, fire place, priest to perform, other attendant needs like proper time, place and day. *Vedic* injunctions prohibit certain rituals for specific. *Varṇas* and *āśramas* and certain other conditions must be fulfilled to undertake the ritual. In essence there are many 'dos and don'ts' which is not there in the study of *Purāṇas*

The ritual is also restricted by the place and time whereas *Purāṇas* do not suffer from these restrictions. It may be studied by all at all times. The rituals are means for mind purification and the study of *Purāṇas* meet that benefit. One goes on pilgrimage in expectation of some merits to occur, they call *puṇyam* which is erroneous in the true sense as pilgrimage gives purification of the mind and *Purāṇas* too meet this objective, even at home.

Percept of *Karma yoga* is renunciation of the expectation of the benefits from the action and to do action as duty or service to the Lord or to the society and take the results as the *Prasād* of the Lord. The corrupt mind does not accept so easily, as business transaction always takes the favorable benefits. It is really a Herculean task to convince the mind and prepare it to accept as such and when we succeed in that again the benefit is going to be the purification of the mind, which is attained through the study of *Purāṇas* and here too we find that the material benefit apart, *karma yoga* becomes easy.

Upāsana is the mental action to make the mind to stay over certain values / features and to concentrate on certain deity through a symbol *[pratīka / pratima]*, whereas the mind runs like a violent race horse. Within a minute it goes all around the world, some times even on filthy thoughts, like a fly. Lord Kṛṣṇa too appreciates the difficulty in controlling the mind, when questioned by his dear disciple Arjuna. It is said that mind control is as difficult as to control the air in the space. The air in the space moves freely without being subjected to any sort of hindrance. Yoga prescribes certain tips such as *dhyāna, dhāraṇa* etc, whereas in the study of *Purāṇas* these difficulties are not insurmountable as the examples and characters are personified and tangible. Moreover the values of meditation depicted are not external to practice of the natural instinct that requires not so much efforts as in the case of meditation on a chosen deity which is not stuffed with blood and flesh as in the human beings. Superlative actions by human body are more convincing over the superior being, of imagination. The actions by the personalities of *Purāṇas* give better evidence of the truth, where there is always the doubt of existence of the divine personalities, far away from the perception of the ken. The heroic deeds, sacrifices and characteristic characters, harness confidence in human beings. Those who study / meditate on *purāṇic* personalities find one self as part and parcel of the episodes and sway therein according to the intuitive tendency of the individual.

To sum up there is shorter distance between the *Purāṇic* characters and divine characters from the stand point of the individual. This shorter distance gives better perception and intimacy, thus good opportunity to subscribe and facilitate to imbibe the values reflected through the stories. Another advantage is that there is less chance of ambiguity due to the language used therein, in different mode. *Purāṇas* use the language of the group in the audience whereas *Śāstras* do not come down so much. To come to *Vedic* ritual, *karma, upāsana, yoga,* some incentives and preparations are required. *Purāṇas* provide that incentive in the form of an urge for fulfillment and also prepare the individual's mind to accept these, the rituals and practices, making it inquisitive.

During the study of *Purāṇas* many other doubts may arise, that need to be addressed beyond this study. Some times it so happens that particular question can not be addressed by the *Purāṇas* and to satisfy the inquirer or to validate that truth some more witnesses are required so in that pursuit the enquirer seeks to study some other scriptures or is emboldened to believe and go to the ritual of *Karma Kāṇḍa.* With the foregoing discussions we come to the conclusion that the study of *Purāṇas* is as much necessary as passing the entrance examination for admission into the college course study.

In rural India even today some orators will move in and narrate the *Purāṇic* episodes to the assembly of farmers and their families, when they have completed the tasks of the day. The skilled orators use the body language as well as musical instruments that explain the charm and also invite better acceptance and attention. In terms of impressions too, they are definite and deeper. Such course also fulfills the urgent need for mental relaxation and amusement after the hard physical work of the day. Thus this single action goes to fulfill double purpose of recreation and learning of the divine values, hand in hand. The study of the *Purāṇas* is the preparatory action, meant for the common people. For individual attention and needs one has to take recourse through individual teacher of *Veda* and *Vedānta.*

This was designed by Maharṣi Vyāsa, when it was felt that the messages of *Vedas and Vedānta* were not reaching the masses, even as an information to the extent that there is something else also beyond the existing activities. To follow the *Veda and Vedānta* enough minds were not available. It is a sort of home study before coming to even elementary school. The *Purānas* fulfill all these requirements and more than what was meant for. Bringing *Purāṇas* into the life of common man is a great service to the nation or even to humanity. *Purāṇas* are being taught by various teachers, under varying circumstances for fulfilling various objectives in the life span of an individual, society and nation.

The Validity

Here in this context, validity means effectiveness, reality and realization.

Effectiveness

Present is the age of scientific advancement and modern living habits, where every answer is weighed on logic and perceptional scale, because the question is so oriented. But can the science question the human value of life? Have we closed our door to the truth, penance [hard effort] and charity? Have the definitions of pain and pleasure changed? Fire and water are still hot and cold. If the answers for all these are 'no' then that must be the effectiveness of *Purāṇas* too. *Purāṇas* continue to inspire millions of life for happy and peaceful living. It continues to govern over the emotion. [Ideal of life- live and let live] - a ladder to reach at the top rung of success. Material enjoyment has failed to bring mental peace and happiness. Mother Jījā bāi made Śivāji, the Śivāji. *Rām nām* given by the parents, inspired Gāndhiji's thoughts, life and even at the point of death. It can be taken for granted that any noble and fine mind has been inspired by the *Purāṇic* values imparted in the early age in some form or other.

It is possible that the avenue might have got shifted from village stage to TV channel but not the menu. The word *Purāṇa* of fourth chapter of *Gīta* stands to denote ancient but ever new, is superimposed on the *Purāṇa* the garland of the legend, bouquet of moral values, as the fragrance of the flowers in the garden of the universe. *Purāṇa* means ancient but ever new, since He is the creator, sustainer and unto Him everything gets resolved. Test of popularity of the *Purāṇas* can be seen by the number and types of people visit the holy places declared by the *Purāṇas* like Vāranāsī, Bṛndāvan, Hardvār, Saṅgam, Kailāś, Mānasarovar, Badri, Kedār, Vaiṣṇodevī etc, celebration of the festivals like *Holi, Divāli, Dasserā, Saṅkrānti and Vaikuṇṭa Ekādaśi etc,* bath in Ganges during *Kumbha melā,* solar, lunar eclipse etc are precept of the *Purāṇas.*

Electronic media too focuses on the *Purāṇas* such as *Rāmāyaṇ, Mahābhārata, Viśṇu Purāṇa* and many more such series are shown in the 21st century, in the age of nuclear bombs, where the conventional weapons have disappeared. *Purāṇas* are the smile of India and one can imagine what happens to one, when one's smile is taken away and how one's face will look without a smile.

Reality

How far there exists the element of truth on these episodes and to what extent they are related to the life over this planet, particularly with reference to the Hindu society of India or the Indians on other lands? Actually we do not know whether such incidents really took place, whether there were such heroic characters and we are not concerned with it as long as the essence and substance serve our purpose. To us the moral lessons look practical and can be inculcated in our life, if not fully at least to that extent, which makes the life worth living. It inspires and brings cheers and gives us the courage to face with the unfavorable, hard situations. As far as the faith in Hindu society is real, the birth and death are real, our relations with the world and its creator are real the *Purāṇas* are also real. We go to see the reality in the purpose less things in content that are beyond our perception and present experience. We prefer to eat the fruits and not count the leaves and trees in the garden.

Realisation

General opinion in the west about Indians, is that we give too much importance to the future over the present, especially with reference to the work of Christian missionaries. It is not correct as we duly care the present too. The *Purāṇas* talk of individual gains; one may derive from it, in turn to the society, to our civilization, fellowship and attitude of service to other less fortunate ones. *Purāṇas* provide a place of pride in the world history and we consider ourselves fortunate to be the part and parcel of such culture and civilization. *Purāṇas* are connected to the *Vedas [Śruti and Smṛti]* as its organ for extending and grossifying its essence and content for general and common understanding of the commandments. The faith in *Purāṇas* automatically brings faith in *Vedas, karmas and upāsanās,* thus what can be gained by *karma yoga, Upāsanās and Bhakti yoga* can be gained through

Purāṇas, if understood properly and practiced with sincerity.

Purāṇas appear before us in every walk of life and the message rings in our ears, the immortal words become the source to have good thoughts. The response ought to have come from the *Karma yoga and Upāsanā. Karma yoga and Upāsanā* benefit us with the purity of mind, and help us in the concentration of the mind which prepares one for *Jnāna yoga,* the science of liberation. *Purāṇas* also bestow the same benefit but less in subtlety. However it definitely opens the door for further progress. The biggest realization from the study [understanding] of the *Purāṇa* is that, it is an antidote to the split personality and instinct, to live in harmony with the physical and mental plane and take step towards the higher plane in this modern society of conflicts and competition. Western society is aggressive to the moral values. In our own country joint family is breaking up and more and more old age homes are springing up. Materialistic life is gaining inroad into the life of simplicity and values. Science of mass destruction is gaining weight over the social and civilized way of life.

Generation is in gloom and the confused parents are not able to provide character building. More and more cases are registered in family courts in the name of socialistic progressive society.

Section II

Date of Purāṇas

Broad consensus has been reached among the scholars about the number of Mahāpurāṇas of *Vedic and Vaidic* characters as 'eighteen'. With regards to the antiquity it is not usually mentioned along with it, as its formation and flowering is independent tradition of *Purāṇic* literature. The original contents were already there before in the fold of *Itihāsa, Śruti* and *Smṛti* as part and parcel of the text, as the functional utility to abide with the programme such as to prepare and support the rituals and austerity or to bring the teacher and the student together as well as to indicate the qualitative measures of the *Triputi* – subject, object and instrument. Therefore the inference of the period of reference has to be imputed in two stages. First with reference to the text to which it belongs and then the period, when that was pulled out, to be put into the fold of *Purāṇas.* As far as we, the *sadhakas* are concerned it makes no difference to us as this is the job related to historians. We are interested in achieving the objectives. We are also not ungrateful to the seers, who gave us the priceless gift to us. We are indeed proud of them and offer our salutations to those great torch bearers for their compassion towards us.

Features of Purāṇas

Following are the features of Purāṇas.

- Creation.
- The intermediate creation.

- Dynasties of the gods and the Patriarchs.
- The fourteen Manus and their periods.
- Genealogy of the kings of the Solar and Lunar dynasty.
- Protection of the world by incarnations.
- Dissolution of the world.
- The cause of creation viz the Jīva and its Karmas.
- Modes of subsistence.
- The refuge – the Brahmān.

Creation

The stages involved in creation are: The *Nirguṇa Brahmān manifests* himself into the *Saguṇa Brahmān.* The *Nirguṇa Brahmāṇ* can not do any creation as it is, since the creation envisages modification and qualifications such as *Satva, Rajas and Tamas.* Pure Brahmān is without any attributes, form, change, parts – whole and special relationship. Brahmān therefore associates with *māyā,* which is not separate from him, but has the three *guṇas* and more predominantly the power of activities and covering [delusions]. These correspond to the *rajas and tamas prakṛti of māyā* – this is the stage of creation. Next is the creation of the five subtle elements and from these subtle elements are created the elemental bodies and subtle worlds. For example the *prāṇa* – the life force, the mind, all the subtle organs, both at individual level and total as well as the space, the wind, the fire, the water and the earth – that supports all, were created.

Thereafter the subtle elements are grossified for creation of the elemental gross bodies and gross worlds. In the beginning some beings were created by Brahmā by mere thoughts – the will power to become the instrument of propagation, i.e., *Prajāpatis and ṛṣis.* Bodies are then channeled through *aṇḍaja* – born from eggs, *svadeja* – born of sweat, *udbhīja* – born of seeds, and *jarāyuja* – *mammals* – human and animals, birds and reptiles, microbes and plant kingdom. These bodies are the essence of the food. They come from food, exist on food and become food at the end.

The intermediate creation

This creation is to sustain the universe and comply with the necessities of the previous creation, in which *Jīvas* have accumulated merits and demerits, born of the matrix of their actions and reactions. It includes the creation of the *Vedas – Rg, Yajur, Sāma and Đīkṣā* to perform the rites and sacrifices, the fee which the priest is entitled for his services, the sacrificer, the materials to be used as oblations, the sun, the moon, the sacrificial fires [*gārhapatya, āhāvanīa and dakṣṇāgni*], days, nights, fortnights, months and years etc. Also created were the rivers, oceans, mountains, herbs and herbal juice to sustain the body – both the gross and subtle bodies. Again proceeded with the creation of seven senses *[Prāṇas],* seven flames, and seven oblations. Further creations are the fourteen worlds [seven upper worlds and seven underworlds], ten directions [east, west, south, north, the intermediary four directions and below and upper] and the presiding gods of the ten directions, *lokpālas,* and *adiṣṭāna devatas.*

Dynasties of gods and Patriarchs

Dakṣa and *Asiknī* had sixty daughters, ten of these were married to the god Dharma, thirteen to the sage Kaśyapa, twenty seven were married to Candra / Soma and the remaining were married to sages Ariṣṭanemi, Vāhuputra,

Aṅgiras, and Kṛśasva. From the ten daughters, married to Dharma, Arundhatī gave birth to objects of the world; Vasu's children were the eight Vasus. Anala's son was Kumāra also known as Kārtikeya, Prabha's son was Viśvakarmā, Sādhya's children were Sādhyadevā and Viśvas' children were Viśvadevās. Kaśyapa had twenty one wives and Dakṣa's daughters married to him were Aditi, Diti, Ariśta, Kālakā, Danāyus, Danu, Simhikā, Krodhā, Pradhā, Viśvā, Vinatā, Kapilā, Muni and Kadru. Among them Diti was the mother of gods, Aditi was the mother Hiraṇyākṣa and Hiraṇyakaśipu, who were demons. Tāmra was the mother of all birds. Vinata was the mother of Aruṇa and Garuda, Garuda was the vehicle of Viṣṇu. Surasā was the mother of snakes. Kadru was the mother of *nāgas, like Ananta, Vāsuki, and Takṣaka* etc. Krodhavaśā was the mother of *rākśasas.* Surabhi gave birth to all cattle. Muni became the mother of *apsarās,* Ariṣta was the mother of *gandharvas,* and Ila was the mother of trees and herbs. Yakṣas were born of Tviśa.

Manvantaras

It is a time principle as our days, nights, fortnight, month and years are to be related to our activities of the past and hope for tomorrow. There are relative differences from the part of sun rise and setting at different part of time even in our world, from one country to another. Manvantara is the time scale, in which activities of creation, sustenance and resolution is specified and comparable to our human years. There are four Yugas, Satya yuga of 17, 28,000 years, Dvāpara Yuga of 12,96,000 years, Treta Yuga of 8,64,00 years and Kali yuga of 4,32.000 years and each of this cycle is called *Mahā Yuga*. The *Mahāyuga* comprises of 12,000 years of god's equivalent 43, 20,000 years of human. 71 *Mahāyugas* constitute a Manvantara and 14 Manvantaras constitute a cycle [*kalpa*]. One *Kalpa* is one day of Brahmā. Each of the Manvantara is ruled by a Manu. In the present *kalpa* six manvantaras are already over and the past Manus were Svāymbhuva, Svārociṣa Uttama, Tāmasa, Raivata and Cākṣuṣa. The seventh Manu is *Vaivasvata.* From *Manvantara* to *Manvantara Indras* and gods change. The Manvantaras are as below.

Manu	Gods	Indra
Svāyambhuva	Yama	Sācipati
Svārociṣa	Parvata, Tuśita	Vipaṣcita
Uttama	Sudhama, Satya, Śiva & Pratardana	Suśanti
Tāmasa	Surupa, Hari, Supta & Sudhi	Sibi
Raivata	Amitabha	Ṛbhu
Cākṣuṣa	Adya	Manojava
Vaivasvata	Āditya, Vasus & Rudra	Purandara
Sāvarṇi	Sutapa	Bali
Dakṣasāvarṇi	Paravata	Adbhuta
Brahmāsāvarṇi	Vāmana	Śānti
Dharmasāvarṇi	Vihaṅgama	Vṛṣa
Rudrasāvarṇi	Haritā	Ṛtadhāma
Raucyadevasāvarṇi	Sūtramā	Divaspati
Indrasāvarṇi	Cākṣuṣa	Śuci

The age of the universe is 184, 03, 20,000 years, the 28th cycle out of 71

Caturyugas. The Iron age i.e. in the Kali Yuga 4976 years are over and the balance is 427024 years. The age of creation is 1960852076 years [approx. 2 billion years]. The seventh deluge may occur after 176187029 years. The scientific conclusion is: "the universe began to expand – two billion years ago." – ('The universe and Dr, Einstein', page 115. "Bibliography of the earth" Prof. Gamow – page 2.)

Scientific data basis:

- An interesting data is that the salinity of the ocean water – the rivers must have been on work for about 300 million years, for its salinity of 3%.
- From the relation between stellar masses and stellar life span, that most of the stars forming the milking way system is three billion years of age.
- Thus there is no permanent and unchanging universe.
- There is considerably coincidence about the age of the creation, calculated by the scientists and that of our scripture based data.

Genelolgy of the Kings of Solar and Lunar Dynasties

Sage Kaśyapa and Aditi had a son named Vivaśvana also known as Sūrya Devata / Mārtāṇda, who was married to Samjña, the daughter of Viśvakarma and had two sons and a daughter. First son was the Vaivasvata Manu, the second was Yama, god of death and the daughter was Yamunā. Unable to bear the energy of her husband Sūrya, Samjña created from her own body a substitute, known as Chāyā and left. She was not very much welcome in her parents' house, so she left for a land named Uttara Kuru and lived there in the form of a mare. Sūrya when he came to know about this, he joined her in the form of a horse and had two sons, who were named Asvinikumāras, the physicians of gods. Sūrya and Chāyā had two sons named Śanīsvar and Sāvarṇi Manu and a daughter called Tapati. After Viśvakarmā chopped off the energy to bearable level, Sūrya and Samjña lived together. After performing sacrifice, Vaivaśvata Manu had many sons and prominent among them were Ikṣvāku, Nṛga, Dhiṣṭa, Dhṛṣṭa Śaryāti, Nariṣyanta, Nabhāga, Pṛṣadhrạ, Ṛṣṭa, Karūṣa and Kavi and by additional offerings to the gods Mitra, Varuṇa and a daughter , named Ila were born. When Vaivasvata Manu died, his ten children divided the earth among themselves. Ikṣvāku ruled the central region and had hundred sons. After Ikṣvāku, his son Vikukśi ruled his father's kingdom [Ayodhyā]. Vikukśi's son was Kakutstha and Sri Rama of Ramāyāṇa belonged to the lineage.

Lunar Dynasty

The energy from the penance of sage Atri gave birth to *Soma or Candra* [moon god]. Candra also performed very difficult penance and Brahmā appointed him the lord for the seeds, herbs, Brāhmaṇas and the oceans. Candra abducted the wife of Bṛhaspati, the preceptor of the gods. There was a terrible war over Tārā, the wife of Bṛhaspati and on Brahmā's intervention, when Candra returned Tārā; she already had a son, named Budha. Budha married Ila and had a son named Purūrava. There were several descendants from the lunar dynasty. Nahuśa married Virajā and they had six sons, namely Yati, Yayāti, Samyāti, Āyati, Ayati and Dhruva. Yayāti was crowned after king Nahuśa and Yayāti had two wives, Devayānī – daughter of Śukrācārya and Śarmiṣṭhā, daughter of *danava* king – Vṛṣaparva. Devayānī had two sons, Yadu and Turvasu and Śarmiṣṭhā had three sons, Druhya, Anu and Puru. Puru succeeded central part of Yayāti's kingdom and his descendant was King Bharata and then the Kuru dynasty. The descendants of Turvasu were the kings of Kerala, Pāṇdya, Kola and chola. Kings of Gāndhara were the descendants of Druhya and Yadu's descendants were Haihayas and famous among them was Kartavīrya Arjuna, who had thousand arms.

Incarnation for the Protection of the Good

When the *Avatāra Puruṣa* himself says on 'protection' it remains no more speculative narration but a promise. Lord Kṛṣṇa says "Though I am unborn, imperishable and the Lord of all the beings, yet, subjugating my *Prakṛti,* I come into being by my own *Māyā.* Whenever there is a decay of *dharma* and rise of *adharma* then I embody myself, O Bharata! For the protection of the good, for the destruction of the wicked and for the establishment of *dharma* I am born age after age".

Dissolution of the Universe

From unmanifestation to manifestation again manifestation to unmanifestation like the day and night again, is the cycle order of this universe. Gītā mentions "Those who know that the day of Brahmā lasts a thousand *Yugas* and that his night lasts a thousand *Yugas*, they are the knower of day and night. At the coming of the day all manifested beings proceed from the unmanifested and at the coming of the night they merge again into the same is called manifested dissolution [*Pralaya*]. This multitude of beings, O Partha! Coming forth again and again, merge in spite of them, at the approach of night and remanifest themselves at the approach of the day". There are other two stages – *laya and atyantika pralaya.* A *jnāni* attains *atyantika pralaya* and does not manifest but permanently merge with Brahmān whereas the ignorant one comes again and again as one from the deep sleep [dream less] to waking world.

The cause of creation

Karma determines the longevity, type and quality of the body, the house of enjoyment and sufferings that have to be exchanged. And this unexhausted *karmas,* have to be exhausted in new creation. The bodies are destroyed, but the individual *Jīvas* retain its identity with unfinished *karmas* in potent form during deluge. Thus the creation comes into being for the *Jīva* to start and continue from the point left at, as the individual continues after a night's sleep. "Below and above, spread its branches, nourished by the *guṇas*, sense objects are the birds and below in the world of men stretch forth the roots engendering actions".

Modes of Subsistence

Four *varṇas* and four *aśramas:* "The duties of *Brāhmaṇas, Kṣatriyas,Vaiśyas as also of Śūdras*, O Scorcher of foes, are distributed according to the *guṇas* born of their own nature, serenity, self-restraint, purity, forgiveness etc, - these are the nature. Thus learning and teaching are the duties of *Brāhmaṇas*. Heroism, vigor, generosity, lordship, not running away from battle are the nature of Kṣatriyas. Protection of the country, ruling and protection of the rights of other *varṇas* are the duties of *Kṣatriyas.* Agriculture, cattle rearing and trade are the duties of *Vaiśyas,* born of their nature. The action consisting of service is the duty of *Śūdra,* born of their nature. Thus engaged in their own duties, they attain perfection as well as the goal of life and living."

The Refuge or Brahmān

He is very luminous without form, and is both within and without, unborn, without *Prāṇa*, without mind, pure, greater than the great, indestructible one. Īśvara [Brahmān with Māyā] is the creator, sustainer and resolver of the universe. Īśvara is the material and intelligent cause of the universe. Example is the spider, that produces the web from the material within it and withdraws unto itself. Another example is the dream – dreamer and waker.

Tradition of Purāṇas, Handed Over / Came to us Through the Teacher – Taught

Glorious are the teachers and the students as the Purāṇa is glorious. A teacher can not be a teacher if he did not happen to be a student. Any amount of learning one may have, he can not be a teacher, if he had not been a student. It is dangerous to learn from such a teacher, who had not been a student.

- The original Purāṇa *Samhitā* [hymns] was taught by Veda Vyāsa to Romaharṣaṇa.
- Romaharṣaṇa had six disciples – Sumati, Agnivarcas, Mitrāyus, Śamśapāyana, Akṛtavarṇa and Śāvarṇi. Each one of these disciples composed a Purāṇa on the basis of Purāṇa Samhitā. Viṣṇu Purāṇa was written after Padma Purāṇa and is specific to glory of Lord Viṣṇu. But there is a variation here. Viṣṇu Purāṇa recounts that the knowledge of Purāṇa was given by Brahmā to sage Ripu.

The teacher	The student
Ripu	Priyavrata
Priyavrata	Bhaguri

Bhaguri	Stavamitra
Stavamitra	Dadhīci
Dadhici	Sarasvata
Sarasvata	Bhṛgu
Bhṛgu	Purkutsa
Purkutsa	Narmada
Naramada	Dhṛtarāṣṭra and Purāṇa
Dhṛtarāṣṭra and Purāṇa	Vāsuki
Vāsuk	Vatsa
Vatsa	Aśvatara
Aśvatara	Kambala
Kambala	Elapatra

The sage Vedaśiras acquired the knowledge of the Purāṇas from the underworld and gave it to Pramāti and Pramāti gave it to Jatukarṇa, who in turn passed on to many sages. Sage Parāśara had had learnt of the Purāṇas from Vasiṣṭha, then it came to Maitreya and he taught to sage Śamika. There may be many more such parallel streams where one or more links might have missed by the passage of time or through oral communication. The idea is that, it is a tested knowledge and had served in the past and there is no reason that it will not benefit us.

CHAPTER II

Moral Values Revealed

Vows, charities, austerities, sacrifices, righteousness, pilgrimage, duties of *Varṇāśramas* and Yoga are merely for heaven. One attains godhood through sacrifice, the world of Brahmā through austerities and various kinds of enjoyment through charities. But not liberation and compared to liberation these are insignificant. Liberation calls for knowledge. Bhagavad-Gītā [9-21] validates as "Having enjoyed the extensive heavenly sphere, when their virtues are exhausted, they enter the mortal world. Thus, those who take refuge in the religion of the Vedas, desirous of enjoyments, go and come". Here in the following episodes, the values of *Vedas* [*Karma kāṇḍa*] that have been elaborated in *Smṛtis, granthas* like Manu, Yajñavlakya and Parāśara, where *dharma Śāstras* have been personified, given physical body in the Purāṇas, so that it can also be the body of everybody.

Brahmā Purāṇa-1

The selfless dove couples

Lesson: Glory of Godāvarī holy bath. *[Ch. 70 – 175]*

The female pigeon was in captivity of a hunter, who happened to rest for the night under the tree, where the said female pigeon and her husband lived together. Having arrived at that place, the female pigeon asked her mate to perform the house holder's duty of honoring the guest, the very hunter who intended to kill her. The male pigeon arranged a fire place for the hunter to protect him from the cold with which he was afflicted and more from the separation from his house.

To satisfy the hunger of the guest the male pigeon jumped into the fire, before him, to be eaten, by the hunter and seeing this, the hunter was wonder struck and he released the female pigeon. When the female pigeon was free, she also followed the suit and jumped into the fire. The hunter then saw to his surprise that the two pigeons had turned into god and goddess. The hunter then begged them to release him from the sins he had committed so far. He was advised to take bath in the river Godāvarī and by doing so he became the citizen of the abode named "Goloka". It is said that on the bank of the river "Pilgrimage pigeon" is still popular. The lesson more significantly emphasizes to follow our traditional obligation and also the efficacy of the bath, in the river Godāvarī.

A hurried conclusion would be that this story is to teach the worship of the guest, appears to be remote. Relationship of the guest stands between same species. Man can not learn from the birds or animals, whose intention and relation are not known. We can infer from the instinct but not the conduct. Man learns from man, so the Lord takes incarnation in the human form to prevail upon the human beings to follow his path. Here the lesson is the penance – that is bath in holy river Godāvarī, which was taught to the hunter, through the self sacrifice in the fire, by the pigeons. In both the cases, it is the merit of penance that benefited from lower body to higher one." *Kath I – ii – 8.*

How the tradition of guest worship came into being. "*Atithi devo bhava.*" *– Tai..*

The guest refers to the unexpected arrival of known or unknown and calls for hospitality. Earlier the means of travel was only by foot and the journey involved was of several days or even months especially for the pilgrimage. There were no hotels or motels available and for halt after the sun set people used to seek shelter in the nearby houses, in the village from where further journey was not possible. The accepted ethics of house holder was to provide them with food and shelter. The rule for the house holder is to cook food for such unexpected arrivals. Cooking for self alone is considered as 'stealing', says Bhagavad-Gītā.

Brahmā Purāṇa-2

Lesson: Desirous of the heaven must sacrifice.

B.G. 4-12 & Ta –XVI- iii. 3

Sacrifice: The Story of the Sage Dadhīci

Long ago there used to be a sage named Dadhīci. His hermitage was near the holy river Gaṅgā and nobody dared to enter that place due to the divinity there. The gods once fought a war with the *Asuras* and won the war. After the war was over, the gods wanted to keep their weapons in a safe place and so they arrived at the hermitage of the sage. When enquired by the sage for their visit, the gods told the sage that they want to keep their weapons in a safe place and they did not find any better place than the hermitage of the sage as no one dared to enter it. Sage Dadhīci agreed to the proposal.

A hundred years passed and the gods did not return to take back their weapons and the weapons started losing their luster. The sage did not know how to preserve the weapons and hence he washed them with holy water.

When washed, all the power stored in the weapons got dissolved into the water and the weapons became totally useless. Dadhīci then drank the washed water. At last after some time when the gods returned to claim their weapons, they found them to be totally of no use. The sage found the situation very uncomfortable and he told them what had happened. The sage continued, "I have swallowed up the energy of the weapons and there is one way out. With my power of my austerities I can give up my life. Then you can request Viśvakarmā to make fine weapons with my bones". As there was no other solution Dadhīci gave up his life and Viśvakarmā made weapons out of his bones which are known as *vajra,* and that was wielded by Indra to defeat the *asuras.*

This story shows the sacrifice of the great sage to keep up his promise. There is a tradition that individual can be spared for the family, a family for the whole village, a village for the nation. This dharma was all along accepted by the society, thus the nation was protected. A sacrifice is a brick and only on that the foundation and the structure of the society stands.

Brahmāṇda Purāṇa

Lesson: Knowledge is luminous. *Kai – 4 & Mu III – ii -6.*

Who was the Best Among the Sages

Janaka was the Emperor of Videha and was a very learned person. He had great respect for the sages and used to give a lot of wealth to them. Once the Emperor performed a great Yajna and wanted to reward the best among the sages. But how to determine, who was the best? He had thousand cows confined in a pen with gold in its horn and declared that whoever was the most erudite among the scholars may drive away the cows. None of the sages dared. But Yājñavalkya, a great learned sage asked his disciple to drive away the cows to his hermitage. The other sages were furious and thought how arrogant was Yājñavalkya to take away the cows. There was a royal priest named Āśvala, who asked Yājñavalkya "are you indeed the best among the scholars?" Yājñavalkya replied with great humility "I bow to the best scholar. I just want the cows". Thereafter Āśvala determined to interrogate Yājñavalkya and put several difficult questions on Scriptures to him. Yājñavalkya meticulously answered all of them. When Āśvala had no more to ask another sage named Arthbhāga started questioning and soon he too had nothing more to ask. Then another sage named Bhujyu started interrogating Yājñavalkya and exhausted his questions. Like this many wanted to defeat Yājñavalkya but could not. When a woman scholar, while asking questions asked some irrelevant question for which Yājñavalkya warned her "Do not, O Gārgi, push your enquiry too far, lest your head should fall off". With this she kept quiet. After questioned by two more persons again Gārgi wanted to ask him two questions and sought the permission from the assembly. Yājñavalkya was able to answer the two questions to the satisfaction of the assembly and they had to admit that Yājñavalkya was the most illumined sage.

Brahmāvaivarta Purāṇa

Lesson: Greatness of feminine principle. *Br. Ch. 47.*

Mahā Gaṇeś

[It is a story of Mahā Gaṇeś. His head was changed to elephant head- here it is not the usual story, where it was cut by his father Lord Śiva but the instrument is the Śani Bhagavān, son of Śūrya. This incident is the result of making fun of Śanī]

Lord Śani was desirous of seeing Lord Gaṇeś. So he went to the Kailāś, where Mother Pārvatī was holding the child. Śani before getting the audience saluted all the Lords - Kṛṣṇa, Śiva, Brhamāji, Dharma and Sun and obtained their permission to visit the baby Gaṇeś. When he was standing before Mother Pārvatī, his head bowed down and was avoiding looking at Mother Pārvatī. Mother asked "why are you not looking at me and my child?" Śanīśvar related a story in which he mentioned that his wife, the daughter of Citraratha, had pronounced a curse that whomsoever he would look would get destroyed, since he forgot to honor her after her out door period, as he was engrossed in the thought of Lord Kṛṣṇa. Having heard this all the gods and dancers broke into laughter and Mother Pārvatī instructed him to see the child. Śanīsvar was in a dilemma and however glanced at the child from the corner of his eyes. Immediately the child's head got separated from the head, went and merged into Sri Kṛṣṇa and the bleeding head less child was in the mother's lap. Everybody was in panic and the mother started weeping bitterly. Lord Kṛṣṇa went to the river Puṣpamudra, where a male elephant was sleeping with its female elephant, keeping its head in the northern direction. These two were surrounded by baby elephants. Lord Kṛṣṇa cut off the head of the elephant with his Sudarśan cakra, put it on his mount, the Garuda. Meanwhile the female elephant got up and addressed Lord Kṛṣṇa, her prayer. Now Lord Kṛṣṇa cut the head of another elephant and put it on the husband elephant's torso. The elephant having touched the feet of the Lord got the blessing of long life of a Kalpa. Then the Lord rushed to Kailāś put the head on the little Gaṇeś and granted the life force. He also consoled Mother Pārvatī, who took back Gaṇeś in this form and nursed.

"*We find that the word of a sati – a chaste woman was always respected by the gods. In fact it is one of the forces that hold the earth in its place, like truth. It is a lesson for us, not to belittle the words of a chaste woman. Disrespect to the creative forces is an insult to the creator of the universe. Everyone is bound by his / her duties towards himself, fellow beings and the nature and negligence attracts punishment, according to the order of cosmos. In this story, there are points in every incident, to be thought over for proper conduct and harmony.*"

Mārkaṇḍeya Purāṇa

Lesson: *"He who abides in Satva go to higher loka and functionary of tamas go to lower world."*

B.G. 14 - 18. & Br – IV – IV – 4 to 6.

Story of Sage Sukṛṣa

It is an interesting tale from the Mārkaṇḍeya Purāṇa, which is not very popular. A mother bird known by the name of Tārkṣī was witnessing the Mahābhārata war and was hit by an arrow of Arjuna and before dying, four eggs from it fell down and miraculously the eggs were not damaged. These eggs got foolproof protection from the bell of an elephant which fell down and protected the eggs. After some time a sage named Śamīk arrived there and heard the noise of the chiks. He lifted the bell and found the four birds. He ordered his disciples to take them to their hermitage, cared well and fed them properly and within three months the birds were able to fly by themselves. Astonishingly, the birds were vigorous. These birds expressed their allegiance to the sage as their mother, father and teacher in gratitude for having saved their life and brought them up, to be independent. When the sage heard the clear human voice from them, he enquired them about their past life and what made them to become a bird. The birds then narrated their story.

A sage named Vipulavān had two sons namely Sukṛṣa and Tumburu. These four birds were the sons of Sukṛṣa and were engaged in the service of their father. Once Indra visited their hermitage in the form of an old bird, with broken wings to test the sage Sukṛṣa. Indra, in the form of the bird said "I am very hungry and so I beg food from you. I am from the mount Viṇdhyācal and fell down as the wings were broken. I became unconscious and came back to consciousness after eight days." The sage asked the bird what sort of food he required for speedy recovery to health and said that he would provide that food. The bird said that he can completely recover if he gets human flesh. The sage told the bird "you are in the evening of your life and at this age generally one gives up all his desires. Why are you so cruel to ask for human flesh? However as I had promised to give you food it becomes my duty to provide you the food." Then the sage called all his four sons and praised them and thereafter told them that they had a debt on him as son as well as that of a teacher. So they had to do as was told. The sons agreed to it and Sage Sukṛṣa said "I have got the duty to honor the guest. Be ready to quench the hunger and thirst of the guest with your flesh and blood". Due to fear the four sons started shivering and said that this could not be done. The sage got angry and said "you have made a promise and now you are breaking that. I curse you to be burnt in the fire and your next birth will be a bird". After this the sage offered himself to the bird as food, after finishing his own last ritual. Indra in the form of the bird said "O sage! I do not eat a living person. So you leave the body by the strength of your power of austerities". When the sage prepared to leave his body Indra revealed his original form and said "Sir, you are a great soul" and blessed him with great spiritual power and accomplishment of Self knowledge. The sons apologized to their father and appeased him. The sage said that the curse could not be undone. But he blessed them that even in the form of a bird they would retain their memory of previous birth.

The birds thus narrated their story of the past and departed to the mount Viṇdyācal.

This narration goes to bring two fold values impact – the honor of the guest wherein the sage was prepared to offer himself as food to the guest, according to the code of conduct prescribed by the scriptures and the second is the dishonor of the instructions of guru/ parents, together going back on the promise, becomes the part of curse, which leads to lower worlds –from human body to the body of the bird *Tai – I – IX – I.*

Vāmana Purāṇa

Lesson: "It is truly Dharmakṣetra." *Bhagavad-Gītā I.I.*

Kurukṣetra – Dharma Kṣetra

King Ṛkṣa who belonged to the Puru dynasty had a son named Samvaraṇa, who was very good in scriptures as he was taught by the sage Vasiṣṭha. One day while hunting, he came across some *apsarās* and he fell in love with one among them. She was the daughter of Sūrya and was known as Tāpati. Having come to know about their liking of each other, Vasiṣṭha got them married. They had a son named Kuru and as his education was also looked after by Vasiṣṭha, he too was very righteous. When he was sixteen, he was crowned as king and was married to Saudāmini. After some time Kuru wanted to do something which would be remembered, by the future generation and he started roaming the whole world. He came across *dvaitavana,* a forest through which, river Sarasvatī flowed. Among the five seats of Brahmā one seat, known as *samantpañcaka* was there. Kuru thought of an idea of ploughing the land near there and he started with a golden plough to which a bull and a buffalo were yoked. While he was on the job Indra came and asked him what was he doing? Kuru replied that he wanted to cultivate the fruits of meditation and righteous living. Then Indra asked about the seeds for which there was no answer and Indra left. Then Viṣṇu arrived and asked him about the seeds. Kuru stretched his right arm and Viṣṇu sliced his arm with *sudarśan cakra.* Then Kuru stretched his left arm and that too was sliced. Then he offered his thighs and finally his head. Pleased with this Viṣṇu granted a boon and Kuru wanted that the ploughed part should become a holy place. Viṣṇu blessed him that Kuru himself would perform great Yajnas there and that place would be known as *Kurukṣetra.* It was here that sage Lomaharṣaṇa narrated the *Vāmana Purāṇa* to other sages.

"*Rightly Dhṛtarāṣṭra called Kurukṣetra as Dharmakṣetra, though unintentionally. Potent was the place with Dharma and Dharma alone prevailed over Adharma in the war of Mahābhārata. The seeds of Dharma always are present.*

It requires the rain water [follower of dharma] to bring out the seedlings, trees and fruits".

Bhaviśya Purāṇa

Lesson: "*Dharma* of a servant and master."

[Respect own duty] BG 3.11.

The Duties

This story glorifies a servant of the king, who sacrificed his family and himself to save the life of the king.

Once in the court of the king Rūpsen of Vardhamān, a man with his wife and son came to ask for livelihood. The king accepted his request and appointed him as guard in the main gate of the palace, known as *simha dvār.* From intelligence agency the king learnt that this person spent all his income for the welfare of the less fortunate. The king became very happy and made him permanent on the post.

One day in the midnight there came a weeping voice from the direction of grave yard. The king came out and asked the guard to find out about that secretly. The king followed from behind. There the guard found a lady, who said that she was the goddess of the kingdom and was weeping as the king would die the next day. The guard asked her the way to avert this calamity and save the life of the king, who was his master. The weeping lady said that the king could be saved if his son's head was sacrificed on the altar of Durgā Devī. Immediately the guard went to his house, awoke his family and brought them to the temple. There he cut off the head of his son as sacrifice. Seeing this ghastly incident his wife died on the spot and the guard too died. The king was watching all this and having seen such sacrifice for his sake, he too decided to kill himself. At that point, when the king was about to kill himself, the goddess stopped him and told the king to ask for a boon. The king was happy and requested the lives of those who had forsaken their life and was granted. The king silently went back to his palace and in the morning the king enquired about the weeping voice in the night. The guard replied that it was nothing as a witch was making the noise. Then the king narrated the entire episode in his court and made the guard, the king of the present Mahārāshtra-Gujarat as reward for his devotion to the duty and to the king, the ruler.

"This is a wonderful narration of the sincerity and devotion to one's own duty, towards the master and the master too responds accordingly. An embodiment of honesty and sincerity to Dharma towards the employer [master] the king [ruler] should be the goal. Sun is beyond Dharma to shine and similarly servant is to serve the interest and well being of the master."

Viṣṇu Purāṇa-1

Lesson: "Whatever is glorious, excellent and permanent verily is the splendour of the Lord." *BG. 10. 41.*

Who is Great?

Viṣṇu Purāṇa glorifies Lord Nārāyaṇa – the Īśvara – the Ultimate refuge, the sustainer, through an incidental dialogue.

Once Nārada came to Lord Kṛṣṇa, who was sitting in the assembly of his ministers and told "O Lord! You are only the great" [glorious and refuge to all]. The Lord replied

“Yes Nārada, I am”. The people in the assembly wanted clarification and Lord Kṛṣṇa asked Nārada to clarify.

Nārada narrated the following: One day morning when Nārada was on a visit to the banks of the Ganges, he saw a big tortoise as big as a mountain and touching the tortoise Nārada said “you are wonderful and lucky to be moving care free in the Ganges.” Before Nārada could finish the conversation the tortoise said, “I am not but the Ganges, who bears with hundreds and thousands of creatures like me and other species in her”. Nārada went to congratulate the goddess of the river with praises but the Ganges replied “I am not entitled to this title but the ocean which takes in hundreds of rivers like me”. Nārada rushed to confer the title of ‘wonderful and great’ to the ocean but the ocean denied it and said that the glory belongs to the earth which shelters many oceans. The earth said that it is the mountain that supports the earth and the mountain said it is Brahmāji and Brahmāji pointed to the lotus stalk which supports him and the lotus stock pointed to the navel of Lord Viṣṇu - Kṛṣṇa and having reached this conclusion Nārada came to Lord to say that He is the only great among all which the Lord had accepted in front of all the audience. Nārada said that his inquisition was over. Having been blessed by the Lord thus, Nārada said “the search of the wonderful, great and glorious one is over”. The idea is that the Lord is the Ultimate and Absolute supporter of all glories and glorious ones.

“The cause and effect analysis from any point, the effect finally always goes to the Lord, the Absolute. He is ‘The Rome’ in the proverb “All the roads lead to Rome”, but one must be careful about the road and not roaming. In the analysis of creation too, we arrive at that point only. A

talk in creation always has this point to bring out to the student.

Viṣṇu Purāṇa–2

Lesson: "Charity and to be true to the promise made."

Tai. I. IX.1.

Mahābali

Mahābali was the grandson of the great devotee of Lord Viṣṇu, Prahlāda and son of Virocana. Mahābali waged war with devas and having defeated them, he drove them out of their realm and brought it under his control. As the whole of heaven came under the sway of Bali, the devas began to leave the place one by one. Everybody was comfortable under Bali's rule but devas and Brāhmaṇas were denied of their privileges, to certain extent. They approached Viṣṇu and represented their grievances. Viṣṇu told them thus: "Bali is devoted to me, but still to redress your grievances I shall take the incarnation of Vāmana shortly". In course of time the Asuras and their countries began to be weakened. Seeing the approach of destruction Bali became thoughtful and approached Prahlāda to learn the reason. Prahlāda told him "Lord Viṣṇu is staying in the womb of Aditi for his incarnation as Vāmana. That is why the country and Asuras are subjected to destruction. Hearing this Bali said "Asuras are more powerful than that Viṣṇu". These haughty words of Bali were despised by Prahlāda, he got angry and cursed Bali "Let your country be destroyed". Bali requested Prahlāda to pardon him. In turn Prahlāda advised Bali "you will get salvation only by devotion to Viṣṇu".

The defeated devas had taken refuge in forests. Aditi, the mother of Devas was very sorry at this. She shed tears before her husband Kaśyapa Prajāpati, who advised his wife to take a fast of twelve days, and taught her the rules and rituals of the fast. She followed his advice, Viṣṇu appeared before her and asked her what boon she wished. She requested Viṣṇu to take birth as her son, to drive away Bali and to restore her sons, the Devas, their kingdom of heaven and the Lord agreed. Aditi became pregnant in due course and gave birth to a son Vāmana, which was the fifth incarnation of Viṣṇu.

Mahābali was performing a sacrifice on the bank of river Narmadā. Vāmana came to the place of sacrifice in the dress of a hermit boy. He told Bali that he was a helpless hermit and that he might be given three steps of ground. Bali was pleased with the boy and told him that he was willing to give the boy even the country called Bhṛngāraka. He was also prepared to forgo the kingly pleasures for the sake of the boy. The hermit boy did not show any desire for them. The teacher Śukrācārya told Bali that the boy was a cheat and that his request should not be granted. But Mahābali decided to stick to his promise and as a preparation he started to offer the boy water from a water pot. Then Śukrācārya got into the mouth of the pot in the shape of a mote and water would not flow freely out of the pot. Knowing this, Vāmana took a blade of *kuśa* grass and pushed it at the mouth of the pot. The grass pierced one eye of Sukrācārya and from that time onwards Śukrācārya had only one eye. Water flowed into the hands of Vāmana. The teacher got angry and cursed Bali. Vāmana began to measure the ground and simultaneously began to grow. The *asuras* who were horrified at this, started attacking Vāmana. Still Vāmana was growing and with one step he measured the whole of earth and with the second step he took the whole of heaven. Then he asked Bali where to place the third step. Mahābali said that he had his body only left, as his own and that Vāmana might take it and complete the third step. Vāmana placed his foot on the head of Bali and pushed him down to Pātāla [the nether world]. Thenceforth the *Asuras* became the inhabitants of *Pātāla.*

"Giving of charity to Brāhmaṇa and teacher was a matter of principle and prestige to the rulers, especially those who were virtuous and Mahābali was among few who deserved the honor of 'dāna Vīra'. Once given the word, those kings kept up the word, even at the cost of whole wealth and even life. Mahābali demonstrated his courage, even to earn the displeasure of his teacher against the honor of his word and Dharma of granting charity to Brāhmaṇa, as a part of sacrificial ritual. Mahābali is worshipped in Kerala in an annual festival – Onam.

Bhāgavata Purāṇa

Lesson: "Austerity and charity to others".

Ranti Deva

Rantideva was a liberal giver and was sincerely involved in offering charity. He used to see that all are fed well before he took his food and that became the norms of his household. Once a severe famine swept the whole country and they did not have anything to eat for several days. One day by chance the family had delicious sweetmeats and other tasty eatables. Rantideva along with his family sat down to partake the food. Just then a Brahmin came, who was hungry. Rantideva fed him and after his departure the available food got apportioned. Then came in, a lower caste person and knocked the door. Rantideva offered to that hungry guest too. The third time when they were ready to take the remaining food, one *caṇḍāla* came in along with his dog for food. The left over was very little and whatever was left over, Rantideva handed over to the new guest. When the guest left, only one glass of water was there. The family was about to divide the water as all of them were very hungry and thirsty but at that moment a beggar, who was very hungry and thirsty dropped at their door steps half unconscious. Rantideva offered the last glass of water to this person. Now the members of the whole family were about to fall unconscious when they saw that the Lord Nārāyaṇa himself was standing along with Śiva and Brahmāji. They praised very much about the charity of Rantideva, even at the point, when he and his own family members had to lose their lives. Blessed are Rantideva and his family members. To face the situation as depicted, one must have His grace, to withstand the tempest and turmoil that demand determination like iron, faith like rock and kindness of a mother.

This is a lesson on charity and honor to the guest.

Nārada Purāṇa -1

Lesson: "Charity, appropriate to the person." *BG. 17.20.*

Efficacy of Dānam

Bhadramati was a poor Brāhmin. The Brāhmin had six wives and two hundred and forty-four daughters. Once hearing the glory of Bhūdāna [giving away the land free to the deserved], he was much impressed and from then onwards he became filled with a strong desire to give land free to the poor. He had no land of his own. But he went to the king Kauśāmbi and begged for some land, which, when received, immediately gave away to the poor Brāhmins as gift. After that he went and bathed in the Pāpanāśana tīrtha situated in the mount of Veṅkatācala. Bhadrmati got salvation by this good deed.

"Donation of land is marked by high value in our tradition and scriptures and given by the kings and rulers, to the Brāhmins, the knower of the scriptures. Receiving and immediately giving away as donation exhibits his control over his greed – a quality, which a guṇa Brāhmin should have."

Nārada Purāṇa-2

Lesson: "Rites due to ancestors is the duty." *Tai. 2.*

Bhagīratha Prayatna. [Difficult Task]

Nārada Purāṇa relates the story of Bhagīrath, who brought the Ganges on the earth, from her abode in heaven.

There was a king named Sagara. He had two wives. The first one was Keśinī and the second was the daughter of the King of Vidarba, named Sumati. Sagara had no issues at all and so he prayed to sage Aurva, who was pleased and said that one of them will have one son and the other will have sixty thousand sons. Keśinī wanted one and the other wanted sixty thousand sons. In due course Keśinī gave birth to a son, named Asamañjasa and the other delivered a gourd inside of which there was a lump of meat. Sixty thousand sons were born from the gourd when that was kept in a pot with ghee. Sagara desired to perform Aśvamedha Yajnā and as practice the sixty thousand sons were made responsible to look after the sacrificial horse.

Indra stole the horse and kept it in the hermitage of sage Kapila, who was doing *tapa* in *Pātāla.* The sixty thousand sons set out in search of the horse and found it in the hermit of the sage. Thinking that Sage Kapila was the culprit they started ill-treating the sage for the theft. Enraged, the sage burnt them to ashes from the fire emanated from his eyes. Sagara entrusted the performance of funeral rites to Asamañjasa and died. Asamañjasa could not perform the rites in the absence of the bodies and asked his son Amśumān and in turn he transferred the responsibility to his son Bhagīratha. Bhagīratha did sever *tapas*, concentrating on mother Gańgā. The Devi appeared before him and asked to choose a boon. He requested the Devi to perform the funeral rites of his ancestors who are in ashes in *Pātāla.* Devi in reply said that the earth may not be able to withstand the powerful flow and he may pray to Lord Śiva to take it onto Him. Bhagīratha went to mount Kailāś and did penance for one thousand years. The Lord appeared in front of him and agreed to receive the rushing flow of Gańgā. Lord Śiva was aware of the conceit of Gańgā and to humble her, contained her in his matted hair. Not finding the flow of water for long Bhagīratha again meditated on Lord Śiva. Thus pleased, the Lord shook his matted hair and thus the Gańgā appeared on the earth. Because of the great effort of Bhagīrath, Gańgā is also known as Bhāgīrathī.

"A son is bound to discharge the debt of parents, by progeny and performance of ritual that saves them from hell. Bhagīratha accomplished his responsibility towards his ancestors and to the society. It was given to Bhagīratha to save millions and billions of souls, placed, in the circumstances in which his ancestors were. Ganges is the strength and life breath of our ***Vedic society****, a gift*

that can not be evaluated and compared. We owe our gratitude to Bhagīratha and proud to be in his lineage."

Garuda Purāṇa

Lesson: "Glorification of rituals." *Bṛ. IV. iv. 4-6.*

Vṛśtosarga Rites

This story of Vīravāhana was told by Lord Viṣṇu himself to Garuda to a question about performing *Vṛśtosarga* and the benefit of it. Vīravāhana was a righteous king and ruled according to scriptural dictates. One day he came to the hermitage of Vasiṣṭha, told him that he was scared of Yama and asked the safe way to overcome. The sage after explaining to the king about the Truth in the scriptures, told him that the best thing is to donate a bull. He said that it is known as *Vṛśtosarga* and on the eleventh day of the death it has to be done. In this connection the sage told him the story of Dharmavatsa. Dharmavatsa was a Brahmin, who was a great devotee of Lord Viṣṇu and highly religious. One day he went to the forest to bring some *Kuśa gras*s for his daily rituals, when four men abducted him and took away to a beautiful city. There he was brought before the king. The king started worshipping him and said that he was blessed. The surprised Brahmin asked the king for clarification. The king said he wanted to see all those who were fit to be worshipped. His minister told him the back ground behind that. In his earlier life, the king was a *Vaiśya,* named Viśvambhara, who worshipped Brahmins, donated alms, and looked after the needy. Once when he was returning from a pilgrimage, he happened to meet sage Lomāśa, and he enquired him about his pilgrimage. The sage also told him that all the pilgrimages are incomplete without *Vṛśtosarga* and asked Viśvambhara to perform the same.

Viśvambhara did as he was told and he had acquired a lot of merits, because of which, he was born as a prosperous king. Since the king could remember his previous birth, he liked the association of all virtuous people and so he asked his people to bring Dharmavatsa. After narrating the story sage Vasiṣṭḥa advised Vīravāhana to organize a *Vṛśtosarga.* Thus the Lord said that this particular ritual has got lots of virtues after leaving the body.

Padma Purāṇa

Lesson: "Blessings of elders and holy persons;

Obedience to the parents." *Tai I. xi. 3. BG. 4-34 & 17-14*

Salutations to the Elders and Superior Persons

Hindu tradition emphasizes to offer salutations to elders, parents, noble persons, monks and virtuous persons as means for fulfillment and is an act of merit. This narration is to illustrate its validity.

Mṛkaṇḍu, son of sage Bhṛgu did not have issues and he was worried as he can not discharge his indebtedness to his father, if he did not have any issues. It is said in the *Vedas* that the son protects the father from going to hell, known by the name '*pum*'. It is only possible when the son carries out the religious dictum of oblation and rituals for the father after his death. So the sage Mḳaṇḍu performed penance for several years to please Lord Śiva to get a son. Śiva appeared before him in person and asked him thus: "Do you desire to have a virtuous, wise and pious son, who would live only up to sixteen years or a dull witted, evil-natured son who would live long?" Mṛkaṇḍu chose the first alternative and soon a son was born. The son was named Mārkaṇḍeya and even from the boyhood the boy mastered all the *Vedas and Śāstras.* His pleasing manners got the approval of his teachers and the boy was liked by one and all. But the parents were sad and whenever they looked at the face of their son a gloom would descend over their face.

When the boy was five years old some holy men came to the sage's hermitage. The child offered salutations to the honored guests. Seeing the boy, the accomplished souls became worried and the sage Mṛkaṇḍu became uncomfortable, seeing the plight of the guests. When pressed for the reason one of the sages said "O sage! Your son is very handsome, intelligent and possesses great wisdom, but his life is short". Though Mṛkaṇḍu knew that, he still pondered over that and immediately performed the thread ceremony for the boy. He instructed him "O son! Whomever you find elder to you, unfailingly offer your salutations to them happily with reverence, whether he is known to you or not". The obedient boy very sincerely carried out the instructions of his father. Some times lapsed and one day by chance ***Saptaṛṣīs*** were passing through. Seeing them the child approached them, offered salutations to them and in the normal course of blessings the sages blessed *"dīrghāyuṣmān bhava"* – may you live long. Then when they saw the boy, they knew that the boy has got a very short life. The age, wealth, death and everything is fixed when the child is in the womb itself by *prārabdha.* Having realized the fact the *Saptharṣīs* propitiated Lord Śiva. The sixteenth year was fast approaching and one day unable to control their grief, the parents wept before the son. Mārkaṇḍeya asked them the reason and Mṛkaṇḍu with tears running down his cheeks told him the story. From that day onwards Mārkaṇḍya started performing penance. The boy was soon engrossed in severe austerities.

The day of his death came and the boy sat before the idol of Lord Śiva in deep meditation. The servants of the god of death could not approach Mārkaṇḍeya for the radiation from him was too hot for them. So Yama, the god of Death, himself came to fetch him. Mārkaṇḍeya cried loudly for help and embraced the *Liṅga* before him. Yama threw his rope in a loop and it went and circled round the *Liṅga* also. Angry Śiva rose from the idol, came down and killed Yama to save the child. Because of this, Śiva got the name Mṛtyuñjaya and Kāla kāla. Thereafter, at the request of the devas, Śiva gave life to Yama again and blessed Mārkaṇḍeya to be of sixteen years for ever.

The theme in this narration is the efficacy of obeying the father sincerely, happily and diligently. Thus one must go by his parents to reap a very rich harvest in future. The other point is that the Lord protects those, who surrender to him with faith and sincerity. One may see the Father of the universe in his own father. This body is the gift of the parents and offer salutations to them and obedience is an expression of gratitude to Lord through the mortal parents and and is a journey from finite to Infinitude.

Varāha Purāṇa

Lesson: "All actions belong to the *Prakṛti* but deluded one thinks 'I am doing'." *BG. III-27.*

Who Am I?

Raibhya and Vasu were the sons of Brahmā. Once both of them along with sage Añgiras went to Bṛhaspati, the teacher of Devas and asked several questions on the attainment of spiritual bliss. One of the questions was whether action was superior or Self Knowledge?

Bṛhaspati, as an answer to the question, narrated a very relevant story.

A pious and religious Brahmin, named *Samyamana,* once went to bathe in the river Ganges. At the spot, where he intended to take bath, a hunter named Niṣturaka was standing and catching the birds. Being a Brāhmin *Samyamana* could not stand the sight and the following conversation took place between the two.

Samyamana: "killing the birds is a cruel act and don't do such acts."

Niṣturaka: "Who am I to perform any act? How can I be a killer? I am the divine soul, which is also in these birds. If I think that I am performing any act, it would be wrong."

Then the hunter put up a fire. When the fire was blazing with several tongues, Niṣturaka asked *Samyamana* to choose one particular flame and put it out. *Samyamana* poured some water and the entire flame got put out. Then the hunter told *Samyamana* "Though the tongues of the flame appear to be different, actually they are one and the same fire only. Similarly, though the universe appears to be of different manifestations, in reality they are from the one Brahmān only and hence can not be differentiated. So, one must go about doing his duty, without the feeling of 'I am the doer'". This story had a tremendous effect on Raibhya and Vasu and they devoted themselves to penance.

"*Action and knowledge are not separable as action leads to the knowledge and are the two sides of the same coin. If there is any difference, it is the mental make up [the perception]. Action prepares for self knowledge, providing necessary base – that is the purity of mind, thus the superiority and inferiority is a misnomer.*

Vāyu Purāṇa

Lesson: "That fool, who outwardly controlling the organs of actions, but keeps dwelling on the sense objects with the mind is a hypocrite," *BG. 3.6.*

Intention and not Action is Important

Suvṛta and Bṛhadratha were the two sons of a Brāhmin named Suśīl. One day both the brothers were walking in heavy rain and happened to take shelter in a house. Unfortunately the house was that of an immoral woman. Both had planned to go to worship Lord Kṛṣṇa as that day happened to be *Janmāṣṭhami.* One of the brothers preferred to stay there and not to go to the temple. So he asked his brother to follow him but the other brother did not share the view and proceeded to the temple, to be blessed. The brother in the house of the immoral woman was mentally imaging the rituals, being conducted at the temple and was cursing himself for the foolish and unfortunate decision he had taken to stay back at the woman's house, to enjoy the filth.

On the other hand, the brother who had proceeded to the temple was constantly thinking about the enjoyment his brother was having and was undergoing the routine of the rituals in the temple mechanically. Next morning when both were returning home, they died on the way due to thunderbolt. The servants of the Lord came to take Suvṛta, who had passed the previous night in the house and the servants of the Lord of death came to pick up Bṛhadratha. Suvṛta told the servants of the Lord that they were mistaken as his brother had spent the night in the temple, doing meritorious acts. The servants of the Lord replied "neither we are doing mistake nor it is injustice. There is a subtle difference in the mental and physical performance. Mental attitude is more substantial and real than the physical, machine like activities. Your brother was though in temple, was mentally engaged in playing with the immoral woman, whereas you, though were physically present in the house, mentally you were in the service of the Lord. Thus you are only the performer of merits and entitled to the end result, to be one with the Lord".

"We have seen our religious teachers giving credit to mental perception and prescription. Karma yoga is a mental fixture; liberation and bondage too are mental attitudes. The whole scripture is meant to own one self, mentally against the background of what we experience and understand in this relative world. Eyes see sun rise and sun set, but the mind knows that it is not true and it is the earth, that rotates and not the sun."

Liṅga Purāṇa

Lesson: "Forgiveness is divine." *Bṛ. 16.3.*

Parāśara

A king named Kalmaṣapāda became a demon due to a curse and a demon named Rudhira entered his body. Once when Śakti, son of sage Vasiṣṭha was walking on a narrow path, Kalmaṣapāda crossed him. When Kalmaṣapāda wanted the way, Śakti told him that he had a right to go first, being a Brāhmaṇa. As a demon, he ate up the son of Vasiṣṭha, and all his brothers. Unable to bear the loss of his sons, sage Vasiṣṭha along with his wife Arundhatī wanted to commit suicide by jumping from the mountain, but the earth, in the form of a woman requested them to desist from such an attempt. Adṛśyantī, wife of Śakti also dissuaded them by telling that she would become the mother of Śakti's son. At that time the baby from the womb started chanting *Vedas*. Lord Viṣṇu also appeared and told Vasiṣṭha that his grandson would be a great devotee of Śiva. The boy was named Parāśara. When the boy grew up, he wanted to know about his father and Vasiṣṭha told him that his father had been eaten up by a demon. Angered by this Parāśara said he would acquire such powers to burn up the universe, but Vasiṣṭha asked him to desist from such ideas. Parāśara prayed to Śiva and Śiva was pleased and granted him some special powers. Parāsara, with these powers could talk to his father. He used his special powers to burn up demons, but Vasiṣṭha told him to stop such destruction. Parāsara followed his advice and was blessed that he would compose Purāṇas. Kṛṣṇa Dvaipāyana was his son – Vyāsācārya.

"Committing sucide is a sin. Patience bears the fruit of peace and justice. Forgiveness is a divine virtue, which is very hard to attain. But if one attains, he has won over the enemies and also hold the key to divine treasures."

Śkanda Purāṇa

Lesson: "He alone is the doer through all hands."

BG. 3.27. & 13. 13.

Lord Jagannāth – Puri Temple

It is said that Viṣṇu is manifest predominantly at Puri. Here is the version of Purāṇa as how the temple of Jagannāth was built. In the solar dynasty there was a king named Indradyumna, who was very devoted and righteous. He had performed many yajñas and always used to see the Lord through his mental eyes, but had a longing to see the Lord, in the form before him. A well studied man suggested to him to go to *Puruṣottama kṣetra,* in Odra [Orissa], along the Nīlgri hills. During the journey through the difficult terrains, he visited so many holy places and finally arrived at *Purṣottama kṣetra.* The king had performed many *Yajnas* there and waited upon to worship the Lord, but the Lord was hidden in the sand, which disappointed the king very much. He decided to go on fast unto death at the foot of the hills. At that time a celestial voice was heard saying "you shall see Him". The king then built a temple and installed the *Narasimha murtī,* brought by sage Nārada. That night he dreamt Lord Viṣṇu. At the dawn, he was informed by his sentries that a fragrant log had been sighted at the sea shore with the marks of *cakra and śańka,* the weapons of Lord Viṣṇu. Sage Nārada, who had come to attend the *yajna,* suggested establishing it on a pedestal. It was done but the king was worried as to who would make the image of Viṣṇu? At that point of time a celestial voice said that the Lord himself would appear in the form of an old carpenter, and suggested that the pedestal may be closed from all the four sides. None should be allowed to see. Next morning an old carpenter appeared, who was allowed to mount the pedestal and do the work in the enclosed area. After fifteen days there were three wooden images, that of Kṛṣṇa, Balarām and Subhadrā. Again a celestial voice suggested that the images should be clothed and then only be worshipped. That is how the wooden image is worshipped in Puri.

'It has been emphasized in Gīta that all actions belong to Prakṛti, the hand maid of Lord. Ignorant one attributes to himself, not knowing that even the thought, memory and their disappearance too are according to His wish. He is the eye of the eyes, ear of the ears and behind all hands and legs." *Bhagavad-Gītā.*

Agni Purāṇa

Lesson: "Thoughts at the time of death influence the next birth. [Type of body]" *BG. 8.6.*

Discussion between Jada Bharata and King Sauvīra:

This is a very famous and often quoted incident of sage Jada Bharata, who was performing penance in the secluded river bank. One day a thirsty pregnant deer came to drink water and hearing the roar of a lion from behind the deer ran for life. Due to fear, the deer delivered a child which fell into the river. Bharata happened to see the new born deer floating in the river and brought it to the *āśrama.* Jada Bharata became very much attached to it. Years went by and Bharata became old and died with the thought of the deer in his mind. Because he died with the thought of the deer, he was reborn as a deer. But even as the deer, he was aware of his previous birth and also the knowledge he had gained and was sorry for having wasted the human life. The deer bathed daily in the river and died in the river bank. The next birth was in the family of a Brāhmin with two wives and was born as the son of the second wife. Bharata became a puppet in the hands of his brothers and was ill treated. One day when he was keeping watch over the field of his brothers the *caṇḍālas* took him away to be offered as *narabali.* Mother Kāli was astounded to find such a learned person and devoured the *caṇḍālas* to release Bharata. While walking back he was picked up by the palanquin bearers of king Sauvīra, to carry the palanquin. As his step was not matching the others, the palanquin was shaking badly and the king got angry. The king asked him "you are hale and healthy. Are you not interested in carrying me [the palanquin]?"

Bharata replied "O king! Neither am I fat nor am I carrying your palanquin, nor tired, nor doing labor. There are two feet, over that there are the thighs and the upper body and over that the palanquin. In that your body is there. Where is the load on me? In reality what you say that you are in the palanquin and I am on the ground is not true. All bodies are caused by the five elements and they too are influenced by the attributes following the stream of flow. From the point of body all are the results of past action. The names and forms all are false. You are king, son of your father, husband of your wife, enemy of your enemy. By what name shall I address you, O king! Are you head, body or leg? None of them. All are separate from you. Now think over and tell me, who am I?"

Having been so addressed by the Brāhmin, one of the bearers of the palanquin [Jada Bharata] the king said to the embodiment of wisdom "O Brāhmin, I was on my way to Kapila muni for liberation. Now you are the same on this earth for me. Kindly instruct me". The Brāhmin said "O king! Please listen. Service to others is the service to the Self. People prostrate to the Gods for wealth, son, kingdom etc. Does that give what is in identity between Self and the God? After getting that there is nothing in the world to be sought. Kindly give your attention to the story of Nidāgha and Ṛbhu.

Ṛbhu was the son of Brahmāji and Nidāgha was the son of sage Pulastya and accepted the discipleship of Nidāgha. On completion of the study under Ṛhbu the student went away to live on the banks of river Devikā. Thousand years passed and one day Ṛbhu went to see

Nidāgha, who after partaking the food from his disciple Balivaiśvadev, said “I am satisfied as the food only grants satisfaction”. And he enquired the other guests also whether they were satisfied. Ṛbhu said “the question of satisfaction arises only to those who are hungry and thirsty. Whereas the Ātmā I am, free from these. Dear disciple! I came to impart some knowledge. Let there be no difference as everything is unto Lord Vāsudeva.”

After one thousand years again, Ṛbhu visited his disciple, he found Nidāgha, standing alone. He enquired “why are you standing alone”? Nidāgha said O Brahmān! There is a crowd standing on the way since the king is entering into the city and so I thought of waiting a little”. Ṛbhu replied “Brahmān, you know all about this place. Kindly tell me who the king is and who are others?” Nidāgha immediately climbed over Ṛbhu and said “I am sitting over you like the king and below me you are standing like elephant”. Ṛhbu said “now what can I say who am I and what I am to you”. Nidādha fell at his feet and said that “you are my teacher”. Ṛhbu said “I came to tell you of Brahmān and Ātmā is not the body and its complexes, it is one and is in everybody’s body.”

“This is a most wonderful talk and through the discussions the Absolute has been revealed. The Ātmā is not the body and body related objects. Atmā is one and in all the bodies. The Consciousness is one and the same in different bodies. The next body is decided by the thoughts one had at the point of leaving the body.”

Ātma-anātma viveka –Upaniśad

Thoughts at the time of death. – Bhagavad-Gītā

Matsya Purāṇa

Lesson: "The varieties in the world are the outcome of men's diverse past work."*Tai. III. iv. 1, also Kath. I. iii. 7-8.*

Goal of Human Life

Sage Kauśikā had seven sons and he sent all his sons to sage Garga to study the scriptures as was the practice, where they serve the teacher and also learn. When they were with their teacher, there was a severe famine and people were finding it difficult even for one meal. The teacher ordered the seven brothers to take the cattle to the forest for grazing. The brothers took the cattle to the forest so that they can graze where some grass could be found. In the forest the brothers felt very hungry and the eldest suggested that they could kill one cow and eat it. The youngest one objected to this and said that at least they should perform the funeral rites and then kill the cow. Other brothers too supported so accordingly they performed the funeral rites of the cow and then ate it. When they returned to the teacher they told him that one cow had been killed by a wild animal and the teacher did not doubt their statement. But killing of a cow is a great sin and they had to suffer for that. So in their next birth they were born as hunters. But they were given to remember their early birth, so they were disgusted in leading the life of a hunter. So they fasted and died. The next birth for them was deer and because of their power to remember their earlier births, they were not interested to be a deer, so fasted and died. Again they were born as birds and four of the brothers remain detached and spent their time in meditation. But the other three were different. Once, the king Vibhraja of Pañcāla had come to the forest for hunting. One of the three brothers was impressed by the power wielded by the king and wanted to be born as a king. The other two brothers were impressed by the ministers and wanted to be born as ministers. So the one who wanted to become a king was born as the son of king Vibhraja, named Brahmādatta and the other two were born as the sons of the ministers. The other four brothers were born as the sons of a brāhmaṇa named Sudaridra. Brahmādatta married Kalyāṇī, who, in her earlier birth, was the same cow whom the seven brothers had slaughtered. Brahmādatta had the knowledge of understanding the languages of all living beings. One day when he was taking a promenade along with his wife, he happened to hear the conversation of a male and female ant. The conversation was like this:

Male ant: "why are you angry with me? Why are you not talking to me?

Female ant: "do not pester me. I don't want to talk to you. Yesterday when you got few grains of sugar, you gave it to the other ant and not to me".

Male ant: "I am awfully sorry, because I thought it was you. I am sorry. I wouldn't do like this in future. Please smile".

When Brahmādatta heard this conversation, he laughed. His wife asked him the reason for his laughing and Brahmādatta told her the entire conversation, but she would not believe him as she thought that he was laughing at her. Any amount of persuasion did not work and it was bothering the king. In his dream Viṣṇu came and told him to wait till tomorrow morning when his mind would be at rest. The other four brothers wanted to go away to forest to meditate but their father objected to it on the pretext that they had to support him. The brothers told Sudaridra to go to the king and ask for wealth and he would give it. They told him to tell the king to remember sage Garga, the hunters, the deer and the birds. It was next morning when the Brahmādatta had the dream. Sudridra approached him and when he heard the Brāhmaṇa, he remembered his early life, which he had forgotten in his material pursuit. He gave enough wealth to Sudridra, handed over the kingdom to his son and left for the forest. The other two brothers, who were the sons of ministers also left with him to pursue the goal of life.

"The incidents are all about the validity of rebirth and that too according to the karma. [Actions of the previous birth] Probably in Satya Yuga, persons with some good samskāras were given the power to remember the earlier births, when sins were of lesser magnitude. But in kali Yuga the prārabdha is complex and sańcita karmas are very heavy and huge. Thus atonement in one birth becomes difficult."

Trust in God and do the right.

Kūrma Purāṇa

Lesson: "Good and bad through the work alone."

Bṛ. III. ii. 13.

King Durjaya and Urvaśī

One can miss the way. Wrong done must be atoned.

Durjaya was a king, who was righteous and learned. He had a beautiful wife. One day the king went to the banks of river Kālindi, there he met an *apsarā* named Urvaśī and he fell in love with her, which resulted in marriage. Durjaya lived with her for many years, forgetting his kingdom, wife etc. Suddenly one day he remembered them and wanted to go, but Urvaśī would not allow.

Finally he was allowed to go on condition that he would not have any connection with any other woman. When Durjaya reached his kingdom, he remembered his promise and avoided his wife. When asked by his wife even persistently, he was evasive, but his wife found out the cause. She told him that he had sinned and so he had to do penance. The king consulted the sage Kaṇva and he suggested that he should go to Himalayas and meditate. On his way to Himalayas he met a *gandharva* king who was wearing a beautiful garland and he remembered Urvaśī. He imagined that the garland would look beautiful on her neck. He fought with the *gandharva,* obtained the garland and went to Kālindi River, but he could not find her. After a great search he found her on the shores of the lake Mānasa. He gave her the garland and started living with her. After some time Urvaśī asked Durjaya about his kingdom and Durjaya told her what happened. Hearing this, she told him that he should go away as otherwise they would be cursed by his wife. The king was so mad after her that he refused. To compel him to go away, Urvaśī made herself an ugly woman and Durjaya got disgusted and left. He did hard penance for twenty four years and went to sage Kaṇva and informed him of everything. Sage Kaṇva appreciated his penance but said that since his sin was severe he had to go to Vārāṇasī and live there. Durjaya obeyed the instructions of the sage and finally got rid of his sins.

"The sense organs are so strong that it can rock the boat and take one to the bottom, if not checked from time to time. The desire for sense pleasures is hidden in the bottom like smoking fire, to consume one's steadfastness in the disciplined life. Lust is the enemy and one must be always alert and never give to its delusion."

CHAPTER III

Section I

Contents in Capsule

The Legends

Introduction

There is something to be known about the actions prescribed and the actions that are prohibited as also about inaction. People seeking fruits of actions worship the Gods, in this world and, for in this world of men the fruits of action come the same way as worshipped. Now it is left to the worshipper, as to what he should worship. He accepts all the ways.

A cricket ball soars up in the sky, to the extent the momentum imparted to it. A tree grows up in time with its inherent vitality. A lotus shoots up along with the rise in the water level in the pond. Similarly man rises in his worth and attainment corresponding to the *Dharma* with which he is endowed with, nothing more or less to it. The characters fuelled through transmigration find their expressions and if it happened to be of far distant part it is Purāṇa. When this is committed to a particular thought, the sectarian way of life, it is *Paurāṇic kathā.*

Purāṇas Devoted to the Exploits of Brahmā

Brahmā Purāṇa

The Brahmā Purāṇa now available appears more as compilation of chapters taken from other Purāṇas like Viṣṇu Purāṇa, Mārkaṇḍeya Purāṇa etc. But still it contains original material also. It deals mainly with the glorification of shrines and holy places. The contents can be summarized as follows: Creation, geography, Dakṣa's sacrifice, places of pilgrimage, story of Śrī Kṛṣṇa, some *avatārs* and Sāṃkhya and yoga philosophy. This Purāṇa is supposed to have about nine thousand verses and the period of composition is – 1300 A.D.

Romaharṣaṇa [Lomaharṣaṇa], a disciple of Veda Vyāsa tells the assembly of sages, who had come to participate in the sacrifice held in *Naimiṣāraṇya* forest. The sacrifice was arranged by the sages [*maharṣīs]* and went on for twelve years. Romaharṣaṇa says "All over water and water, divine being in sleep – *Nāra* – water and *ayana* – bed – Nārāyaṇa. Came out of golden egg by itself [*svayambhu*] after being inside the egg for one year. The creation thus came into being – the earth, the heaven and also sky, directions, time and senses.

The seven sages created were Marīci, Atri, Aṅgīras, Pulastya, Pulaha, Kratu, and Vasiṣṭha together with Rudra and Sanat Kumāra. *Svayambhuva Manu* - the male principle and *Śatarūpā* – the female principle were created. So the descendents from Manu are known as *Mānava.* Vīra, Priyavrata and Uttānpāda, were the three sons of Manu and Śatarūpā. Dhruva was the son of Uttānpāda. Prācīnabarhis who, belong to the Dhruva lineage had ten sons, who were known as Pracetās, were supposed to rule but were not interested and went away to the forest for penance and austerity, thus the earth was left with no one to rule and sufferings surfaced everywhere. Beautiful woman Mārīṣa, daughter of the trees was married to Pracetās, and Dakṣa was born – the Prajāpati. Dakṣa's wife Asiknī gave birth to five thousand sons, known as Haryaṣvas, who went away to explore the earth on the advice of Śri Nārada and did not return. The second batch of five thousand too met with similar instance. Dakṣa was enraged but was calmed down on the formula that his daughter Priyā, when married to Brahmā should bear Śri Nārada as her son. From, sixty daughters of Dakṣa, ten to Dharma, thirteen to the sage Kaśyapa, twenty seven to Soma and the rest were married to the sages Ariṣṭanemi, Bahuputra, Aṅgīras and Kṛśāśva – thus the creation went on. Aditi's sons were twelve gods. Diti's sons were demons, including Hiraṇyākśa and Hiraṇyakaśipu and others.

Marut

Diti, the mother of *Daityas* wanted a son to be born to kill the Indra to avenge the deaths of her own sons but could not keep up with the *Vrata;* prescribed by her husband Kaśyapa, that was washing the feet before going to bed and braiding the hair. Indra managed to cut the child in the womb into seven parts x seven parts and while they were crying, Indra said "mā ruda" meaning 'don't cry' and these forty nine sections came to be known as 'Māruts'. They followed indra, as envisaged in the conditional boon granted to her. *Vam 71.*

King Pṛthu

King Anga was religious but not his son Vena, who picked up evil characters. The sages physically caught hold of Vena. From kneading the right thigh, came Niṣāda – a dwarf and horrible creature and kneading the right arm emerged Pṛthu, a flaming fire and his energy lit up the four quarters, had bow in hand and beautiful armors. On the birth of the Pṛthu Vena died. To anoint Pṛthu all rivers and oceans came with their holy waters and jewels. Gods and sages also came to bless. Brāhmaṇas crowned Pṛthu as the king of the earth and also entrusted the Lordship of other regions, such as Soma was appointed over creepers and herbs, stars, planets etc. Varuṇa as the Lord of the oceans, Kubera as chief of all the Kings, Viṣṇu of the Ādityas, Agni of Vasus, Dakṣa of all Prajāpatis, Indra of Māruts, Prahlāda of Daityas, Śiva of Yakshas, Samudra of rivers and so on. Having come to know the future deeds of Pṛthu, the Sūtas and Magadhas composed many praises. King Pṛthu, with his bow and arrow leveled the barren earth and in the form of cow, made to yield food grains. Agriculture, horticulture and animal husbandry became prosperous. Villages and cities came to stay. There was all round prosperity and happiness. Subjects were given their dues in sustenance and development. With these deeds of Pṛthu only, the earth came to be called as 'Pṛthvī.' *Vis- 18-22.*

Kuvalaśva

He was the son of Bṛhadaśva a descendent of Kakutstha. Bṛhadaśva wanted to retire and hand over the kingdom to his son, but a sage named Utaṅka requested him not to, because a demon named Dhundhu, living under the sand was troubling him very much. But the king said that his son Kuvalaśva was capable of handling the demon and he proceeded to forest. Kuvalaśva went with his hundred sons and fought the demon and killed him. But in the fight Kuvalaśva lost all but three of his sons.*MB – vana parva 201 -205.*

Temple for Sun God

On the shores of the ocean, there is a land called Utkala, now known as Orissa. That land was occupied by Brāhmins and religious people. There is an image of Lord Sūrya and it is known as *Koṇḍāditya*. It is a wonderful temple and though the surroundings are full of sand, still trees grow. It is said that if one prays to Lord Sūrya, according to the prescribed rituals, one can get rid of all the sins.

Witness of the Deluge

Once when the cyclic *Pralaya* took place, by the grace of Lord Viṣṇu, sage Mārkaṇḍeya could witness it. It was darkness all over and there was rain of meteors and fire and all the living beings perished. After that there was continuous hail storm and it spared nothing. Sage Mārkaṇḍeya was meditating on Lord Viṣṇu, but had fear in the mind. Then he heard a voice, telling him not to fear. He continued his meditation and after some time he was surprised to see a small child sleeping on a golden bed on a banyan tree and floating. The child asked the sage to enter him as he was seeking a refuge and before the sage could react, he entered the child. The sage could see all the regions, oceans and the entire creation in the stomach. Baffled he again started praying and then he came out of the boy's mouth and Viṣṇu appeared and blessed. He gave a boon that he would build a temple for Śiva in the *Puruṣottama Kṣetra* and that temple is known as Lord *Bhuvaneśvara.* *Bh. 10-8 to 11.*

Granting life

Satya Yuga was a wonderful period, when people were very happy, there was no infant mortality and people lived for thousand years and more. During the reign of King Śveta, living was all the more pleasant as he was highly religious and was constantly working for the welfare of the people. But unfortunately a sage named Kapālagautama lost his infant child and he brought the dead body to the king and wanted him to give life to the child. The grief stricken king vowed that he would immolate himself if he was not able to bring back the child to life within one week and he prayed to Lord Śiva with one thousand flowers of blue lotus. The boy was brought back to life. King Śveta also had the credit of building a temple for Viṣṇu in Puruṣottam Kṣetra which is known as Śvetamādhava temple. *MB. Sh. 115,153,133.*

Gautamī Gańgā

It is generally known that the river Gañgā was brought to the earth by Bhaghīrath but it is seldom known that a part of it was brought by Sage Gautama. Gañgā was Mother Pāravtī's sister and she wanted that Gañgā should be far off from Lord Śiva. Gaṇeś too wanted that his mother should be happy and schemed to remove Gañgā. There was a severe famine and it was difficult to survive, but Gautama had the river flowing in his hermitage. So he asked other sages also to come and live in his hermitage. Ganeś made good acquaintance with the other sages. He had asked Jayā, companion of Pārvatī to come in the form of a cow and eat the grains. She was also instructed that she should fall and die even with a small beat. When the sage Gautama saw that a cow was eating the grains, he took a stick and just tapped the cow. The cow fell down and died. It was a terrible sin to kill a cow and

Ganeś suggested that Gautama should do penance, by bringing down Gaṅgā and the sages also nodded their heads. Sage Gautama went to Himalayas, did penance, pleased Śiva and brought down the Gaṅgā.

Bath in the Gautamī Gaṅgā

Viṣṇu always sleep in the bed of the serpent named Ananta and he had a son named Maṇīnāg. Garuda is the vehicle of Lord Viṣṇu, but Garuda is the enemy of all snakes. Maṇināga wanted protection from Garuda, so prayed to Śiva and got the boon that Garuda would do no harm to him. Garuda was surprised to see Maṇināga roaming without fear and so kept him under his custody. Śiva's companion Nandi noticed that Maṇīnāga was not to be seen and hence on the advice of Śiva prayed to Lord Viṣnu and Viṣṇu in turn advised Garuda to release Maṇīnāga. Unhappy Garuda told Viṣṇu that, he being his strength it was unfair on the part of Viṣṇu to suggest such things. The Lord agreed that Garuda was his strength and asked him to bear the weight of his little finger and placed it on his neck and Garuda was crushed. Garuda apologized and asked the Lord a way to get his original form. It was suggested to pray to Lord .Śiva and Śiva advised Garuda to bathe in Gautamīgaṅgā and Garuda got back not only his form but also vigor.

Distress Time

Once there was a severe famine and there was nothing to be found to eat. At that time of famine sage Viśvāmitra came to the banks of the river Gautamī Gañgā with his family and disciples. Everyone was very hungry and the sage asked his disciples to look for some food. After searching, the disciples came back with a dead dog and said that they could not find anything else. The sage said that at the time of distress, when there was no alternative, the dog's meat could be consumed. He told them to wash it well, offer it to the gods and ancestors and then can be partaken. Indra could not stand the offering of dog's meat so took the form of a vulture and took away the meat. Viśvāmitra knew and was about to curse Indra, when he brought it back with *amṛta* but the sage refused to accept it, saying that at the time of distress it was not wrong. Seeing that there was no other alternative Indra arranged for rain. *M. B. Śp. Ch. 141.*

Power of Devotion

A Brāhmaṇa named Śveta was an ardent devotee of Lord Śiva and had his hermitage on the banks of the river Gautamī Gaṅgā. Death came over Śveta and the messangers of Lord of death came there, but could not enter the house, as Śiva himself was present there. After waiting for some time Yama sent his assistant named Mṛtyu to find out what had happened. Mṛtyu arrived at the scene and when he saw the Śiva's assistants he told them that he had come to take Śveta and threw the noose around Śveta's body, but he was killed by Śiva's assistants. This led to a full scale war and in the fight yama too was killed by Kārtikeya. Lord Śiva insisted that his devotees would not go to Yama but straight to heaven. As there was no other solution, it was agreed. Then water from Gautamī Gaṅgā was brought and sprinkled over Yama's body and Yama was revived.

Grabbing of Laṅkā

Sage Viśravas had two wives. Kubera was the son of first wife and Rāvaṇa, Kumbhakarṇa and Vibhīṣaṇa were the sons of second wife. Kubera was ruling over Laṅkā and was prosperous, but this was not liked by the second wife, who instigated her sons against Kubera. Rāvaṇa and his brothers did penance to please Brahmā and Brahmā granted them boon that they could win over Laṅkā. Armed with this boon Rāvaṇa won over Kubera and drove him out. He also warned that anybody who gave shelter to Kubera would be punished. Kubera approached his grandfather sage Pulastya. Pulastya advised him to pray to Śiva on the banks of Gautamī Gaṅgā. Śiva pleased with his devotion made him the god of wealth. *MB. Vp. ch 275.*

Further Glory of Gautamī Gaṅgā

Hariścandra was a king from the dynasty of Ikṣvāku. He got a son with the blessings of Varuṇa on the condition that the child would be sacrificed in a yajnā, to be performed to please Varuṇa. But Hariścandra was postponing the sacrifice on some pretext or other. One day Rohit, son of Hariścandra overheard the conversation between his father and Varuṇa and said that he himself wanted to perform a sacrifice in honor of Viṣṇu, so went to perform austerity. But Varuṇa afflicted Hariścandra with stomach ailment. Hearing about father's ailment Rohit bought the third son of a Brāhmaṇa, to be sacrificed in his place, but Hariścandra would not agree to the proposal. But a divine advice came that performing the sacrifice on the banks of Gautamī Gaṅgā did not require any sacrifice,as it is very holy.

Faith in Penance

Vṛddhagautama was the son of sage Gautama. He too was a sage but with physical deformity and hence he would not mingle with anybody. But he knew some *mantras,* which he would always repeat and he also used to worship *Agni devatā.* Due to his physical infirmity, he was moving from place to place. Once, while wandering, he found a beautiful cave and thought that he could make it his place of living. When he entered the cave, he found a very old lady with wasted body, due to rigorous austerity. When he was about to prostrate to her she restrained him, telling he was her guru. Vṛddhagautama being younger, he was confused and asked her the reason for making him *guru,* when he had not seen her at all. She said that she was the daughter of an *apsarā* but unfortunately she had left her in the cave telling that whosoever entered the cave would be her husband. He refused to marry her on the pretext that he was younger than her and also ugly. She threatened to commit suicide and said that because of her *tapasyā* she could make him handsome and a learned one. He married her when he became handsome due to the power of her *tapasyā.* Once many sages came to visit them and among them some taunted them, asking whether Vṛddhagautama was her son or grandson. The couples felt bad and sought the advice of sage Agastya. Agastya suggested to them to bathe in the river Gautamī Gaṅgā and when they had a dip, with prayer to Lord Śiva and Viṣṇu, they became young and pretty.

Revenge for Father's Death

Dadhīci was a highly revered and learned sage and because of his power due to austerity people used to keep off his hermitage. Once gods left their weapons with Dadhīci after victory over the demons and did not claim it for long but when they claimed, the weapons had lost their luster. So the sage had to offer his body to make weapons for gods. Sage Dadhīci's wife Lopāmudrā was very unhappy with this incident and she wanted to immolate herself but restrained as she was pregnant.

After the baby was born, she handed over the child to a pippla tree and committed suicide. The boy was called PIppalāda because he was brought up by the pippala tree. When the boy grew up he wanted to know about his parentage and the tree told him about his parents. Pippalāda wanted to take revenge for his parents' untimely end and consulted Candra. Candra suggested to him to go to the banks of Gautamī Gañgā and pray to Lord Śiva. Having pleased Lord Śiva, he was told by the Lord that when he was able to see his third eye, his wish would be granted. Pippalāda had to continue his austerity again and when he saw Śiva's third eye, a demon appeared from the eye. He wanted to know what was expected of him. Pippalāda told the demon to kill the gods and the demon came to kill him. When asked for the reason, the demon told him because Pippalāda's body was created by gods. Pippalāda ran to Lord Śiva. The Lord told him to go to a certain forest and live there, where the demon can not enter. When gods approached Lord Śiva for protection, the Lord convinced Pippalāda that revenge would not serve any purpose and Pippalāda agreed and he wanted to see his parents. By Śiva's grace, he could see them and had their blessings.

MB. Ch -100.

Prince in the form of a Snake

Śūrasena was the king, who had a son after a lot of austerities, but the son had the form of a snake. The parents were very remorse about it but they kept it a secret. The son who was in the form of a snake was named as Nāgeśvar. But Nāgeśvar was able to converse like humans and he became fully lẹarned. He became desirous of getting married. With the help of the minister Nageśvar was married to a princess without telling her that he had the form of a snake. The marriage was held as per the custom of Kṣhatriyas and the marriage was performed with his sword. After the marriage, when the princess arrived at the palace, she was told by a maid that her husband was god and now was in the form of a snake. When Nāgeśvar saw the princess Bhogavati he remembered his past life that he was a snake as a companion of Śiva and due to a curse he was sent to the earth. He recounted this to his wife and she too remembered her past. Both of them went, bathed in Goutamī Gañgā; and obtained a handsome and divine form. *Brah. 111.*

Brahmā's Fifth Head

Once there was a war between gods and demons in which gods were defeated. They went to Śiva on the advice of Brahmā. Śiva drove the demons to the end of earth. During the fight, whenever a drop of sweat fell from Śiva's forehead, an ogress appeared, known as *matris,* who too fought the demons and drove them away. While the demons were running Brahmā's fifth head, which had the shape of a donkey's head asked them to come and fight and that he would help them. Alarmed by the change of events, the gods ran to Viṣṇu and asked him to cut off the fifth head of Brahmā but Viṣṇu said that only Śiva could do it. Śiva cut off the fifth head of Brahmā but the earth refused to bear the chopped off head and so Śiva had to bear it.

Fight Between Birds

A pair of owl and a pair of dove had long standing enmity and always quarreled among themselves. The doves were supported by Yama and the owls by Agni. They were supplied weapons by both the gods and when the quarrel threatened to destroy peace, both yama and Agni intervened and made them to forget their enmity. The place where they lived is known as *yamyatirtha and agnitirtha.*

True devotion

A sage named Veda used to worship a Śivaliṅga, everyday till afternoon and then went to beg for alms. There was also a hunter by name Bhilla who used to make offerings to the Liṅga by way of whatever he had hunted. Veda was surprised to see that everyday his offering to the Liṅga was scattered away and a piece of meat was found. As both of them never met each other Veda was curious to find out and one day he was hiding to see what was happening. As usual Bhilla came with his offerings and Śiva appeared before him and asked "why are you late? I was waiting for you". Veda became furious and after Bhilla left he asked Śiva "this is great injustice. He is a hunter and a cruel man. I performed austerity for so many years and you never appeared. I am going to break the Śiva liṅga". The Lord said "you wait till tomorrow". The next day Bhilla came and found that blood was oozing out from the *liṅga* for which he considered himself to be responsible. He started hurting himself with the arrow. Then the Lord appeared and said "you see the difference. You gave me offerings, but Bhilla has offered his whole soul". The place where Bhilla used to pray is known as *bhillatirtha.*

Friendship

Gautama was a Brāhmin and Maṇikuṇḍala a Vaiśya. The latter was a follower of *dharma,* whereas Gautama had opposite opinion about *dharma.* Gautama's aim was to cheat his friend so he suggested that they go to other places for trade and Maṇikuṇḍala agreed reluctantly. On the way Gautama was always telling that those who follow *dharma* suffer, but Maṇikuṇḍala would not agree. To resolve this, they had a bet that whoever loses the bet should surrender their wealth. They asked many people and the opinion was that those who follow *dharma* suffer and Maṇikuṇḍala gave away all his wealth. The friends had two more bets on the same point and Maṇikuṇḍala lost the bet and lost his hands and eyes, but he would not change his opinion about *dharma*. Gautama left his friend alone and Maṇikuṇḍala was lying on the banks of Gautamī Gañgā. There was a Viṣṇu temple where Vibhīṣaṇa used to come every evening for prayer and his son found Maṇikuṇḍala. Vibhīṣaṇa knew the herb, which brought back to life Lakṣmaṇa and with the same herbs Maṇikuṇḍala could get back his eyes and arms. Now Maṇikuṇḍala could travel and he came to a city, where the princess was blind. The king wanted her to be cured. Maṇikuṇḍala could cure her with the same herbs and was married to the princess. Many years later Gautama was caught by the soldiers for committing some crime and was brought before Maṇikuṇḍala and he could recognize his friend. He was pardoned and was given some wealth too.

Power of Delusion

Kaṇḍu was the name of a great sage, who had a hermitage on the banks of Gautamī Gañgā and he performed severe austerities, irrespective of the climatic conditions. Indra sent a nymph named Pramloca to Kaṇḍu to distract him from the penance. Pramloca with her enticing manners won the heart of the sage The sage married her and went to Mandāra to live. A hundred years passed away and Pramloca sought the permission of the sage to go back, but the sage asked her to stay for some more time. Like this centuries passed away but the sage did not lose the amour. One evening the sage stepped out of his hermitage and Pramloca asked him where was he going.

The sage: "The sun is going to set. I am going to do my evening prayer. I don't want a break in that."

Pramloca: "Is the sun setting for you only today? Sun set of hundreds of years have gone by."

Sage: "Dear, you have come only this morning. I have seen you today only. What is the truth?"

Pramloca: "it is nine hundred years since I came here".

The sage became angry and scolded Pramloca. He understood the time wasted and asked her to go back. She was pregnant at that time and when she was traveling on the sky, the embryo fell on the trees and that child was *Māriṣa*. *Vis Ch. 15.*

Caṇdāla and Brahmā Rākṣasa

A *caṇdāla* is an outcaste. Once there was a *caṇdāla* but he was very much devoted to Viṣṇu. He used to fast on the eleventh lunar day and sing praises of Lord in the night. On one such *Ekādaśi d*ay after fasting he went to the bank of river Kṣiprā to pluck flowers, where a *Brahmārākṣasa* [demon] was living and he wanted to eat the *caṇdāla*. *Caṇdāla* promised to come back after finishing his prayer in the temple and he kept up his promise. The demon was surprised at his arrival and asked for some of the *Puṇya* he had accumulated. The demon told him his story that he was a *Brāhmaṇa,* but born as a demon because he performed the duties of a priest without having the sacred thread and as such became a demon. The *caṇḍāla* parted with part of his *Puṇya* and the demon was freed. After some time the *caṇḍāla* went on a pilgrimage. During that time he remembered his past life that he was a learned Brāhmin but had to be born as a *caṇḍāla,* as he threw away the alms he had collected. He performed penance and was pardoned.

Brahmāṇḍa Purāṇa.

The Brahmāṇḍa Purāṇa has been divided into four parts, known as *"Prakriyāpāda, Anuṣaṅgapāda, Upodghātapāda and Upasamhārapāda".* This is followed by *Lalitopākhyāna* of forty chapters. This Purāṇa is said to have been taught by Brahmā himself, to the sages assembled in the *naimīśāraṇya,* at the time of performing *Sattrayāga*. First two parts deal with creation, geography of earth, the *manvantaras, Vyāsa and Vedic śākhās.* The third section deals with the funeral rites, Gaṅgā coming to the earth, Āyurveda etc. The fourth part deals with Manus, *Kalpa pralaya,* description of the fourteen worlds etc. *Lalitopākhyāna* deals with the famous *Lalita sahasranāma.* It is said that *Adhyātma Ramāyaṇa* is part of Brahmāṇda Purāṇa. Many verses of this Purāṇa are also found in the *Vāyu Purāṇa* and many scholars are of the opinion that these two Purāṇas were originally called as *Vāyavīya-Brahmāṇda Purāṇa* which would have been separated around B.C. 400. This Purāṇa has 12,000 verses. This Purāṇa is also found in the Balineese language of Bali island of Indonesia.

Animal Sacrifice

Once Indra performed a great *aśvamedha Yajna* and many sages were invited to the *Yajna.* Too great a number of animals were sacrificed and the gods partook of the offerings. The number of animals, sacrificed was so huge, that the sages were very unhappy. They expressed their opinion to Indra that violence on so many animals can not be dharma and it was a sin, but the gods argued that it was permissible. And the argument acquired significance. A mediator was appointed and he was Uparicaravasu, who had learnt the techniques of Yajna from Uttānpāda and was considered an authority on the subject. But the Vasu was a friend of Indra, and he had got an aerial chariot from Indra. So he sided with the gods that such huge sacrifice was permissible. However the sages felt that Vasu was telling lie and cursed him to enter the earth and live in the underworld. The gods blessed him that whatever offerings are made in the form of clarified butter in Yajnas would go to Vasu. In a Yajńa the final offerings in which clarified butter is poured is called *Vasordhāra,* the flow of clarified butter.

Mat.Ch. 152.

Kārtavīryārjuna

Kārtavīryārjuna belonged to the Hehaya dynasty and was the son of Kṛtavīrya. He was ruling from his capital Māhiṣmatī. On the advice of Nārada, the king performed ***"Bhadradīpa Pratiṣṭhā"*** rite, to attain both material pleasures and salvation on the banks of the river Narmadā. At the conclusion of the rite, he got a number of boons from Dattātreya, one of them being that he would have thousand hands. He ruled for 86,000 years. Kārtavīryārjuna while returning jubilantly heard a celestial voice saying, "You fool, don't you know that a brāhmaṇa is superior to a Kṣatriya? A Kṣhatriya rules in alliance with the Brāhmaṇa." On hearing this, Kārtavīryā became angry as he understood that Vāyu was behind the message and argued that Kṣatriya was superior. Vāyu warned him that he would be cursed by a Brāhmaṇa. A sage called Āpava cursed him. Once when Paraśurāma was fourteen years old, his father Jamadagni went to the forest to bring *samit*. His mother Reṇukā went to fetch water. When she reached the rive bank, she saw Kārtavīryā indulging in amorous pleasure with his wives. She waited unobserved on the banks for some time and stepped into the river, when they left. Finding the water to be muddy, she had to go to another place and there she found Citraratha with his wives. She had to wait again and it was very late when she arrived at the *āśrama*. Sage Jamadagni, who was waiting impatiently for the arrival of Reṇukā, in a fit of fury, asked Paraśurāma to cut off his mother's head and he obeyed the father. Subsequently on a request from Paraśurāma Reṇukā was brought back to life.

Kārtavīrya subdued all the kings and a big list is given including Trayyāruna, Hariścandra etc. Fully bloated with pride, Kārtavīrya went to the seashore and challenged the ocean. He started killing the animals. When God Varuṇa asked him what he wanted, he asked Varuṇa to name some one, who can fight with him. Varuṇa said Paraśurāma son of Jamadagni was the fit person. Kārtavīrya once went for a hunt. While returning, he found the *āśram* of Jamadagni. He went alone and paid his obeisance to the sage. The sage welcomed him and asked him to call his followers also. They had a sumptuous food and after night halt, they returned. Candragupta, minister of Kārtavīrya told him that Jamadagni had a divine cow which yielded all the food for the guests. He also offered to go and get the cow for him. The king agreed and Candragupta went with a few men and asked Jamadagni to part with the cow, for which the sage refused, telling the cow was Suśīla, the sister of

Kāmadhenu. When the minister wanted to take the cow forcibly, the cow vanished. They tried to capture the calf but Jamadagni prevented it and was beaten to death by Candragupta.

When Paraśurāma returned to the *āśram,* along with the disciple Akṛtavraṇa he found his father lying dead on the floor. Paraśurāma cried aloud and Reṇukā beat her chest twenty one times. Paraśurāma took a vow that he would go round the world twenty one times and annihilate the Kṣhatriya kings. Sage Śukra appeared there with the cow Suśilā and restored Jamadagni back to life. Now Paraśurām had turned himself an embodiment of revenge. In the company of Akṛtavraṇa he took his position at the palace gate and challenged Kārtavīryārjuna for a fight. Kārtavīrya came out with a huge army. In the terrible fight that ensued, Paraśurāma himself chopped the thousand arms of Kārtavīrya. All his sons were killed. Kārtavīrya was beheaded and that was the end of Hehaya dynasty.

Chapter:16, 44, 58, 67-70, 81.

Geography

It was mentioned earlier that the earth was divided into seven *dvipas* and Jambudvīpa was one of them, in which *Bhāratavarṣa* is situated. Agnidhra was the ruler of the Jambudvīpa. He had nine sons and so this was divided into nine. Each of the regions came to be known after their names and the regions are: Nabhi, Kimpurusa, Hari, Ilavrita, Ramya, Hiranvana, Kuru, Bhadrasva and Ketumala. Jambudvīpa has six major mountain regions and they are Himalayan range, Hemakuta region, Nisada, Nila, Srngavana and Vaiduryamaya. South of Himalayas is Bhāṛatavarṣa, Kimpurusavarsa adjoins Hemakuta,

Harivarsa is the present China, is right of Nisada range, Ilavritavarsa surrounds Sumeru. Ramyakavarsa is farther down, Hiranvanavarsa is Mancuria, Kuruvarsa is Siberia, Bhadrashvavarsa is China and Ketumalavarsa is Iran / Afghanistan. Mount Sumeru is in the centre, like a stem. Sumeru can not be described by human beings. Its peak, it is said is laden with gold and gems. It has within it many caves, palaces and is full of riches.

Mount Kailāś

Mount Kailāś is as white as snow and has several peaks, having vast area. It is place of Śiva. The middle peak is where Kubera resides. As he is the god of wealth, his palace also reflects prosperity. It has also its own aerial vehicle. Kubera's associates also reside there. River Mandākinī flows through Kailāś. There are also Alkānanda and Nanda rivers. Mother Pārvatī performed penance here to get married to Lord Śiva.

Bhāratvarṣa

India is known as Bhāratvarṣa. It is bounded by Himālayas in the north and by ocean in the south. This land is known as *karmabhūmī,* because here it is a way of life. It has been divided into nine regions and they are: Indradvīpa, Kaseru, Tāmraparṇa, Gabhastimāna, Nāgadvīpa, Saumya, Gandharva, and Varuṇaī. It has many mountains and they are Mahendra, Malaya, Śuktimāna, Ṛkśa, Vindhya and Pāripatra. The major rivers are Gaṅgā, Sindhu, Sarasvati, Śatadru, Candrabhāgā, Yamunā, Sarayu, Irāvatī, Vipāś•, Gomati etc.

Astronomy

There are fourteen *lokas,* six are above the earth and seven are below. The *lokas* above are Buvar, Suvar, Mahar, Jana, Tapa and Satya *lokas.* The seven *lokas* below are Atala, Sutala, Nitala, Gabhastala, Mahatala, Śritala and Pātala. Atala has dark color land with host of demons, snakes like Kabhanda and Kaliya. The pale earth of Sutala too is the house of demons and snakes like Nāmuci, Mahananda and Takśa etc. Nitala has earth like blood in color and there live demons like Prahlāda, Anuhlāda, Agnimukha and snakes like Hemaka, Ulkamukah etc. The land in Gabhastala is yellow in color and Kālanemi, Gajakarṇa etc live there. Mahātala is covered with sugar, where Virocana and snakes like Svastika etc live there. The sixth underworld is Śritala, which is the residing place for snakes like Vāsuki etc. Let us have a look at sky with stars, the part of constellation 'Little bear, Dhruva [pole star] etc. All the stars and planets revolve around Dhruva. Sun rays make the water to evaporate from the oceans and rivers to form cloud to rain, thunder and lightning. The Ājneya clouds are large formations of water from ocean for heavy shower with no lightning or thunder. Brāhmaja clouds cause rain with thunder and lightning and the third type of cloud is known as Paṅkaja clouds. These clouds are light clouds with or without rain. The chariot of the Sun is drawn by seven horses and they are Gāyatrī, Uṣnik, Trṣtubh, Anuṣtubh, Jagatī, Paṅktī and Bṛhatī. From the twelve Ādityas two Ādityas ride every two months in the chariot, having six groups. The horses of the chariot of Sun are yellow in color whereas the horses of moon are white in color and the chariot and horses of the moon appeared from the ocean. It has ten horses. During *Śukla Pakṣa* moon gets the juices from the sun to be consumed by gods during *Kṛṣṇa Pakṣa.*

Lalitopākhyānam

This section has got the famous *Lalita Sahasranāma,* one thousand names of the Mother of the Universe, which endowed with mystical powers. This work depicts the Mother both in the *saguna* and *nirguna* form. In most of the verses in one line she is depicted in *saguna form* and the next line she is depicted in the *nirguna* form. It is in the form of conversation between sages Haygriva and Agastya and it was taught by sage Hayagriva to Sage Agastya.

Taitrīya

Yājñavalkya was the disciple of Vaiśampāyana. Once Vaiśampāyana had to perform a difficult Yajña, and so he called all his disciples to help him. Yājñavalkya suggested that he can assist him all alone and there was no need for others. The teacher took it as arrogance and told Yājñavalkya that he would not like his disciples to be arrogant and asked him to surrender whatever he had learnt from him. Yājñavalkya vomited all his knowledge and that was absorbed by the other disciples in the form of *Tiitri* birds and that was how it came to be known as the famous *Taitrīya.*

Brahmāvaivarta Purāṇa

This Purāṇa is considered to be a more ancient work – probably earlier than A.D. 300, since the Viṣṇu Purāṇa has mentioned it among the Mahāpurāṇas. But the text in print form might have been evolved during the period A.D. 800- 1600. As the cause of the creation is known as '*vivarta*' – meaning 'appearance' this Purāṇa has been named as Brahmāvaivarta Purāṇa.

The first section declares the evolution of the universe from the four faced Brahmā, who is also Śri Kṛṣṇa himself. The second chapter outlines the manifestation of Durgā, Lakṣmī, Sarasvatī, Sāvitrī, and Rādhā from the *Mūlaprakṛti* as per the command of Sri Kṛṣṇa. Ganeś kāṇḍa describes the birth and exploits of the two sons of Śiva and Pārvati. Sri Kṛṣṇajanma kāṇḍa dwells on the story of Kṛṣṇa and Rādhā. There is also mention of Āyurveda, rituals, importance of Sālagrāma and its worship, Kaliyuga, greatness of Tulsi leaves. This Purāṇa has about 18,000 verses.

This Purāṇa was narrated by Sage Śauti, son of Romaharṣaṇa to several sages who had assembled in the forest named *naimīṣa.* In an act of glorification of Sri Kṛṣṇa, this Purāṇa depicts Sri Kṛṣṇa as Brahmān. It was dark and empty everywhere, Kṛṣṇa had a desire to create and thus the creation began. From Kṛṣṇa's right emerged Nārāyaṇa. Śiva emerged from the left side of Kṛṣṇa. From the lotus which emerged from Kṛṣṇa's naval emerged Brahmā. From his chest emerged *Dharma*, the god of righteousness. From his mouth appeared Sarasvatī, from his mind Mahālakṣmī who is also known as Svargalakṣmī and Rajalakṣmī. From his thoughts emerged Durgā, who carries all sorts of weapons. Sāvitrī emerged from his tongue, the god of love, known as Madan emerged from his consciousness. Then all other gods were created. Now as mentioned in other Purāṇas, from the Brahmāṇḍa the other creations came out. While continuing the creation, when Kṛṣṇa was in *rāsamaṇḍala* a beautiful girl emerged from Kṛṣṇa's left and she was to be known as Rādhā. From Rādhā's body came out one hundred thousand crore women, known as *Gopīs*. From Kṛṣṇa's body more gopīs and all other living beings like cows, bulls etc appeared. From that Śiva was given a bull, Brahmā a swan, Dharma a white stallion and Durgā a lion.

Further Creation

As per the advice of Kṛṣṇa, Brahmā created further things like lokas, countries, cities, Vedas etc. From Brahmā's naval appeared the heavenly architect Viśvakarmā, Vasus and the sages, Sanaka, Sanandana, Sanātana and Sanatkumāra. Brahmā asked these sons to carry on the creation, but they refused and went away to the forest for meditation. Infuriated Brahmā issued fire from his forehead out of which *Rudra* appeared.

In relationship the Purāṇa quotes that fourteen women should be considered as mothers. Mother, father's other wives, father's mother and so on.

Upavarhaṇa

Due to a curse Nārada was born as a *gandharva* and Vasiṣṭha named the boy as Upavarhaṇa, meaning the boy would be shown reverence. When he became a youth, fifty daughters of the *gandharva* king wanted to marry him and he married all of them. Once when he went to Brahmā, saw Rambhā dancing and he wanted to marry her. Enraged Brahmā cursed him to die. Upavarhaṇa's chief wife Mālāvati wanted to curse gods, Brahmā etc and the gods ran to Viṣṇu. Viṣṇu adopted the form of a Brāhmin youth, told Mālāvati about inevitability of death, sickness etc and Upavarhaṇa was brought back to life. After living a normal life Upavarhaṇa and Mālāvati died and she was born in the lineage of Manu. She could remember her early life and Uapavarhaṇa was born to

Kalāvati, the queen of Kānyakubja and he was named Nārada because his birth brought rains.

Even as a young boy Nārada meditated upon Kṛṣṇa and he was delighted when Kṛṣṇa appeared, but started weeping when Kṛṣṇa disappeared. Then a voice from above assured that when he gave up the body he would see Kṛṣṇa again. Once Brahmā compelled Nārada to get married to Mālāvati and that time Brahmā spoke about the four *varṇas*. After hearing the advice, Nārada went to Śivaloka. Lord Śiva gave some important advice on leading a righteous life and told him about what should be done and what not. From there Nārada went to the sage Nārāyaṇa in the forest of Badrīvana. The sage narrated the exploits of Sri Kṛṣṇa to Nārada. *Bh. Skanda 7.*

Prakṛti

Sage Nārāyaṇa explained to Nārada the five basic *Prakṛtīs*. Here it indicates the goddesses who excel in creation and they are Durgā, Rādhā, Lakṣmī, Sarasvatī and Sāvitrī. Other goddesses derive their power from them. The women are born of these and an insult to the woman is an insult to the goddesses. These Prakṛtis have the three guṇas in them – Satva, rajas and tamas. At the beginning Kṛṣṇa divided himself into two – one half male and the other half, female, Rādhā.

Goddesses

Nārada was told by the sage that Sarasvatī should be prayed on the fifth day of lunar fortnight in the month of *Māgha*. It appears that Lakṣmī, Sarasvatī and Gaṅgā were the wives of Nārāyaṇa but after a quarrel, Sarasvatī cursed Lakṣmī to become a tree and a river, Gaṅgā to become a river and Gaṅgā cursed Sarasvatī to become a river. Lakṣmī became Tulsi and river Padmāvati; Gaṅgā became a river and Sarsvatī too. Nārāyaṇa sent Gañgā to Śiva, Sarasvatī to Brahmā and retained Lakṣmī only.

Mother Earth

The goddess of earth is known as *Vasundharā / Medhinī / Pṛthvī.* The earth was brought up by Viṣṇu, in the form of boar, from the ocean. Thus the earth is conceived to be the wife of Viṣṇu. One should worship the earth before starting anything connected with the earth just as building a house, cultivating etc.

Tulsi

Tulsi was the daughter of Kuśadvaja and right from the young age she started doing *tapasyā.* She pleased Brahmā with her devotion. Brahmā told her that in the present birth she would marry a demon named Śaṅkacūda and in the next birth she would attain Kṛṣṇa. As Tulsi could remember her earlier birth, she knew that she was a gopī in goloka and fell in love with Kṛṣṇa but Rādhā cursed her to be born on the earth. Brahmā also told her that Śaṅkacūda was a gopa and was in love with her but was cursed by Rādhā that he would be born as a demon. Brahmā also taught her a *mantra* to appease Rādhā. Once she met Śaṅkacūda and married him. As a demon, Śaṅkacūda was a terror to the gods and they went to Kṛṣṇa and appealed. The demon had a talismān, given by Kṛṣṇa and to kill him it was necessary to take it out from him. Also he had a boon from Brahmā that he could be killed when his wife starts living with another one. Kṛṣṇa gave a weapon to Śiva to kill him, Kṛṣṇa himself went in the form of a brāhmaṇa to Śaṅkacūda and got the talisman as a charity. Then he took the form of Śaṅkacūda and lived with Tulsi so that Śiva could kill him. When Tulsi came to know the happenings she cursed

Kṛṣṇa that he would take the form of a stone, the Sālagrāma. Kṛṣṇa consoled her that she would be able to go to Vaikuṇtha and she would become the sacred river Gandaki. Her hair would grow as sacred leaves – Tulsi [basil]. *De. Bh. Skanda 9.*

Power of a Chaste Woman

King Aśvapati was the father of the chastest woman, Sāvitrī. For eighteen years he worshipped the goddess Sāvitrī and got a maiden from *Agnihotra,* whom he named as Sāvitrī. Sāvitrī grew up very beautiful but nobody came forward to marry her. The king advised her to travel in the outside world and select a husband for her. According to the king's advice, she took some elderly ministers with her and traveled through the forests in which hermits lived. Once Nārada happened to visit the palace and was talking to the king, when Sāvitrī returned from her sojourn. She prostrated to Nārada and her father. Nārada enquired about her marriage and the king said that she was just coming back from the search. Sāvitrī replied that she had accepted prince Satyavān as her husband. Satyavān was the son of Dyumatsena, who had become blind and due to this disadvantage he was conquered by his enemies. So he had to leave for the forest. Nārada was all in praise of Satyavān. When asked by the king whether there was any negative point against him Nārada said that Satyavān would die within one year. The king felt miserable on hearing this but Sāvitrī said that she had accepted him as her husband and she would not change her decision. Aśvapati agreed and the marriage was performed. The king left Sāvitrī behind and returned. Sāvitrī discarded all her jewelleries and started living with her husband and in-laws. Nearly a year passed, when there were only four days left, Sāvitrī undertook penance by total fasting and the third day she kept awoke the whole day. The next day Satyavān took his axe and was leaving for the forest to cut wood, when Sāvitrī insisted that she would accompany him. Both of them went to the forest, collected roots and fruits and Satyavān started cutting wood. But soon he felt weak and wanted to lie down. Sāvitrī put his head on her lap. Then she saw a person, clad in red and coming towards her husband. He came and stopped near them. Realizing that it was Yama – god of death, she stood up and bowed before him.

Savitrī asked him "Who are you lord?"

Yama: "I am Yama and have come to take away the life of your husband".

Sāvitrī: "Generally only your messengers come. Why have you come?"

Yama: "Because your husband is a righteous person, and in such cases, I come personally." Then Yama cast his rope and took out the soul and Sāvitrī saw her husband lying on the floor life less. She followed Yama, who was going on the southern direction and Sāvitrī followed him. Yama advised her to go back and conduct the funerals of her husband.

Savitrī "I am coming to the place, where my husband is being taken away. When I have the merits of a dutiful wife, have the merits of fast vow and purity and your blessings what can hamper me?"

Realizing that it would be difficult to send her back Yama asked her to ask for a boon except the life of her husband. She asked for recovery of the sight of her father-in-law and it was granted. Still Sāvitrī followed Yama. Now Yama asked her to ask for one more boon.

This time she asked him for the recovery of the kingdom and it was granted. But she continued to follow Yama and Yama was ready to grant a third boon which was for hundred sons to her father and that too was granted. But Sāvitrī did not seem to be giving up and followed Yama. Now Yama was willing to give a fourth boon and she asked that she may have hundred sons born through Satyavān. Yama realized that she would not give up unless Satyavān was given life. Yama was pleased with her devotion towards her husband and Satyavān was brought back to life. Satyavān rose and they were about to go home, when Dyumatsena, having got back his eye sight came in search of the children. Sāvitrī recounted the entire happenings and everybody was happy. In the meantime some people from Salva came to request Dyumatsena to take over the kingdom as the minister had killed the king and people had expelled the minister. They all returned to the kingdom. *MB. Vp. Ch 293-299.*

Rādhā

Rādhā was born to Vṛṣabānu in Gokula. Her marriage was arranged with Rāyaṇa but she did not want to marry, so she left her shadow in the body and went away to Goloka. After fourteen years Kṛṣṇa was born and Rāyaṇa was his maternal uncle. Once Kṛṣṇa was playing with a gopi named Virajā and when Rādhā came to know about it she rushed to that place. Sudāmā heard the sound of approaching chariot, warned Kṛṣṇa and all of them ran away. Virajā, due to fear of Rādhā committed suicide and became a river, circling Goloka. Rādhā could not find anybody and went back. Later when she met them she rebuked them and cursed Sudāmā that he would be born as a demon. Sudāmā felt that the curse was unreasonable and cursed Rādhā that she would be away from Kṛṣṇa for hundred years. This curse had its effect in *bhūloka.*

Divinities

Svāhā is the burning power of fire and goddess Svāhā was created so that the oblations reached the gods. In any ritual the word *Svāhā* should be uttered. *Agni* married *Svāhā* and their three sons were the three kinds of fires, Dakṣiṇā, Gārhapatya and Āhavanīya. In order to ensure that the offerings made by brāhmaṇas reached the pitṛs, *Svadhā* came into being. Dakṣiṇā is the goddess, who ensures that the fruits of the sacrifices performed, are granted and Yajña Deva married her. Ṣasthīdevī was born out of one sixth part of *Mūlaprakṛtī* and so the name. Also called Devasenā, she is the patron deity of children. She grants them life and protects them and always remains by the side of the children. She gave life to the born dead baby of King Priyavrata. Maṅgalacaṇdikā is born of Durgā and always showers blessings on her devotees. She appeared in front of Śiva and increased his prowess in burning *Tripura.*

Gaṇeś Kāṇda

Nārada asked sage Nārāyaṇa that, why had the misfortune of losing the head occurred to Gaṇeṣ for which Nārāyaṇa said that it was because of the curse of sage Kaśyapa, as once Śiva happened to hit Kaśyapa's son, Sūrya with his trident.

Once Paraśurām wanted to see Śiva in Kailāś, but Gaṇeś, standing in the gate stopped him and a scuffle broke out. When Paraśurām wanted to hurl his *Paraśu* at Gaṇeṣ, Gaṇeś wounded him around with his trunk and threw him into the sea. Then picked him up from there and threw him on the earth. Now Paraśurām hurled his

Paraśu, which was given by Śiva to Paraśurām and so it could not be repelled totally. It broke the left tusk of Gaṇeś and that is how he became *ekadanta.* Both Śiva and Pārvati arrived at the scene and Paraśurām apologized and worshipped Gaṇeś. Sage Nārāyaṇa told Nārada that Gaṇeṣ should not be worshipped with *tulsi.* The reason for that: Once Tulsi met Gaṇeś and expressed her desire to marry him, but Gaṇeś refused and she cursed Gaṇeś that he would not be able to remain unmarried. In turn Gaṇeś cursed her that she would fall into the hands of a demon and then become a shrub. When Tulsi tried to appease Gaṇeś, he blessed her that she would be the most holy shrub, but refused to accept as an offering for himself. *Bh. Ch. 83.*

Kṛṣṇa Kāṇda

Releasing the Wives of *Saptaṛṣīs* from Curse

Once the cowherds, who were with Kṛṣṇa were feeling very hungry and thirsty and Kṛṣṇa suggested to them to go to the nearby place, where some Brāhmins were performing sacrifice so they could get something to eat. When the boys approached the Brāhmins they were too indifferent and the boys approached the wives of the Brāhmins. The wives of the Brāhmins treated them very warmly, gave them plate full of rice, sweet meats etc. They also told the cowherds that they longed to be with Kṛṣṇa always and did not want to be in the hermitage. Kṛṣṇa immediately blessed them and sent them to *Goloka,* leaving their shadows there. These were the wives of *Saptaṛṣīs,* who were cursed by sage Aṅgīras having been touched by the unholy fire while cooking.

Multiple Brahmā

A nymph, by the name Mohini wanted to marry Brahmā, but he rejected the idea and he was cursed by her that all worship of Brahmā would stop. Brahmā rushed to Nārāyaṇa for help. There Brahmā saw that Brāhmas with hundred faces and thousand faces were waiting to see Nārāyaṇa. When enquired by Brahmā about them, Nārāyaṇa said that they belonged to other universes and there were several of them. Brahmā felt humbled. Nārāyaṇa advised Brahmā to bathe in the Gaṅgā and be rid of the curse of Mohini.

Result of Insulting the Teacher

Once Indra neglected the goddess Pṛthvī and the goddess cursed him that he would be cursed by his own guru. It so happened that once Indra did not show due respect to Bṛhaspati and he was cursed to lose all his power and glory. After great suffering Indra appeased Bṛhaspati and got back his kingdom. When he arrived at his kingdom after long spell of absence, his kingdom was in a pretty bad shape and he asked Viśvakarmā to rebuild it. In spite of doing good work he was going on keeping pressure on Viśvakaramā and the architect of the gods was not able to do anything else. He went to Nārāyaṇa for help and the Lord took the form of a small brāhmaṇa boy and visited Indra. He appreciated his mansion and said that no other Indra had such a wonderful city and also no other Viśvakarmā did such a wonderful job. Indra asked the boy how many Indras and Viśvakarmās he had seen. The boy replied "count less number of Indras. Twenty eight Indras were born in one day of Brahmā." Then the boy showed a row of ants moving and said "all these ants were created by me and all of them were Indras and I made sure that they are reborn as ants." Indra realized his insignificance. *MB. Śā.p. Ch. 84.*

End of Rādhā's Separation

Once Kṛṣṇa sent Uddhava to find out how were his people in Bṛndāvan. Uddhava came back with the message that Rādhā was in pretty bad condition and that he had told them that Kṛṣṇa would come and meet them. To keep up the promise of Uddhava, Kṛṣṇa met all of them in their dreams.In a hermitage named Siddhāśrama Rādhā prayed to Gaṇeś and Pārvati. The Mother appeared and said that the curse of Sudāmā was over and that she would unite with Kṛṣna. [In other place the purāṇa states the place as Prabhāsa]. Rādhā returned to Gokula and Kṛṣṇa went and met her there. Kṛṣṇa and Rādhā climbed on to a chariot and came to Bṛndāvan and met Nanda, Yaśodā and other gopas and gopis. They saw Kṛṣṇa in the form of eleven years old boy. Kṛṣṇa told them that in this universe everything is illusion. He also told them that Kali is fast approaching, when the world would be full of evils. An aerial cart came down and as per instructions from Kṛṣṇa all the gopis and gopas mounted the chariot and went to Goloka. [This account of Kṛṣṇa, leaving the earth is different from what is said in other Purāṇas.]

The entire Brahmāvaivarta Purāṇa was recounted by sage Nārāyaṇa to Nārada and Nārada felt very happy. He wanted to go to Himalayas to meditate but the sage said that earlier Nārada had been a king of *gandharvas* and had fifty wives and one among them had taken rebirth only to marry him. It was his duty to marry her. So Nārada married her and forgot Nārāyaṇa. Sanatkumar shook Nārada out of his slumber. He made him to leave his wife and wander. Eventually he merged into Nārāyaṇa.

Mārkaṇḍeya Purāṇa

This is probably one of the few Purāṇas which has retained much of the more ancient materials composed probably around A.D.300. Though it is said to contain 9,000 verses, the printed texts available now have only 7,000 verses. The Purāṇa starts with the questions put by sage Jaimini to the sage Mārkaṇdeya, who directed him to four Cātaka birds for the answers, living in the Vindhayācala hills. The birds later on referred to the teachings of Mārkaṇdeya, given to Krausṭuki. The well known Devīmāhātmya, also known as Saptaśati and Lalita Sahasranāma are part of this Purāṇa only. In this Purāṇa, the Vedic deities like Brahmā, Agni, and Sūrya get greater coverage than Viṣṇu or Śiva. This Purāṇa gives equal importance to the *Śrauta Smārta* rites which started dwindling. The Purāṇa also deals with legends such as Hariścandra, Kārtavīrya etc.

Jaimini was a disciple of Vedavyāsa, who taught him Sāma Veda. Once he came to sage Mārkaṇdeya and wanted to know answer for his questions, which were disturbing his mind. Mārkaṇdeya apologized to the sage telling that he really had no time and that answers for the questions would be given by four birds, named Piṅgākśa, Vivodha, Suputra and Sumukha, which were living in the Vindhyācal Mountains. Astonished by this answer Jaimini wanted to know the back ground of those birds and Mārkaṇdeya recounted the following: Vapus was an apsarā who wanted to prove to Nārada that she was the best among apsarās both in beauty and intelligence and so she went ahead to disturb sage Durvāsā's meditation. She took the form of a bird and started singing. Duravāsā understood the purpose and cursed her that she would be born as a bird and live for sixteen years. She would also have four sons. Vapus was born as a bird named Tārkśi, and while flying over Kurukṣetra she was hit by Arjuna's arrow and was killed but four eggs fell out of her stomach and a sage called Śamīka brought up these birds, which have been mentioned earlier in the story of Śamīka.

Jaimini with the Birds

Jaimini went to Vindhyācal and he heard the birds, chanting Vedas. Jaimini put his three questions, answers to which he wanted from Mārkaṇḍeya before.

- Viṣṇu has no forms and is the Lord of everything. Why was he born as human in the form of Kṛṣṇa?
- Why was it that Draupadī had to marry five Paṇḍavas at the same time?
- Why did Draupadī's five sons had to die, while sleeping and not in the battle field?

The birds gave Jamini the following answers. Triśiras, son of the sage Tvaṣṭā performed a severe penance by hanging himself upside down. Indra was scared about his position and killed him. So Indra lost a portion of his energy which was absorbed by Dharma. Tvaṣṭā was very angry and created Vṛtra, a demon, pulling out a hair from his body, to kill Indra. Indra made peace with Vṛtra and killed him unawares. Indra again lost a portion of his energy which was taken by Vāyu. By posing himself as sage Gautama he appeared before Ahalyā for which he lost his energy further and was taken by Aśvinikumārs. When the Lord had taken avatār to destroy the sinners, gods had also taken birth on the Pṛtvī. From the energy of Indra, taken by Dharma was born Yudhiṣṭhira, from what Vāyu had taken was born Bhīma, Arjuna was from Indra's own energy and from the energy taken by Aśvinikumārs were born Nakula and Sahadeva. Indra's wife Śacī was born as Draupadī and as five Pandavas were born from the energy of Indra alone, she had to marry all the five.

Sage Viśvāmitra had taken the entire kingdom of Hariścandra and drove him out of the kingdom. When Hariścandra's wife was walking slowly while going out of the kingdom Viśvāmitra beat her with a stick. The Viśvadevas felt very much hurt by this treatment, meted out to the queen and said 'shame, shame'. Viśvāmitra cursed them to be born as human beings. When they begged for mercy he said that they would not have the attachments, what human beings have with family etc. So they were born as the sons of Draupadī and were killed by Aśvatthāma, while they were sleeping.

Viṣṇu has no forms, but he had taken the form of human beings to deal with human beings and their related problems. *Ch. 1, 2, 41, 49, 56.*

Agony of the Sage

When Hariścandra was deprived of his kingdom, Vasiṣṭha, who was the court priest, was away when Hariścandra lost his kingdom. When he came back he cursed Viśvāmitra to become a bird. In turn Viśvāmitra too cursed Vasiṣṭha to become a bird. These two, thus having become gigantic birds fought with each other in the sky. It turned out to be a big war and all natural calamities started occurring. Brahmā tried to advice them, but when they were in no mood to heed them he took off their birds form and granted them their original form. He told Vasiṣṭha that Hariścandra was in heaven. So the two sages gave up their fight.

Tapaśśakti of Anasūyā

Sumati was the son of a brāhmaṇa named Mahāmati and the father advised the son several times to lead a spiritual life, leading to liberation, but the son would not answer and the father kept on repeating. One day Sumati told his father that he remembered all his past lives and he had studied all Śāstras. He explained to the father about the fruits of good and bad deeds and also explained various hells. He also narrated the story of Anasūyā. There is no other woman in the Purāṇas, who surpasses Śilāvatī in her fidelity. In order to enable Ugraśravas, her husband, to satisfy his passion, she once carried him on her own shoulders to a prostitute's house. On the way Māṇḍvya Muni pronounced a curse that Ugraśravas should die at sunrise, as his leg touched the sage. The grief stricken Śīlāvatī pronounced a counter curse that the sun should not rise on the next day. As the sun failed to rise, the Trimūrtis accompanied by Anasūyā persuaded Śīlāvatī to withdraw her curse. The curse was withdrawn on the promise that her husband would be revived. Happy with the accomplishment of the mission Trimūrtis asked Anasūyā to ask for a boon. Anasūyā expressed her wish that Trimūrtis should be born as her sons. It was agreed. Viṣṇu was born as Dattātreya, Śiva as Durvāsā and Brahmā as Candra to Anasūyā. At that time a demon named Jambha was the leader of the *asuras,* who fought with the gods and gods were driven out. Under the advice from Bṛhaspati, the gods pleased Dattātreya and Dattātreya suggested that when the war took place under his glance, the demons would lose their powers. The gods summoned the demons for another war and at that time they fled towards Dattātreya's āśram. There the demons happened to see Lakṣmī and they wanted to take her away. They had put Lakṣmī in a palanquin and carried her away and at that time Dattātreya advised the gods to attack them. When Lakṣmī was on one's head she would forsake him. Thus the gods attacked the demons and destroyed them. At that time a king named Kṛtavīrya wanted to go to forest and meditate and hence handed over the kingdom to his son Arjuna, but he did not want to become a king unless he could be the best. Sage Gārga advised him to go to Dattātreya and pray. Arjuna went to Dattātreya and got several advices as to how to be a benevolent king. *Brah. Ch. 39 – 43.*

Mother's Teachings to the Son

A king named Śatṛujit had a handsome son, named Ṛtadvaja and he was very good in every art. He was attracted by one and all. Once the two sons of the Nāga king Aśvatara adopted the form of Brāhmin boys and started playing with Ṛtadvaja. They got attached to him so much that they could not be away from him and they visited him daily. When questioned by their father, they told him about the quality of Ṛtadvaja. Aśvatra suggested that they could take some gift for the prince. Then they narrated the story of the prince, as they heard from Ṛtadvaja himself. Once a sage named Galava brought a horse to the king Śatrujīt and said that a demon was disturbing his *tapasyā* by taking many forms such as lion etc and suddenly a horse fell from above, which could travel anywhere in the world. Its name was Kuvalaya. The brāhmaṇa gave the king the horse and asked for protection. Śatrujīt accepted the horse and gave it to Ṛtadvaja to control the demon. Because of the horse Kuvalya the prince came to be known as Kuvalayāśva. When Rṭadvaja reached the hermitage, the demon adopted the form of a boar and attacked. Ṛtadvaja shot an arrow and the demon was hurt but fled into the forest.

He was chased by the prince. The demon entered a deep pit on the earth. Ṛtadvaja followed him and to his surprise found a city with golden palaces. On a golden seat he found a beautiful woman sitting and they fell in love with each other. Her name was Madālasā, daughter of the king of *gandharvas,* but had been kidnapped by a demon named Pātālaketu and was threatening to marry her. Ṛtadvaja married her there itself, but the demons started attacking them. The prince could easily destroy them and came back to Śatrujīt. Śatrjīt was very happy. The prince, on the advice of his father, protected the sages, who performed Yajnas. Once the prince came across, Tālaketu, brother of Pātālaketu, whom the prince could not recognize but the demon recognized him as the killer of his brother. In the form of a sage he told Ṛtadvaja that he wanted to perform Yajna but had no money and asked ıor the necklace, he was wearing. The prince gladly gave away the necklace he was wearing. The demon also asked the prince to wait in his hermitage so that he could have his bath and come back. When the prince was waiting Talaketu went and told Satrujit that the prince had died in fighting the demons and showed the necklace as a proof. Hearing this Madālasā died and the king performed the death rites of his daughter in law. On his return the prince learnt what had happened and from that day he pined to see Madālasā only.

Having learnt about the sad story of Ṛtadvaja, Aśvatara, the Nāga king performed *tapasyā* in Plakṣāvataraṇa, the place of origin of river Sarasvatī, and prayed to Sarasvatī that he and his brother should become excellent singers. With this boon, pleased Śiva, who granted them a boon. Aśvatara asked for the boon that Madālasā should be born as his daughter, in the same form as she died and she should remember her past. With Śiva's blessings, she was born from one of his hoods. He kept Madālasā hidden from the view of his sons too and asked them to bring one day, the prince Ṛtadvaja. Accompanied by the two, Ṛtadvaja came to the world of Nāgas and the prince was surprised to see their prosperity. King Aśvatara received the prince respectfully and extended great hospitality. Finally the king asked the prince what gift he would like to have for which the prince replied that he did not need anything except his blessings. The king said he would get him what he wanted most and brought Madālasā. Though at first, the prince thought it to be an illusion, but then his joys knew no bounds and he returned to his kingdom, with his wife. After the death of Śatṛujit he became the king and had three sons but with the teachings of Madālasā, none of them wanted to become king. When the fourth son was born, Ṛtadvaja did not want Madālasā to teach, what she taught to the other sons. So Madālasā taught the fourth son, known as Alarka about Dharma.

After a number of years had passed, Ṛtadvaja went to forest with his wife, leaving the kingdom to the care of Alarka. Before leaving, Madālasā gave him a ring and told him that there was a letter in the ring, which he may read only at the time of great distress. Though Alarka ruled well, attachment to possessions did not leave him. One of his brothers, named Suvāhu, who had become a saint wanted to teach his brother the true knowledge and he made a plan in association with the king of Kāśī. A letter was sent by the king of Kāśī asking him to hand over the kingdom to his brother Suvāhu. Alarka refused and a war was started in which, Alarka had to face defeat. Alarka was feeling depressed. Then he remembered the letter in the ring, given by his mother. The letter read as follows: **"Give up the company of other people. If you can not,**

associate only with those, who are good. Give up all desires". He accepted his mother's suggestion and went to Dattātreya. He told Dattātreya "Sir, I am very unhappy. Please tell me what I should do"? Dattātreya replied "Tell me why you are unhappy"? Then Alarka realized that unhappiness belongs to the body and he was not the body, but Ātmā. All depend upon the state of the mind and mind is not Ātmā. Alarka told Dattatreya "I have realized the true knowledge. But my mind is greatly disturbed. Tell me how to avoid rebirth"? Then Dattātreya taught him about Yoga and blessed him. Alarka told the King of Kāśī that he can take away his kingdom. The king was surprised and told him about the plan, his brother made to make him realize what the Truth was. Then Alarka made his eldest son the king and retired to forest. Hearing the story, Sumati and his father Mahāmati too retired to forest. *Vam. Ch. 59 & 60.*

Svārociṣa

There was a handsome Brāhmin who had a desire to go around the world. Once he met a person, who had the technique to go places by herbs. He helped him with his technique and he went to Himālayas. While he was enjoying the place, the herbal paste on his feet got washed off, so he could not return to his place and was looking for a way out. Then an *apsarā* named Varūthinī saw him and fell in love with him, but the Brāhmin was interested only in going back home and prayed to the *Agni devatā*, who helped him to get back home. A *gandharva* named Kali wanted to marry Varūthinī but she would not agree. He came to know that Varūthinī was in love with the Brāhmin and took the form of the Brāhmin. Now Varūthinī was delighted to marry him, not realizing that it was Kali. Kali had put a condition that she would not look at his face when they were in forest. They married and had a son named Svārociṣa. Kali left as soon as the son was born. Svārocisa grew up as a good scholar in Vedas etc. Once Svārocisa went to Mount Māndāra where a frightened woman came running and requested to save her. She told him that her name was Manoramā and once she and her two friends Vibhāvari and Kalāvati went to Mount Kailāś.There they met a sage who had become too thin due to severity of tapasyā and she made fun of him. The sage got angry and pronounced a curse that she would be captured by a demon. When the other two friends expressed that a sage should not have cursed for trifles, they were too cursed to become a leper and the other a tuberculosis patient. Since then a terrible demon was chasing her and she asked him for protection. Manoramā had in her possession a powerful weapon, and she taught Svārocisa how to use it. Immedtiately the demon arrived and Svārocisa waited till she was captured and was about to release the weapon, when the demon requested not to release the weapon. He recounted his story that his name was Indivara and was Manoramā's father. He had become a demon due to the curse of sage Brahmāmitra and the sage had said that he would be released from the curse when he was about to eat his own daughter. The curse was given because he tried to collect the details of Āyurveda medicine without the knowledge of the teacher. Indivara taught the knowledge of Āyurveda to Svārocisa and with this he was able to treat Manoramā's friends also and he married all the three.

Svārocisa learnt the language of all beings from his wife Vibhāvari and Padmini vidyā – from his wife Kalāvatī. One day he heard ducks, discussing among themselves that Svārociṣa was a very happy man, when the other duck said that how a man with three wives could be happy? Though Svārociṣa was unhappy, but forgot the conversation soon. He had three sons and was happy. After a while, he heard the same converstion from some deer. Svārociṣa was ashamed but soon forgot it. One day Svārociṣa went for hunting and while he was about to release an arrow at a boar, a deer appeared and asked him to shoot her instead of the boar. When asked the reason the deer said that she was in love with and wanted to marry him. The deer asked him to embrace her and when Svārociṣa embraced, the deer became a beautiful woman. She told him that she was the goddess of forest and he married her. They had a son born and was named as Dyutimān, who became the Svārociṣa Manu. *Ch. 61.*

Mārkaṇdeya Purāṇa contains one of the most important glories of Devī, which is known as "Devī Mahātmyam" and it is also known as "Sapta Śati" because it contains seven hundred verses, in thirteen chapters. It is preceded and succeeded by glories of Devī for daily chanting.

Madhu, Kaiṭabha and Mahāmāyā

The Devī Mahātmyam had been narrated in a story form in which the sage Medhā describes the glory of Devī to a king, named Suratha, who had lost his kingdom and came to stay in the hermitage and a Vaiśya, who had been driven out by his family. In spite of their separation from the family, they continued to think about them and the sage said that it was known as Mahāmāyā, illusion. Devī created this illusion to prevent beings from going to true knowledge. Then the sage told them the story of Madhu and Kaiṭabha. At the end of the cycle Viṣṇu was sleeping known as *'yoga nidrā'* and there was everywhere water only. Two terrible demons emerged from his ear wax and tried to kill Brahmā. [In Mahābhārata, Śanti parva, it is mentioned that these two demons appeared from the two drops of water of the lotus, one was sweet and the other hard] Brahmā prayed to Mahāmāyā, who always is present in Viṣṇu's eyes, and pleased with his prayers, she entered Viṣṇu and awoke him. Viṣṇu fought with the two demons for long and by the illusion created by Mahāmāyā they asked Viṣṇu to ask for a boon and Viṣṇu said that except their death what else could he ask? Having realized that they had been cheated, they told Viṣṇu that they could be killed, where there was no water. Viṣṇu placed the demons between his thighs and slit their heads with Sudarśan cakra. *De.Bh. Skanda 1.*

Mahīśāsura Vadha

In the second and third chapter sage Medha narrated the story of killing Mahīśāsura, who had deprived Indra and the other gods of their positions. Hearing about the fate of the gods, Viṣṇu and Śiva were so angry that from that anger came out the form of a woman. The energy of all the gods was associated in the formations of the limbs and all the gods gave special jewelleries and special weapons. The goddess thus armed, mounted on the lion and roared. Various generals of the demon fought the goddess and were killed. Seeing that all his men were being killed, Mahīśāsura himself came to fight, taking the form of a buffalo. When the buffalo came under the noose of the goddess, he took the form of a lion and then he tried to adopt various other forms. The goddess started drinking and with blood shot eyes jumped on to the buffalo. The buffalo could not escape and she cut its head with the sword. Thus the end of Mahīśāsura brought cheers into all the three worlds.

The fourth chapter is devoted to the praise and glorification of the Devī and chapters five to eight are devoted to the slaying of Śumbha and Niśumbha.

De. Bh. Skanda 5.

Slaying of Śumbha and Niśumbha

Śumbha and Niśumbha were two demon brothers, who conquered the three worlds and drove out the gods from the heaven. The gods prayed to Devī to grant them succor. When the gods were praising Devī, Pārvatī was going to bathe in the Ganges and she asked them, whom they were praying? Then a Devī came out of the body of Pārvatī and said that they were praying to her. Because she came out of the body of Pārvatī she was called 'Kauśikī'. Two servants of the demons, named Caṇda and Muṇda saw Devī and told Śumbha and Niśumbha that Devī was fit to be their wife. Śumbha sent Sugrīva as an emissary to bring Devī. When approached by Sugrīva Devī told him that she had made a vow that she would marry only him, who defeated her in the war. Angered by this, the demons sent their assistant named Dhūmralocana with a huge army with instructions to bring Devi. But the army was destroyed within no time and Dhūmralocana was also killed. Hearing the news, Śumbha sent Caṇda and Muṇda to bring Devī, dragging her by the hair. Seeing them Devī was furious and a dark woman with garlands of skull appeared, who was called Kāli and scourged the army. The soldiers were nullified like chaff and Caṇda and Muṇda themselves entered the fray. Climbing on the lion she cut off the head of both Caṇda and Muṇda and brought them to Devī. Devī blessed her that she would be known by the name Cāmuṇḍā as she killed both of them. Now the king of the demons sent a huge army to capture Devi. Kauśikī sent Lord Śiva as a messenger to convince the demons to return the kingdom to devas but Śumbha was furious.

Another general of Sumbha named Raktabīja came for fighting. Devī hit him and blood was flowing like a river from his body. From the blood demons identical to him sprung up and within no time the war field was full of them. Caṇdikā requested Kālī to open her mouth and take in the blood coming out from his body and also the demons coming out. Kālī swallowed everything and with loss of blood he became weak and was killed. Then Niśumbha took a big army and gave a fight but ultimately was killed. Now only Śumbha was left out and he took whatever army was there and entered the war. But his army was destroyed in no time and Śumbha, having lost his chariot and weapons started hitting Devī. Devī slapped him on the chest and he fell down. He lifted Devī into the sky and there fierce fight went on and ultimately Devī lifted him and threw him on the earth and before he could get up he was killed by Devī. All gods from the heaven rained flowers on Devī.

The next chapter is devoted to praises of the Mother and in the last two chapters' the king after praying to Mother got back his kingdom and the Vaiśya got knowledge of Self. *De. Bh. Skanda 5.*

King's Concern for Citizens

Rājyavardhana was an ideal king, who was ruling the world well and there was no drought or misery among the citizens. He performed many Yajnas and ruled for thousand years. He had a wife named Mānini. One day when she was applying oil to the king's hair, a drop of tear fell on his hand. Asked about the reason for weeping, the queen said she saw a grey hair. The king decided that it was time to go to forest but even his citizens would not allow him to retire. Instructed by a *gandharva*, the citizens went to a place called Kāmarūpa and prayed to the Sun god for three months. When the god appeared they asked for a boon that Rājyavardhana should live for ten thousand years and the boon was granted. Hearing about the boon the king became very unhappy. When asked about the reason for his unhappiness by his wife, he said that there was no fun in living longer when the other lovable ones had gone away. Realizing about the fact, the king went to the forest with his wife and meditated upon the Sun god. The Sun god appeared after one year of prayer. The king asked for a boon that all his citizens should live for ten thousand years and the boon was granted.

Karaṇdhāmana

Khanitra was a righteous king and ruled well. He had four brothers and he gave each one of them separate kingdom to rule. But the brothers plotted to kill Khanitra by creating demons out of a yajna but Khanitra had lot of *puṇyas,* so the demons could not go near him and instead killed the priests, who performed the rtuals for the brothers. Having come to know about the plot from Sage Vasiśṭha, Khanitra went to forest and meditated till his death. Then his son Kṣupa became the king. Being a good ruler his period of rule was golden and his son, Vivimsa and grandson Khaninetra were also good rulers. One day Khaninetra went for hunting. Seeing him all the deer fled, but one deer came and told him to kill it. When asked for the reason, the deer said, it had no children. Khaninetra wanted deer meat for performing a Yajna and while the conversation was going on another deer came and told him not to kill the first deer as it had no children and instead kill the second one as it had many sons. When asked about the reason the second deer said that it had sons and it did not want to live as it was always worried about their safety. Khaninetra decided that he would not kill either of them but to do *tapasyā* for a son. He meditated on the banks of Gomatī and prayed to Indra. He got a son, named Vālakāśva, whom he taught the art of warfare. When he became the king, all the kings jointly attacked him. Worried about the situation, he covered his face and was thinking; many soldiers emerged from his hands and defeated the enemies. Because of this he came to be known as Karaṇdhāma.

Avikṣita

Avikṣita was the son of Karaṇdhāma and from the astrologers he knew that his son would become famous. Since Avikṣita was very handsome and had very good qualities many princesses married him. He also fought with many kings and married their daughters. Once he fought with the king of Viśāla, but in the fight other kings joined and fought a war of *adharma.* They tied him and brought him before the king Viśāla. Having come to know about his son's capture, Karaṇdhāma came to his rescue and defeated the king of Viśāla. Karaṇdhāma wanted his son to marry the daughter of the king of Viśāla but he refused and came back. But the princess of Viśāla was adamant to marry Avikṣita and went to forest to do *tapasyā* to attain him. She did so strenuous penance that in three months, she was about to die. The gods came rushing and promised that she would marry Avikṣita. One day when Avikṣita went to forest for hunting he heard some woman crying and found that a demon was carrying away the princess. He killed the demon and married her. He had a son named Marutta.

Marutta was very intelligent and was taught warfare by none other than Bhārgava. As Avikṣita had no desire to rule, the kingdom was handed over to Marutta. Marutta ruled and performed yajnas so much that he became more powerful than Indra himself. Once a sage came to Marutta and complained that snakes were disturbing their pursuit. Seven sages had died and sought protection. Marutta went to the hermitage of the sage and found seven sages were dead. He released a divine weapon, which burnt all the snakes. The snakes went and sought protection to the mother of Marutta. Avikṣita came to the rescue of the snakes and advised his son to stop, but the son said that since they had committed sin he would not stop. At this point Avikṣita let loose a terrible weapon, but the sages came and stopped the dual after the snakes promised to bring back the seven sages to life. Father and son embraced each other. *MB. Aś. Ch. 3-10.*

Nariṣyanta was the eldest son of Marutta. Marutta ruled over the world for seventeen thousand years and then handed over to the son. Nariṣyanta once performed a yajna, the kind of which had never been performed and he gave away so much to the Brāhmins that, when he wanted to perform a second yajna no Brāhmin was willing to be the priest as they had received enough. Dama was his son and in strength he was like Indra and in calmness he was like a sage. Once in the *svayamvara* of Suman, daughter of Cārukarma, she selected Dama, but there were three other princes who wanted to marry her and they abducted her. In the dual that ensued Dama killed Mahānanda, defeated Vapuṣmana and rescued Suman. When Nariṣyanta became old he handed over the kingdom to Dama and retired to forest. Vapuṣmana came to the *asrama* of Nariṣyanta and grabbed him by the hair and cut off his head. The sages who were by the side protested but he paid no attention. When the news reached Dama, he vowed to feed the flesh of Vapuṣmana to demons; otherwise he would jump into the fire. A fierce fight began and seeing his generals being killed Vapuṣmana started fleeing but Dama called him back to fight like a Kṣhatriya. He killed all his seven sons, grabbed Vapuṣmana by hair and killed him also. *Ch. 4.*

Hariścandra

Hariścandra was the king of solar dynasty, very much reputed for his unique truthfulness and integrity. In order to keep up his word and for the sake of truth, Hariśchandra gifted away his kingdom to Viśvāmitra. In spite of handing over the kingdom, Viśvmitra claimed *guru dakṣiṇā,* and to pay that he sold his wife Candramatī and son Rohitāśva and finally himself. He earned his livelihood by cremating corpses and himself doing the duty of the guard in the burning *ghāt* as a slave to a *Caṇḍāla.* Then the *Trimūrthīs,* Brahmā, Viṣṇu and Śiva appeared and granted many boons and rewarded him with all honors. *De. Bh. Skanda 7*

The entire Purāṇa was narrated by the birds to Sage Jaimini.

Bhaviṣya Purāṇa

The text of this Purāṇa consists of two parts *Pūrvārdha* and *Uttarārdha.* But many scholars consider that the latter half as an independent treatise and call it as *Bhaviṣyottara Purāṇa.* This Purāṇa is a veritable store house of topics such as the samskāras, rules on studying Vedas, vratas, glorification and worship of Sūrya devata etc. Interestingly this Purāṇa mentions about bringing of the Maga brāhmaṇas from the Śakadvipa into our country by Sāmba, son of Sri Kṛṣṇa and getting them settled on the banks of the river Candrabhāgā. They are supposed to be Zorostrians from Persia. The boost to Sun worship in our country is due to them. This is called Bhaviṣya Purāṇa because it gives the genealogy of the kings, who will come in the future. This contains 14,500 verses.

Brahmā

This Purāṇa gives more importance to Brahmā and it is known as *rajasic Purāṇa,* as Brahmā is always connected with creation. Some sages approached Sage Śatānīka, a disciple of Vedavyāsa to tell them about the righteous conduct, and on the advice of Vedavyāsa, Śatānīka approached another brother disciple, named Sumantu. And the discussions between them form the substance of this Purāṇa. It was Brahmā who created the universe and from his powers he created the sages Marīci, Atri, Angīras, Pulastya, Pulaha, Kratu, Vasiśṭha, Bhṛgu, Dakṣa and Nārada.

Gaṇeś

Earlier human efforts gave the desired results and there was no need for divine grace. And people had become over confident. Brahmā did not like this and he wanted to somehow stop this. He created a god named Gaṇeś, whom everybody has to worship, if success was desired. He is the first god to be invoked for starting anything. [All the Purāṇas speak uniformly Gaṇeś as the son of Śiva and Pārvatī, but in this Purāṇa this is unique, which attributes Gaṇeś to Brahmā]

Worship of Sun

There are three classes of Sun worshippers. They are known as sun-worshipping Magas, fire-worshipping Magas and the sun-worshipping Bhojakas. The word 'ma' indicates sun and maga means sun worshippers. Magas hail from Śakadvīpa. The son of Kṛṣṇa, Sāmbha had a curse that he would have leprosy and the remedy for that was to worship Sun. He constructed a temple for Sun on the banks of the river Candrabhāgā. The priests from Śakadvīpa were well versed in sun worship and hence he brought the Magas and settled them here. The Maga brāhamaṇas are said to be the descendants of Sun and the story goes like this. Sujihva was a devotee of fire god and he had a daughter named Nikṣuba. She secretly married Sun and when the father came to know about this he cursed her that his son would be a 'good-for-nothing'. Nikṣuba prayed to the Sun god and she was told that though he could not undo the curse, he blessed that his descendants would study Vedas and wear holy thread. These are Maga Brāhmins. [It is suggested by scholars that Maga Brāhmins were from Iran. The ancient Iranians were worshippers of the fire and Sun.] This Purāṇa mentions five types of fire and the Iranian sacred books have five kinds of fire. Like Magas, Bhojakas too hail from Śakadvīpa. They too wear the sacred thread, which was known as *avyańga.* They believed that Viṣṇu always reside at the base, Brahmā in the middle and Śiva at the top of *avyañga*. The devotion of the Bhojakas was far superior to Magas. The Bojakas serve Sun as a wife serves her husband. It is said that for Bhojakas, there was none equal to Sūrya. The Bhojakas were born to be priest for Sun god and the story goes like this. King Priyavrata, son of Svaymbhuva Manu built a temple for Sun in Śakadvīpa with a golden idol but could not find a priest to perform the rituals in the temple and so prayed to Sūrya. As per the request of Priyavrata Sūrya created eight men out of his own body, two were from the forehead, two from the arms two from the legs and two from the rays of the Sun. These were Bhojakas and were put in charge of the rituals at that temple.

Brahmā Parva 66, 72, 73.

Temples

Bhaviṣya Purāṇa deals elaborately on building of temples, types of temples, suitable places for temples etc. The lands where bones, coal, hair etc are found are not suitable for building temple. Different types of soils are suitable for people from different *Varṇas* to build temple. White earth is suitable for Brāhmins, red earth for Kṣatriyas, yellow for Vaiśyas and black for the fourth class. The quality of the ground is tested. First a pit is dug and the pit is then filled up. After filling, if mud is left over, the land is most suitable. If it just fills the pit, it is medium type. If the pit is not filled, the place is not suitable. There are said to be twenty types of temples, beginning from Meru, which is a multiple storied to single story with sixteen sides. Elaborately dealt topics are about the type of idols, material used, size, shapes etc. Defective images invoke their wrath.

Religious Rites. [*Vratas*]

A vrata is defined as willful denial of bodily comforts to prove the control over the mind. It is performed to please the gods for some favor and also to have mastery over the mind. The benefits accrued from the rites are passed on to others. The following story makes it clear. Ūrmila was a poor woman, living in Mithilā and as she could not make her livelihood there, she went to Avanti. Once her children were very hungry and she had to steal some grains from her master's granary. Her daughter, named Śyamala was very beautiful and was married to Yama. Yama told Śyamala that though she was free to go anywhere in the house but she should neither enter nor open the locks of seven rooms. In the meantime Ūrmila died. Though Śyamala obeyed her husband's instructions, curiosity made her to open one of the rooms and peep inside. She saw that her mother was being tortured by *yamadūtas*. One by one, she found that in all the rooms her mother was being tortured. She immediately ran to yama and told him that she had disobeyed him but wanted to know why her mother was being tortured? Yama replied that it was because she stole some grains from her master who was brāhmaṇa and stealing from a brāhmaṇa was a big sin. Śyamala wanted somehow to save her mother and asked how she could save her mother. Yama replied that as she had accumulated lot of *puṇyas* by observing *budhāṣtami* – a religious vow observed on the eighth lunar day, which falls on a Wednesday, she could transfer some to her mother. Thus Śyamala saved her mother from the torments.

Sharing of Merits

On the sandy stretch of the river Vetrāvati, a Brāhmin was walking and while walking, he found a ghost getting roasted in the hot sands and the ghost was crying of agony. When enquired for the reason for the pitiable condition, the ghost said that in its previous birth, it was a *Vaiśya,* who had accumulated a lot of wealth but neither donated anything nor ever worshipped the gods.The only aim in his life was material pursuit, and now suffering for that. The ghost requested the Brāhmin to save him. The Brāhmin transferred some of the *puṇyas* he had accumulated due to observing *śukra- dvādaśī –vrata,* the twelfth lunar day which falls on a Friday, and relieved the ghost from the agony.

Vratas

Bhaviṣya Purāṇa has a number of vratas for propitiating the gods, such as *ubhaya dvādaśi vrata, tilaka vrata, jatismara vrata, rasakalyāni vrata, ardranandakāri vrata,* etc. It has a number of vratas to propitiate the Sun god, like *abhaya pakṣa saptami, ananta saptami* etc and there are about thirty three vratas. A great number of vratas are there to propitiate other gods, like Viṣṇu, Kārtikeya etc.

Charities

This Purāṇa gives lot of importance to the performance of charities also. Wealth used in donation gets multiplied only, and never gets depleted. There are rules about how much *dakṣiṇā* should be given to the priest for performing a yajna and how much charities should be given. There are many types of charities and they are like donating cows, ox, land, she-buffalo, utensils, house, food, plate, bed, drinking water and many more.

Guru

A teacher, who has knowledge, should transfer it to eligible students and one who does not fulfill this condition is not eligible to be maintained by the states. There are four types of teachers:

- *Ācārya* is one who teaches the secret knowledge of the Vedas.
- *Upādhyāya* is one who teaches Vedas for his livelihood.
- *Guru* is one with whom the students stay and learn. The teacher provides the student the food and shelter.
- *Ṛtvija* is one who performs sacrifices as a profession.
- *Mahāguru* is one who is supreme among all of them and who is well versed with the entire *Vedas.*

Wages

To ensure proper remuneration for different type of jobs, rules regarding, how much wages should be given for different types of jobs performed were laid down. Several jobs like brick laying, well digging, sweeping, making copper vessels, bronze vessels, blacksmith etc are in the list.

Marriage

There are four categories of girls, a seven year old is called *gauri,* a ten year old is *nagnika*, a twelve year as *kanyaka* and above that a *rajasvalā.* The best one for marriage is *gauri,* next is *nagnika and kanyaka, rajasvalā* is the worst. There were eight forms of marriage.

- *Brahmā* is that form of marriage in which the bride is dressed in valuable jewellary is given away to noble family.
- *Daiva* is a marriage in which the bride is married to a groom of good conduct in the presence of priests.
- *Ārśa* is the one in which the daughter is given away after performing Vedic rituals and donating a cow or a bull.
- *Prājapatya* is the marriage in which the girl's father instructs the pair to discharge their religious duties.
- *Asura* is the marriage in which the bride's parents give the bride after receiving a price.
- *Gandharva* is the marriage in which they get married after falling in love.
- *Rākṣasa* is the one where the bride is abducted and married.
- *Paiśāca* is one where the abduction is done by force or deceit, without the consent of the bride.

The Purāṇa states that a wife is half of the husband and where women are not revered, they are destroyed. It deals elaborately as to how a woman should behave. It can be seen that divorce is permitted, if any one is not satisfied with the other or the woman is barren. It recommends that the husband wait for eight years and in case of divorce the *strīdhana* received must be returned.

The Future

The uniqueness of the Bhaviṣya Purāṇa is what it says about the future. It gives the complete details of the dynasty in Kali Yuga. Though this is found in all the Purāṇas, Matsya and Vāyu Purāṇas mention that this has originated from Bhaviṣya Purāṇa only. The Purāṇas say that after Sri Kṛṣṇa gave up his mortal body Kali Yuga had started. The dynasty of Kali Yuga would be: The Pauravas of Pāṇdavas dynasty, Ikṣvāku dynasty, Barhadratas of Magadh, Pradyotas, Śiṣunāgas, The Nandas, The Mauryas, The Sungas, The Kaṇvas, and The Andhras. After Andhras, the ruling will be taken over by their servants. There will be Vidiṣ dynasty of nāga king Śeṣa also.In fact attempt has been made to fix the period of Mahābhārata war by the number of kings and work backward up to Parikṣit, and the approximate period has been fixed between 1500 and 1000 B.C.

Different Aspects of Sun

Bhaviṣya Purāṇa extols Sun god very much. Sun has got twelve aspects. In each of the twelve months one aspect of the Sūrya is manifested. The chariot of the Sun is made out of gold and was built by Brahmā him self and the charioteer is known as Anuru. It is drawn by seven golden color horses and always two *adityas, two sages, two apsarās, two gandharvas and two nagas* ride on the chariot.

Vāmana Purāṇa.

Vāmana Purāṇa had been taught by sage Pulastya to Nārada. In this work, the ten incarnations of Viṣṇu has been dealt, especially the *Vāmana avatāra.* This Purāṇa also deals with the other topics. It is said that this Purāṇa was in two parts and the second part is known as *Bṛhadvāmana purāṇa,* which is no more available. This Purāṇa has ten thousand verses. The scene of Śiva marrying Pārvatī is vividly described. This Purāṇa is said to be similar to Varāha Purāṇa.

Nārada once went to sage Pulastya and wanted to know about the Vāmana Purāṇa. Pārvatī complained to Śiva that she would like to have a house as the monsoon was fast approaching, but Śiva suggested that they could go and live in the clouds, as he was not in a position to have a house. Then the sage Pulastya recounted the story of Brahmā losing a head, with variation, which had been already dealt with.The Yajna performed by Dakṣa is also described.

Urvaśī

Two sages Nara and Nārāyaṇa were meditating and Indra as usual, decided that their meditations should be disturbed. So he deputed the god of love – Madana and Rambhā, a nymph for this purpose. When Nārāyaṇa saw them he understood the purpose of their visit. He asked Madana to sit down and while they were discussing; the sage took out a bunch of flowers and started kneading on his thigh. From that a very beautiful woman appeared. She was named as *Urvaśī,* as she appeared from *'uru'* meaning thigh. Nārāyana presented her to Madana and told him that Indra could use her as an *apsarā*. Seeing the power of the sage, Madana ran from there.

De. Bh. Skanda 4.

Once Prahlāda went to bathe in the Naimīśatīrtha and after that he went for a hunt. Near the river Sarasvatī, he found a tree fully pierced with arrows. A little further he found two sages, sitting and meditating. They had bow and arrow with them. Prahlāda decided that they could not be sages. He told them that they did not look like sages. The reply to that was that they were doing what was in their power. Prahlāda, being a king told them that they could not be having any power, independent of him. The sages replied "We are Nara and Nārāyaṇa and there is no equal to our power." Prahlāda became wild with anger and asked his soldiers to attack the two sages. Nara and Prahlāda fought with each other and the fight became fiery. Helplessly Prahlāda shot the divine weapon, *Brahmāstra,* which was repelled by *nārāyaṇāstra.* Then Prahlāda released still superior divine weapon, which was also made null and void by Nara. Now Nārāyaṇa relieved Nara and started the fight, but soon Prahlāda was hit by an arrow and fell unconscious. He was taken away by his soldiers. Prahlāda came back the next day and the fight continued for long but in vain. Prahlāda prayed to Viṣṇu.The Lord appeared and advised Prahlāda that Nara and Nārāyaṇa being his incarnation, nobody can defeat them. The lord suggested to him to win over them by devotion. Prahlāda handed over his kingdom to Andhaka, another demon and started praying in *Badrikāśrama.* Pleased with his devotion Nara and Nārāyaṇa offered him a boon, Prahlāda wanted that the sin committed by fighting with them should be absolved and it was granted. He also wanted that he should ever remain a devotee of Viṣṇu. The two sages blessed Prahlāda that he would be invincible. *Ch. 8.*

Demon King Following Dharma

Sukeśa, son of Vidyutkeśa was a demon king and by difficult penance he had obtained a wonderful city, which could fly in the sky, a boon from Śiva. Once Sukeśa happened to go to a forest, where cluster of hermitages were there and he asked the sages to give him some good advice. The sages described about *dharma,* creation, geography, sins, hells etc. After hearing the advices, Sukeśa ordered his citizens to follow *dharma*, as laid down by the scriptures. By practicing this, the energy of the demons increased and their city was shining like sun in the day and like moon in the night. The Sun god was unhappy, because his glory started diminishing. He gazed at their city with rage and the city fell down. Hearing the wail of the demons, Sukeśa prayed to Lord Śiva and the Lord having known the reason gazed at Sun. The Sun started falling, so Sūrya appealed to the sages and the sages suggested to him to fall on the city of *Vāraṇāsi.* Sūrya fell on the city of *Vāraṇāsi* and bathed in both the rivers, *Vāraṇa and Asi.* As the people on the earth started suffering without sun, Brahmā suggested the people to pray to Śiva. Śiva was merciful and established the sun in its place and Brahmā established the city of Sukeśa in its place. *Ch. 15.*

Vindhya Mountain

The peak of the Vindhya Mountain was so tall that it was touching the sky and prevented the sun rays, falling on the ground. The sun went to the sage Agastya and requested him to do something. Sage Agastya adopted the form of an old man and went to the Vindhya peaks.

He requested the peak to lower its height as he wanted to pass through for going to a *tīrtha.* The peak obliged and lowered its peak so that he can pass it. After passing, the sage Agastya told the mountain to keep its peak lowered as he would return by the same route. He also threatened that if not, he will curse the mountain. The fear of curse made the Vindhya to keep its peak lowered, but sage Agastya never returned by the route. *De. Bh. Skanda 10.*

Why Viṣṇu is Called 'Murāri"?

Sage Nārada wanted to know from sage Pulastya, why Viṣṇu is called Murāri. Sage Kaśyap had a son named Mura. Mura was wondering why always the *asuras* get beatings from gods? To stop this he did penance and got a boon from Brahmā that whomsoever Mura touched in a fight, he would die. Armed with the wonderful weapon Mura defeated all the gods including Indra. Once on his visit to earth, he found King Raghu, performing a Yajña and challenged the king. Sage Vasiṣṭha, who happened to be there, told Mura that humans have already been defeated by him and suggested to go and fight with Yama. Mura went and challenged Yama and Yama fled to Viṣṇu. Viṣṇu told Yama to send Mura to him. Accordingly Yama told Mura that Viṣṇu was waiting for him to fight. When Mura appeared before Viṣṇu, Viṣṇu asked him why he was frightened so much. He said he could not fight with a man whose heart was trembling. Viṣṇu told him to put his hand on the heart to see how his heart was trembling. Mura put his hand on his heart and died. In Sanskrit *'ari'* means enemy and Viṣṇu was Mura's enemy and so he is called *'Murāri'.* *Ch. 60.*

How *Daṇḍakāraṇya* Came into Being

Daṇḍa was the name of a prosperous king, who was the son of Ikṣvāku. In the course of a hunting expedition, Daṇḍa happened to see Arajas, the daughter of Śukrācārya and he was very much fascinated. He committed rape on her and she told her father about the attack by Daṇḍa. Śukrācārya asked his daughter to do *tapas* and he told her that he would burn Daṇḍa's kingdom by a rain of fire. Arajas did penance as suggested by her father. At the behest of Śukrācārya Indra destroyed Daṇḍa's kingdom by a rain of fire. Afterwards the place had become a terrible forest where even birds and animals did not live and came to be known as *Daṇḍakāraṇya*. *Utt. Rā.*

Another Dwarf

There is another story of Viṣṇu adopting the form of a dwarf in *Vāmana Purāṇa*. Dhundu was a demon who had acquired the boon from Brahmā that gods including Indra would be unable to kill him. He drove away the gods and they had taken shelter in Brahmā loka. Dhundu wanted to go to Brahmāloka and drive away them from there also, but to go to Brahmāloka he had to perform hundred horse sacrifices and he made ready to carry out the sacrifice on the banks of river Devikā. Frightened gods appealed to Viṣṇu. Viṣṇu knew that Dhundu could not be killed and so he adopted the form of a dwarf and started floating in the waters of Devikā. The demons rescued him and asked him how did this happen? The dwarf explained that in a property dispute his brother had thrown him into the river. Taking pity Dhundu asked the dwarf whether he would like to have some property. The dwarf declined and wanted land as big as his three feet. When Dhundu agreed, the dwarf took a giant form, measured the world in one step, second step all the regions including heaven and the third step he put on Dhundu's back, pushed him down into a pit. Having measured in three steps Viṣṇu is called *'trivikrama'*. -

Earlier Births of Purūrava

The first king of lunar dynasty was Purūravas. Dharma was a Vaiśya and was rich enough, but he was righteous. Being a trader he moved about a lot and once he had to travel to Saurāstra region. While traveling through a desert all his belongings were looted and was left alone. Disgusted he lied down under a tree, which was the only tree seen in the desert. When he woke up he found himself surrounded by a number of ghosts. The leader of the ghosts asked Dharma what he was doing there. Dharma explained his condition. Taking pity on him the leader of the demons, asked the others to arrange for food and water, which was arranged immediately. After having his stomach full, Dharma asked the ghost about its past. The ghost recounted its past. It was Somaśarma and had a rich neighbor named Somaśrava, a devotee of Viṣṇu. Somaśarma was evil and miser. Once Somaśarma happened to go, with other people on a pilgrimage and it so happened that he donated little food to a brāhmaṇa, but that food was not suitable for giving as it was meant for the ghosts. So after his death he became a ghost. Having given some food, he had no problem for food. Dharma performed the final rites for Somaśarma at Gayā and he was freed. Dharma lived a righteous life and was born as a king and he continued to be righteous and so in his next birth he was born as a brāhmaṇa but ugly and after praying to Viṣṇu he became handsome. Then his succeeding birth was king Purūravas.

Penitence Converts Evil to Good

There was a great ascetic and erudite scholar, called Kośakāra, son of sage Mudgala. A son was born to him an idiot, deaf and dumb and the child was forsaken at the gates. An evil minded Rākṣasa woman replaced the child with her own. Hearing the cries of the child, Kośakāra's wife picked up the child, thinking it as her own. In the meantime the husband of the Rākṣasa woman asked her to leave the child from where she had picked up. She put back the child, but could not pick up her child as it was tied by a *mantra* by Kośakāra. They brought up both the children, Divākara was the name of the Rākṣasa child and Niśākara was the name of Kośakāra's own son. At the age of seven, both the children were invested with the sacred thread. Divākara learned the Vedas, but Niśākara did not and he was despised by all. His father pushed him into a well and covered its mouth with stone. Niśākara lived in the well for many years. The fruits of a cluster of plants in the well, served as his food. Some ten years later when Niśākara's mother found the mouth of the well closed, she asked as to who did so and from the well came reply "mother, it was father who covered it." The mother asked who was in the well and the answer was that it was her son. His mother rolled away the stone and took the boy home. The boy told the parents that it was a good penance for him to be in the well and he felt sorry for his indifference to studies. He wanted to lead a religious life. The boy could remember his earlier births and told his parents as why was he born as dumb and deaf. He told them that because of repeated evil acts he was shunting from hell to different births, from bird to animal and that was why he had to be born as dumb and deaf as left over part of sins. *Ch. 91.*

Section II

Purāṇas Dealing with the Exploits of Viṣṇu

Viṣṇu Purāṇa

Viṣṇu Purāṇa fairly touches the points of general features of the Purāṇas and contains the usual topics of creation, deities, Manus, the Vedas, four *varṇas* and personification of Kali Yuga, the Purānic geography, time, genealogies, ethic, vratas, temple and temple rituals, bhakti and other instructions and information. This Purāṇa belongs to A.D.300 and has around 23,000 verses. The description of the Kali Yuga, the age in which we are living now, seems to be astonishingly accurate.

The Creation

The creation has been described as having emerged from the egg which contains every object in potential form, including Brahmā as given in Brahmā Purāṇa.

Curse of Durvāsā - Churning of the Ocean

Sage Durvāsā, once got a beautiful and fragrant garland from a lady and with the garland on his head he went to Indra's place. He found Indra sitting on his elephant and he threw the garland to Indra. Indra caught it and put it on the elephant's head. When the elephant lifted its trunk, the garland fell on the ground. The sage took it as an insult and cursed Indra that Lakṣmī, goddess of wealth will leave his kingdom. So not only Indra's place but all the three worlds lost the lustre. This was the chance; the demons were waiting for and attacked the Devas. On the advice of Brahmā the Devas prayed to Viṣṇu and the Lord advised them to have a truce with the demons, so that the ocean can be churned along with them, by which *amṛta* was expected, which would make them immortal. The demons did not know the background and readily agreed. The snake Vāsuki was used as a rope and mount Mandāra as the churning rod. Viṣṇu adopted the form of a large turtle to support the mountain. From the churning wonderful things came out, just like the cow Surabhi, Vāruṇī, Pārijāta tree, the apsarās, the moon etc. Some bad things also came out such as poison. Then Dhanvantari came out with the pot of *amṛta* in his hands. Lakṣmī emerged in a lotus, holding a lotus in her hand. Sages chanted hymns, eight elephants protected and gave her bath, the ocean gave her garland of lotus flowers [unfading] and Viśvakarmā provided jewels. Lakṣmī embraced Viṣṇu. The demons somehow managed to get the pot of *amṛta*. Viṣṇu took the form of a female, charmed the demons and took to distribute the *amṛta* and gave all to the gods and thus they became immortal and stronger. The demons fled to the underworld. Gods began to rule the heaven, sun came back to the old path, and so the stars. Indra pleased Lakṣmī, who gave him boons that she would never leave the three worlds; she would never turn away from anyone who prays to her with the same prayer, which Indra used.

Dhruva

Manu had two righteous sons, namely Priyavrata and Uttānapāda. Uttānapāda had two wives Suruci and Sunīti. Suruci's son was Uttama and Sunīti's son was Dhruva. Once when Uttama was sitting on the lap of Uttānapāda,

Dhruva also climbed on to his lap. Suruci scolded Dhruva and said that he should not aspire for the throne as it was always for Uttama. Dhruva was very much hurt and complained to his mother, who comforted him, that human beings suffer or prosper according to their past *karmas* and thus not to be unhappy but do religious, righteous and selfless work. Dhruva resolved to attain the highest place in the world and left the house to do penance. In the forest he met the seven sages [*saptaṛṣīs*] and told them his resolve to attain the highest place, neither wealth nor kingdom. He got the advice to pray to Viṣṇu and gave him a *mantra.* Dhruva went to the banks of Yamunā [madhuvani]. His penance was so great that the gods started worrying about their positions. The Lord assured the gods that Dhruva's penance was not for any position and appeared before Dhruva. The Lord narrated to him about Dhruva's previous birth of brāhmaṇa, a devotee of the Lord and wanted to be a prince so he was now. Dhruva was placed in the middle of the sky and all the stars revolve around him. His place is near the constellation of seven sages forming the great bear.

Amsa 1. Ch. 11&12.

The Pracetas

Emperor Pṛthu had two sons named Antardhāna and Vādī. Antardhāna got a son named Havirdhāna. His wife was from the race of Agni, named Dhiṣaṇa, gave birth to six sons. They were Prācīnabarhis, Sukra, Gaya, Kṛṣṇa, Vraja and Ajina. Prācīanbarhis had ten sons and named Pracetās. The ten sons did hard penance for ten thousand years to fulfill the instructions of their father and through the grace of Lord Viṣṇu completed the task of filling the world with people. *VP - 75.*

Prahlāda

Hiraṇyakaśipu was protected under the boon from Brahmā that his death may neither be in the day nor in the night, from any animal nor man, nor with any instruments etc. Armed with this strength he conquered the three worlds and also assumed the title of Indra, Savitā, Vāyu and Agni. Everyone had to worship him and had a palace created out of crystal to live in, had full enjoyment of drink and dance etc. Hiraṇyakaśipu begot of Kayādhu five sons, Prahlāda, Samhlāda, Anuhlāda, Sibi and Bāskala. Young Prahlāda was sent to study under a guru [teacher] and Hiraṇyakaśipu wanted to know what his son had learnt The reply was that he had learnt to worship Viṣṇu. Hiraṇyakaśipu was furious. He asked the teacher why did he teach this and the reply was that he had not. Prahlāda said that he had learnt it from the teacher of the teachers - Viṣṇu. He was sent back to the teacher to undo what he had learnt. After many years Prahlāda came back, he was asked by his father what he had learnt and the reply was "to pray to Viṣṇu". He ordered his son to be killed and hundreds of demons attacked him but no harm could be done to Prahlāda. Many snakes were let loose on Prahlāda but no harm could come to him· because he had the protection of Viṣṇu. Many elephants were ordered to stamp him but their tusks broke. Fire was lit around him but fire could not do any harm. On the request of his priests Prahlāda was sent again to school and whenever he found time, he used to pray to Viṣṇu. Hearing this, Hiraṇyakaśipu instructed his cooks to poison his food but as his mind was always on Viṣṇu the poison had no effect. Then the priests created a fierce demon and the demon attacked Prahlāda with a *trisūl* but it broke into pieces so the demon started attacking the priests and killed them but because of Prahlāda's prayer they were brought back to life. Hiraṇyakaśipu asked Prahlāda from where he was getting these powers and the answer was that they were the powers of Viṣṇu. He asked his servants to take Prahlāda to the top of the palace and throw him down, but nothing happened. Then he called Sambarāsura, who was well versed in the art of māyā to create illusion around Prahlāda, but Viṣṇu's *Sudarśan cakra* destroyed all the illusions. One day Hiraṇyakaśipu was so wild that he took out his sword and asked Prahlāda where his Viṣṇu was. The reply was that Viṣṇu was everywhere. Hiraṇyakaśipu struck the nearby pillar when Viṣṇu in the form of a fierce man-lion form appeared. The man-lion jumped on the body of Hiraṇyakaśipu, put him on his lap, tore the intestines and killed him. Moved by the devotion of Prahlāda Viṣṇu appeared in his normal form and asked him to ask for boons. Prahlāda wanted that he should be ever faithful to Viṣṇu. Prahlāda became the king and ruled for a long time. *Skanda. 7.*

Priyavrata and Bharata

The eldest son of Svāyambhuva Manu, Priyavrata married Barhiṣmatī, daughter of Viśvakarmā and had ten sons. Three of the sons were not interested in kingdom and became sages. Then the world was divided into seven regions and each one was given one region to rule. The regions and the kings were:

Name of king	Region
Agnīdhra	Jambūdvīpa.
Vapuṣmān	Śālmalidvīpa.
Dyuti-mān	Krauñcadvīpa.
Medhātithi	Plakṣadvīpa.
Bhavya	Śākadvīpa.

Śavāna	Puṣkaradvīpa.
Jyotiṣmān	Kuśadvīpa.

Agnīdhra had nine sons and he divided the Jambudvipa among them and Nābhi got the region which ultimately became Bhāratavarṣa. Nabhi's grandson was Bharata after whom the country was called Bhāratavarṣa.

Geographical description: The seven dvipas were surrounded by seven oceans. In the middle of the Jambudvipa is the golden hued Mount Meru. River Gañga originates from the feet of the Lord Viṣṇu.

Astronomy: Worlds of the sun and moon, Stars -Mercury, Venus, Jupiter, Saturn, the Saptaṛṣīs and Dhruva come under astronomy. Lokas are Bhūh, Bhuvah, Svah, Mahah, Tapo, Satya and Brahmāloka. There are also seven underworlds.

Vedavyāsa

In each age Viṣṇu in the form of Vedavyāsa divides the Vedas. In the present Manvantara the Veda had already been divided 28 times. The next Vedavyāsa will be Aśvatthāma. The disciples of Vedavyāsa, who had learnt all the four Vedas, are: Paila who was taught Rg Veda, Vaiśampāyana, the Yajur Veda, Jaimini, the Sāma Veda and Sumantu, the Atharva Veda.

Teacher's Anger

Once a famous gathering was organized by *ṛṣīs* and stipulated that whoever did not attend the gathering would commit the crime of killing a Brāhmaṇa. Vaiśampāyana did not attend the gathering and on the seventh day, by mistake he stamped his nephew and killed him, which was a terrible sin. Vaiśampāyana divided the Yajur Veda into twenty-seven parts and distributed these parts among his disciples and one among them was Yājñavalkya. He told his disciples that since he had committed the crime of killing a Brāhmaṇa, he wanted to do atonement and requested them to organize a sacrifice. Yājñavalkya said "I will organize myself for the sacrifice as others do not have the powers". This angered Vaiśampāyana and he asked him to return whatever he had learnt. Yājñavalkya vomited whatever he had learnt and other disciples ate it in the form of birds. In Yajur Veda there is a branch named '*taitirīya*' after the name of the bird Tittira. Since Yājñavalkya wanted to learn Yajurveda he prayed to Sun god and finally in the form of a horse Sun taught him Yajur Veda which even Vaiśampāyana did not know.

MB. Śā. Ch. 318.

Purāṇas

Purāṇas existed in the form of '*Samhita*', the original text that was taught by Vedavyāsa to his disciple Romaharṣaṇa. Romaharṣaṇa had six disciples, namely Sumati, Agnivarcas, Mitrāyus, Śāmśapāyana, Akṛtavaraṇa, and Sāvarṇi. It was on this basis that Viṣṇu Purāṇa was brought out after Padma Purāṇa, the glory of Lord Viṣṇu.

Yama

He is the authority to award punishment for the omission and commission by the *jīvas* and one can not escape him except those who are devoted to Lord Viṣṇu. He performs according to the dictates, laid down by the Scriptures. This question was answered to Nakula by Bhīṣma. Bhīṣma's friend had heard the conversation from Jatismara sage that had taken place between Yama and Yama's servant. Yama told his servants not to touch the devotees of Viṣṇu as he also works under the direction of Viṣṇu.

Rituals

These are scriptural code of conduct to be observed in particular situations and events such as at the time of birth of a son, marriage etc. Each *Varṇa* has its own specific contents. The rituals govern every aspect of life from birth to death. The priest class is the authority to perform these rites.

Māyāmoha

It was a new religion, especially created for the demons and *daityas* so that they give up the Vedas and righteous path, in order they lose their power and capability, which led the Devas to win the war, since they followed vedic dictates.

Sin of Even Speaking to Evil Persons

Śatadhanu and his wife Śaibyā were committed to Viṣṇu and spent their time in meditation on the banks of river Bhāgīrathī. One day Śatadhanu happened to speak to a fraudulent teacher and his wife avoided him. After death, because he talked to the fraudulent teacher he was born as a dog and Śaibyā was born as a Jatismara daughter of King of Kāśī. Having known that her husband was born as a dog, she refused marriage and located the dog and reminded to it its previous birth. The dog fell from a mountain and died and its next birth was of a jackal. Having been reminded about its previous birth, the jackal died and was born as a wolf, then a vulture, a crow, and a peacock. Finally when King Janaka was performing an *aśvamedha Yajña*, the peacock had a bath at the time of sacrifice. When Śaibyā reminded it about its earlier life, the peacock died and then was born as a son of Janaka. Śaibyā married him and when he died she died on the funeral pyre and both of them attained heaven.

Dynasties – Manus

First in the line of Manus was Brahmā. [Visnu came out of Brahmāṇḍa – the Brahmān]. From the Brahmā's finger was born Dakṣa Prajāpati and his daughter was Aditi. Aditi's son was Sūrya and Sūrya's son was Manu. Through a Yajna to Mitra and Varuṇa, a daughter named Ilā came out. As Manu wanted a son, so Ilā became a son for some time, named Sudyumna. Budha, Chandra's son married Ilā and they had a son called Purūravā. Sudyumna performed yajna to become a man and after becoming a man he had three sons, Utkala, Gaya and Vinata. In this lineage there was king called Marut who performed a wonderful yajña. Further down the family, there was a king named Śaryati, who had a daughter Sukanyā and she was married to sage Cyavana. They had a son Anarta and Anarta's son Revata had hundred sons and the eldest son Kakudmi had a daughter Revati. He was not sure to whom he should marry his daughter and went to Brahmā to consult. On the way he heard gandharvas singing and spent some time, listening to it. Finally when he approached Brahmā, Brahmā said that several thousand years had passed, since he was listening to the music and his city was named as Dvārakā. Brahmā further stated that Viṣṇu was born as Baladeva there. He married Revati to Baladeva. As Revati was taller than him Baladeva pulled down her height, with his plough.

Ikṣvāku and Others

From the spittle of Manu came out a son, named Ikṣvāku and his son was Vikukṣi. He wanted to perform *Mahāpralayaśrāddha* and sent his son to get some meat. Vikukṣi hunted many deers and he was hungry, so ate some of them. When this was offered to Vasiṣṭha he said it was unclean. Ikṣvāku banished his son, though he ruled the country after his death. Vikukṣi's son was Purañjaya, who was brave. When devas were defeated by the demons Viṣṇu told the Devas that he would be born as Purañjaya and defeat the demons. So Devas approached Purañjaya and riding on Indra's shoulders he defeated the demons. So he was known as Kakutstha. In his lineage was born Yuvanāśva. As he had no son, he performed a ceremony, which lasted till midnight and the priests had kept the sacred water in a pot, to be given to his wife. Not knowing this, Yuvanāśva drank the water and a child was born from his right side. Indra agreed to be the mother of the child and the child was known as Māndhātā. During Māndhātā's time there was a sage named Saubhari, who lived under the water and once he saw a king fish playing with its children. So the sage desired that he too should have a family. He wanted Māndhātā to give one of his fifty daughters in marriage. Though the king did not want his daughters to be married to him as he was ugly he was afraid of his curse. So he said that it was his daughters' right to choose their husbands. Saubhari requested one chance and if all of them refused to marry him, he would go away. The king agreed and all the fifty daughters wanted to marry him because Saubhari, being a powerful sage, transformed himself into a very handsome man. So he married all the fifty and asked Viśvakarmā to make individual palace for all of them. After some time, Māndhātā wanted to find out how his daughters were and he was surprised to find all of them happy as Saubhari created fifty different forms of himself. *Ch. 2-4*

Sagara

One of the descendants of Māndhātā was Purukutsa. Viṣṇu had entered him so that he could defeat the *gandharvas,* who had occupied *nāga world.* In the same dynasty was king Subāhu who lost a war and went to the forest with his wife. When she was about to deliver, Subāhu's another wife gave her poison and the child remained in the womb for seven years. When Subāhu died in the hermitage of sage Aurva, his wife wanted to die on the same funeral pyre but Aurva prevented her, telling that his son would be the bravest. This child was Sagara. Having learnt all warfare from Aurva, Sagara gained back the kingdom lost by his father. *Ch. 16 & 17.*

In the dynasty of Bhagīratha, there was a king named Saudāsa. One day while hunting, he saw two tigers and he killed one of them, which became a demon before dying and the other one vowed of revenge. Later the king performed a yajna in which Vasiṣṭha was the priest. When Vasiṣṭha had gone out, the demon took the form of Vasiṣṭha and asked the king to make some meat and rice. Then the demon took the form of the cook and prepared human meat and served. Vasiṣṭha understood it to be a human meat and cursed Saudāsa to become a demon. Having realized that it was not the mistake of the king he reduced the curse to twelve years. But the king felt that he had been cursed unnecessarily and wanted to curse the sage. So he took water to curse back the sage but his wife prevented it and he had to pour the water on his feet because of which his feet became diseased and black. Because of this he came to be known as Kalmāṣapāda. As a demon he was eating human beings. Once he met a brāhmaṇa, going with his wife and wanted to eat them. The wife of the brāhmaṇa begged for mercy but when he did not relent, she cursed him that as soon as he met his wife he would die. So even after twelve years, when he got back his original forn, he did not meet his wife. In this lineage Sri Rāma was born. *MB. Ādi. 176.*

Curse to become Bodiless

Nimi was Iksāvaku's son and he performed a yajna which lasted for five hundred years. He wanted Vasiṣṭha to preside over the yajna but Vasiṣṭha said he was already performing one for Indra which would last for five hundred years and asked him to wait till then. Nimi came away and performed, with sage Gautama as the chief priest. After finishing the yajna at Indra's place, Vasiṣṭha came to Nimi's place, only to find that the Yajña was being performed. He cursed Nimi that he would become body less. Nimi too cursed Vasiṣṭha that he too would be body less, but Vasiṣṭha got another body by the grace of Mitra and Varuṇa. When the yajna was completed, Indra etc offered to give him a body but Nimi refused and only wanted that he should be in everybody's eyes and that is why blinking of eyes is called *nimisha.* As Nimi did not have a son the sages pounded Nimi's dead body and brought out a son, who was called Janaka- means father and because his father did not have a body, he was also called *Videha-* bodiless. When Janaka was ploughing the field he got a daughter who was known as Sītā.

De. Bh. Skanda 6.

Candra

[King of lunar dynasty]. Brahmā's son was Atri and Atri's son was Candra. He is the ruler of stars and plants. Because he performed *Rajasūya yajna* he became arrogant and he kidnapped Tārā, the wife of Bṛhaspati, *guru* of devas. In spite of repeated requests from Bṛhaspati, he did not return Tārā and so a war ensued. It was a terrible war and it came to a halt only with Brahmā's intervention and Tārā was returned. Candra and Tārā had a son, known as Budha.

Once Urvaśī was cursed by Mitra and Varuṇa and she had to come to the earth. She married Purūravā, but as gandharvas were feeling lonely they plotted to separate Urvaśī. They had six sons. In the lineage of Purūravā there was a king name Jāhnu, who found that his bowl, used for yajna was filled with Gaṅgā water and he drank the entire Gaṅgā but restored it on the request of *Devarṣīs* and so Gaṅgā is also known as *Jāhnavī.* In that dynasty, Gādhi had a daughter named Satyavati, who was married to sage Ṛcīka who gave Gādhi thousand horses in exchange. Satyavati wanted a son and also for her mother. Sage Ṛcīka performed a *homa* and after that he made two balls of rice and gave them to Satyavatī. He advised her to eat one of them and to give the other to her mother. Ṛcīka had put "Brahmātejas" [brilliance of Brāhmin] in the first rice ball and "Kṣātratejas' [brilliance of Kṣatriyas] in the other. When Satyavatī and her mother ate the rice balls, it so happened that the rice ball intended for her mother was eaten by Satyavatī and the one intended for Satyavatī was eaten by the mother. Later Ṛcīka came to know of the mistake. In due course Satyavatī and her mother gave birth to sons; Satyavatī's son was named Jamadagni. Satyavatī begged her husband and requested that her grandson should be brave and violent and not the son and that was what happened. Satyavatī's mother gave birth to Viśvāmitra. Jamadagni's son Parśurām killed many Kṣatriyas.

Brh. Ch. 57.

Rāji

Purūravā had a grandson named Rāji, who had five hundred brave sons. Once when war broke between *Devas* and *asuras*, both went to Brahmā to know who will win the war and Brahmā said, that side in which Rāji fights will win. Both approached Rāji. Rāji had put a condition that he should be made Indra. As Devas agreed to the condition he fought for them and won the war. But Rāji allowed Indra to continue but when he died his sons demanded to become Indra so a war was started in which they defeated Indra. On the request of Indra, Bṛhaspati performed yajna and made them unrighteous so they were defeated ultimately. *Mat. Ch. 24.*

The Jewel Syamantaka

Lord Kṛṣṇa's consort Satyabhāmā's father was Satrājit. Once he prayed to Sūrya and got a famous jewel Syamantaka and wherever the jewel was, disease, poverty would not be there. Kṛṣṇa wished that it should be with King Ugrasena. Fearing that he may have to part with the jewel, Satrājit gave it to his brother Prasena, who was killed by a lion, when he went for a hunt. The jewel came into the hands of Jāmbavān, who gave it to his son. The citizens of Dvāraka thought that Kṛṣṇa might have killed Prasena and to remove the wrong impression, Kṛṣṇa followed the trail. Finally came to Jāmbavān and there was terrible fight for twenty one days. As Kṛṣṇa did not return for eight, nine days the rumors were afloat that Kṛṣṇa had been killed, so his friends performed *Śrāddha,* which increased Kṛṣṇa's strength. Finally Kṛṣṇa won the war, got back the jewel and also married Jāmabavān's daughter, Jāmbavatī. Kṛṣṇa returned the jewel to Satrājit, who felt ashamed and gave his daughter Satyabhāmā in marriage. But some Yadavas like Akrūra, Kṛtavarmā and

Śatadhanvā also wanted to marry Satyabhāmā and they were waiting for an opportunity. When Kṛṣṇa went away to Pāṇdavas, while they were in Vāraṇāvata, Śatadanvā killed Satrājit. Satyabhāmā became furious and went to Vāranāvata to tell Kṛṣṇa about her father. Kṛṣṇa came back and with Balarām fought Śatadanvā. Śatadanvā ran for help to Akrūra and Kṛtavarmā but both refused but Akrūra agreed to keep the jewel provided Śatadanvā did not tell anyone. Both Kṛṣṇa and Balarāma chased Śatadanvā and he started running but Kṛṣṇa went behind him and killed him. But Kṛṣṇa could not find the jewel. Baladeva did not believe this and went away to Mithilā. After a lot of convincing, Baladeva returned home. In one of the meetings in the assembly, Kṛṣṇa told Akrūra that Baladeva believed that he had the jewel. He requested him to show the jewel to assembly and Akrūra showed. It was decided that it can remain with Akrūra. *Pad. Ch. 13.*

Śiśupāla

Jaya and Vijaya were the gate keepers at Vaikuṇṭha and were born thrice in asura womb, because of a curse by sage like Sanaka. In earlier life Śiśupāla had been Hiraṇyakaśipu. His mother was the sister of Vāsudeva. Śiśupāla was born with three eyes and four hands and brayed like an ass. The parents wanted to abandon the child but a ghost appeared and said that the child would grow to be very strong and powerful. It further said that as soon as the child saw the person, born to kill him, he would lose his third eye and when the child was seated on the lap of the person two of his four hands would be lost. The child was put on the lap of many persons, but nothing happened. One day Kṛṣṇa and Balrarām came to see the child. When the child was placed on Kṛṣṇa's lap, the third eye and two hands of the child vanished. Kṛṣṇa's aunt, the child's mother prayed to Kṛṣṇa not to kill the child. Kṛṣṇa promised that he would forgive him one hundred times. While Śiśupāla grew up he always maintained enemity with Kṛṣṇa. He abducted the daughter of his uncle, king of Viśālā and in the battle that followed he was killed by Kṛṣṇa and after his death, his effulgence was absorbed in Kṛṣṇa. *MB. Sab. Ch. 43.*

King Pratīpa

In the dynasty of Kuru there was a king named Pratīpa. He had three sons – Devāpi, Śāntanu and Bāhlīka. One day when he was worshipping Sūrya Devatā in the waters of Gaṅgā, a beautiful maiden rose from the waters and sat on his right thigh. The king was embarrassed and told her that the right thigh was for the daughter and daughter-in-law. He said that she would become his son's wife. She ultimately married his second son Śāntanu. Devāpi was not interested in ruling and went over to the forest. Śāntanu became the king, but there was no rain for twelve years and the Brāhamaṇas were of the opinion that the eldest son only should have become the king. Śāntanu's minister sent someone to preach all wrong things to Devāpi and so he became a sinner. He no longer was eligible to become the king and so Śāntanu continued as a king. His son was Bhīṣma.

Kali

Purāṇas state that there will be a king in future, who will be known as Mahāpadmananda, who will destroy Kṣatriyas. Śūdras then will become kings. He will have eight sons and he and his sons will rule the earth. A brāhmaṇa named Kautilya would kill all of them and the Śūdra kings known as Maurya would rule and Kautilya would make Candragupta, king. Then Sunga kings would rule, subsequent rulers would be Kaṇva, Andhra kings etc. Kali era will be a terrible one, people will not have the basic needs, and Dharma will be destroyed and Viṣṇu will be born again as Kalki.

Vāsudeva and Devakī

Vāsudeva married Devakī and Kamsa drove the chariot for them. Then a voice from the ether said "the eighth child of this woman will kill you". When Kamsa heard this, he wanted to kill Devakī, but Vāsudeva said that he would hand over the child whenever it was born. At that time the Pṛthvī Devatā went and complained at Sumeru to the gods that demons were creating havoc. It was too much for her to bear. Brahmā suggested going to the northern shores of the ocean and praying to Lord Viṣṇu. On hearing the prayers, Viṣṇu pulled out two hairs from his head, said that those two demons born out of the hairs would destroy the demons and that he would be born to Devakī as the eighth child. Hearing all these from Nārada, Kamsa imprisoned both Vāsudeva and Devakī. The seventh child was transferred to Rohiṇī, another wife of Vāsudeva without anybody's knowledge. Lord Kṛṣṇa was born on the eighth day of waning of the moon. By the grace of the Lord, the prison doors opened, the chain fell down. Vāsudeva took the child and crossed the swelling Yamuna. Vāsuki held up its hood to protect the child and Vāsudeva and the child was taken to Nanda, where his wife Yasoda had given birth to another child, a daughter known as Yogamāyā. Kṛṣṇa was placed there and Yogamāyā was brought back to the prison. The guards reported the birth of the child to Kamsa. Kamsa picked up, but the child slipped away from his hands, rose up and adopted the form of a goddess. While flying away it said that he who would kill him was already born. Kamsa called all his friends and said that all the babies which were born unduly strong should be killed. He released Vāsudeva and Devakī from the prison, telling that there was no use keeping them there.

End of Pūtanā

Once when Nanda happened to come to Mathurā, Vāsudeva congratulated him for the birth of the son as Nanda was not aware of the exchange of the babies and requested him to take care of his own child as well Rohiṇī's child. One night Pūtanā, a demoness came to breast feed Kṛṣṇa. The limbs of any child got destroyed, when the child took milk from Pūtanā. But Kṛṣṇa drank the life out of her and she fell down with a big noise. Once when Kṛṣṇa felt hungry, he was kicking his small legs. As a result of his kicking of the legs, the cart under which he was lying overturned. Everybody came running and was wondering how the cart had overturned.

Sage Gārga named the children. Nanda's child was named as Kṛṣṇa and Rohiṇī's son as Balarāma. Once Yaśodā, unable to bear the mischief of Kṛṣṇa, tied him to a thresher. Kṛṣṇa pulled the thresher and he got stuck in between two trees and the trees got uprooted. Without knowing that all these were Kṛṣṇa's mischief, everybody thought all these, to be bad omen. All cowherds shifted to Bṛndāvan. Balarāma and Kṛṣṇa grew up there.

Kāliya

Kāliya was a huge snake, living on the banks of Yamunā. It was a menace to everyone, as it was poisoning the water and causing death to many. Kṛṣṇa knew that Kāliya was none other than the one which was defeated by Garuda and wanted to kill the snake. Kṛṣṇą jumped into the water while Kāliya was moving towards Kṛṣṇa and all the snakes coiled around Kṛṣṇa and bit him. When the cowherds saw this, they rushed to inform his parents and they came running. Kṛṣṇa shook off the snakes, lowered Kāliya's hood, climbed over the hood and danced. The hood started bleeding. On prayers from Kāliya's wives he spared Kāliya but on the promise that he would go back to the ocean.

Dhenuka and Pralamba

Dhenuka was a fierce Rākṣasa in the figure of a donkey. He lived on deer meat. Kṛṣṇa and Balarām once came across him. There the trees were full of fruits and the cowherds wanted to enjoy the fruits. Kṛṣṇa and Balarām started plucking the fruits and hearing the sound the Rākṣasa came and started kicking Balarāma with his hind legs. Balarām caught hold of the legs and started twirling the demon and the demon died. While they were playing, another demon named Pralamba took the form of a cowherd and joined them. Pralamba and Balarām raced and Balarām won the race, so Pralamba had to carry Balarām on his shoulder. But when Balarām climbed on his shoulder he assumed a huge form like mountain and started running. Balarām beat down the demon's head and killed him.

Govardhana

The family decided to perform *a yajna* in honor of Indra but Kṛṣṇa suggested to worship the mountain Govardhana. Govardhana is a mountain of Ambādi [Gokula]. This was believed to be a form of Kṛṣṇa. The residents of Ambādi used to worship it from time immemorial. So as per the suggestion of Kṛṣṇa worship of Govardhana started. Indra got annoyed at this and ordered the clouds to destroy the herds.Torrential rain started pouring and the cattle started dying. In order to protect the unfortunate ones, Kṛṣṇa plucked the Govardhana and balance it on his little finger, thus gave all of them refuge and humbled Indra.

Ariṣṭa was an asura servant of Kamsa. Once, at the instance of Kamsa he went to Gokula disguised as an ox to kill Kṛṣṇa. The ox instilled terror in people by tearing to pieces hills and mountains with its horns, bellowing like hell. But Kṛṣṇa faced the beast, rained blows on it and was thrown away. Thus the *asura* died.

All these incidents were narrated to Kamsa by Nārada and Kamsa decided to kill Balarām and Kṛṣṇa. So he sent a demon named Keśī, who adopted the form of a horse, to kill Kṛṣṇa. He caused terror among people. Kṛṣṇa pulled out the teeth of the horse and tore it up. That is why Kṛṣṇa is called Keśava. Kamsa planning to kill Balarām and Kṛṣṇa, conducted a festival called *Cāpapūjā* [worship of the bow]. It was Akrūra whom Kamsa sent to bring Balarām and Kṛṣṇa for the festival. Akrūra understood the plot, informed Kṛṣṇa about it and also advised Kṛṣṇa to kill Kamsa. Kṛṣṇa and Balarām accepted the invitation and Akrūra brought them in a chariot. Kṛṣṇa and Balarām reached Mathurā and on the way they took some clothes from a washerman. They took some garlands and also Kṛṣṇa corrected the hunch of a woman. Having heard that both the brothers had arrived, Kamsa instructed Cāṇūra and Muṣṭika to kill both of them. A huge elephant named Kuvalayāpīda was also let loose, at the entrance. Arrangements were made for the wrestling. Nanda and Vāsudeva were also present. At the entrance Kṛṣna and Balarām had killed the elephant and they were carrying their tusks. The wrestling started with Kṛṣṇa wrestling with Cāṇūra. It was a terrible fight and finally Kṛṣṇa raised Cāṇūra's body, rotated it hundred times and threw it on the ground. Cāṇūra died. Balarām while fighting grasped Muṣṭika so hard that the life force went out of his body. Kamsa ordered his guards to capture both of them but Kṛṣṇa jumped on to the stage and caught Kamsa's hair. He threw him down and killed him. Balarām also killed Sumāli, Kamsa's brother, when he came to fight. Ugrasena, Kamsa's father, who had been kept in prison, was set free.

After this Kṛṣṇa and Balarām went to their guru named Sāndīpani, who lived in Kāśī. They learned from him all the Vedas, art of drawing, astronomy, gāndharva veda, medicine, training elephants and horses and archery. The study lasted only sixty four days. On the eve of completing their education an asura named Pañcaja carried away the son of the sage, while the child was bathing in the Prabhāsatīrtha and kept him inside a conch where the *asura* lived. The sage, greatly grief-stricken, asked his disciples Kṛṣṇa and Balarām to get him back as guru dakṣiṇā [fees for the preceptor]. Kṛṣṇa and Balarām went to the banks of the river and prayed to Varuṇa. Varuṇa appeared before them and they told him about the mishap. With the help of Varuṇa they killed the asura Pañcaja and got back the son of the guru. The conch in which the asura lived was taken by Kṛṣṇa. Because the conch belonged to Pañcaja the conch got the name Pāñcajanya.

Jarāsandha

Asti and prāpti, the two wives of Kamsa, were daughters of Jarāsandha. When Kṛṣṇa killed Kamsa, the two daughters went to their father and shed tears before him. Jarāsandha became angry and with a mighty army surrounded the city of Mathurā. A fierce battle was fought between Kṛṣṇa and Jarāsandha. At last Balarām caught hold of Jarāsandha and was about to kill him, when an ethereal voice said that Balarāma was not the person to kill Jarāsandha and Jarāsandha was set free.

Kālayavana

A brāhmana named Garga was insulted by Yādavas and he started *tapasyā* on the shores of the ocean to get a son who can defeat Yādavas. Mahādeva gave the boon. The son was black and as the king of Yavanas had no son; he adopted the son who came to be known as Kālayavana. Having obtained the names of the powerful kings, he collected a huge army and attacked Mathurā. As Kṛṣṇa felt that Yadavas may find it too difficult to fight either Jarāsandha or Kālayavana, he built a fort on the shores of ocean which came to be known as Dvārakā. All the citizens were brought to Dvārakā from Mathurā. Kṛṣṇa then appeared before Kālayavana and led him into a dark cave in which a powerful king known as Mucukunda was sleeping. Thinking that it was Kṛṣṇa Kālayavana kicked him. Mucukunda was furious and burnt up Kālayavana. Once Mucukunda fought for devas and desired a boon that he should sleep long. The boon was that whoever awoke him would be burnt up.

Once Balarām was drunk and wanted the river Yamunā to come to him to take bath and when Yamunā ignored, he pulled Yamunā and the river changed its course.

Bh. Śkanda. 10.

Rukmiṇī and Rukmī

Bhīṣmaka was the king of Vidarbha who had a son named Rukmi and daughter Rukmiṇī. Rukmiṇī and Kṛṣṇa wanted to marry but Rukmī did not like Kṛṣṇa. Bhīṣmaka was also an ally of Jarāsandha and so decided to marry

Rukmiṇī to Śiśupāla. All went to Vidarbha to witness the marriage and Kṛṣṇa along with Yādavas was also there. One day before the marriage Kṛṣṇa abducted Rukmiṇī. All the kings joined and attacked Yādavas, but were defeated by Balarām.

Rukmī vowed not to return to Vidarbha without killing Kṛṣṇa and collected huge army, but Kṛṣṇa easily defeated him. Kṛṣṇa was about to kill him but Rukminį prayed to spare his life. So Rukmī had to build a new city because of his vow.

Pradyumna

Pradyumna was Kāmadeva, who was burnt by Śiva and was born as the son of Kṛṣṇa and Rukmiṇī. He was kidnapped as soon as he was born, by Śambarasura as he knew that Pradyumna is destined to kill him and threw the baby into the ocean. A fish swallowed the baby and the fish was caught and brought to Śambarāsura's kitchen. Śambara called his wife Māyāvatī [Māyāvatī was Kāmadeva's wife] and asked her to get the fish cooked. When Māyāvatī cut open the fish, she found a beautiful child inside it. She had a liking for the child and brought it up as her own. When Pradyumna grew up he had all the charm of Kāmadeva. One day Nārada revealed to Māyāvatī that Pradyumna was the incarnation of Kāmadeva. When Pradyumna noticed that Māyāvatī's love was changing into one of passion, he questioned her. Māyāvatī told him everything and Pradyumana decided to kill Śambara. In a fierce battle Pradyumna killed Śambara and took Māyāvatī to Dvāraka. Kṛṣṇa was told then about everything.

Narakāsura

Narakāsura was born when Hiraṇyākṣa was carrying the earth down the ocean, his tusks came in contact with goddess of earth and she became pregnant. This was Narkāsura. Once Indra came to Kṛṣṇa and complained to him about the atrocities of Narakāsura. Kṛṣṇa rode on his vehicle Garuda with Satyabhāmā to Prāgjyotiṣa. They flew over the city and understood the layout. The battle began after the reconnaissance. They fought with the asuras and all of them were killed. A fierce battle ensued in which Narakāsura was killed. The Nārāyanāstra, which was in possesson of Narakāsura was given to his son Bhagadatta. Kṛṣṇa and Satyabhāmā went to the world of gods and returned the ear rings of Aditi and the umbrella of Indra, which Narakāsura had stolen. *Bh. Skanda.10.*

Pārijāta

Kṛṣṇa arrived at heaven to return the loot of Narkāsura and Satybhāmā happened to see the Pārijāta flower. She wanted the tree in Dvāraka. Kṛṣna uprooted the tree and put it on Gaurda, but the guards of Indra objected, telling that it belonged to Śacī, Indra's wife. Satyabhāmā got angry and told the guards to tell Śacī that she was taking the tree. Incited by Śacī Indra attacked Kṛṣṇa with Vajra, his weapon. Kṛṣṇa blew his conch shell and let loose thousands of arrows. Indra used his vajra, Kṛṣṇa simply caught it and Indra started running away. At this Satyabhāmā made fun of Indra and offered back the Parijātā tree. Indra apologized and refused to take back the Parijātā tree.

Aniruddha

Aniruddha was Kṛṣṇa's grandson and son of Pradyumna. Among Krsna's sons Pradyumna and his son Aniruddha were the best. One of the stories about this handsome prince refers to his being kidnapped by Uṣa, daughter of Bāṇāsura. Bāṇāsura was the son of Mahābali and had one thousand hands. Śiva pleased by the sacrificial devotion of Bāṇāsura granted the boon that Śiva himself and Pārvatī would guard his fort. So no one had the prowess, to attack him. Overflowing with conceit he challenged Śiva for a fight. Śiva foretold him that, the day his flagstaff would be broken, he would have a chance for a fierce fight. Uṣā, daughter of Bāṇāsura, asked Mother Pārvatī about her husband and Mother told her that she would see somebody in dream a handsome prince, who would be her husband. She saw a prince in the dream but could not recognize the prince. Her companion Citralekhā drew the pictures of all the princes, known to her and Uṣā recognized Aniruddha. Citralekhā, by the power of her mantra, brought Aniruddha from Dvārakā into Uṣā's room. Bāṇāsura got the scent of it as the flagstaff was broken and took Aniruddha into custody. Nārada reached Dvārakā and gave details of Aniruddha. Kṛṣṇa and Pradyumna in all rage encircled the palace with a strong army. The fierce fight ended in the defeat of Bāṇāsura. Aniruddha married Uṣā.

Pauṇḍraka

King Pauṇḍraka was the king of ancient Kārūṣa, had the illusion that he was Kṛṣṇa, the incarnation. He adopted the name Vāsudeva and sent messengers to Kṛṣṇa thus: "Oh Kṛṣṇa, I am the real Vāsudeva. Therefore put down all your royal emblems and robes, come and worship at my feet". As soon as Kṛṣṇa got it, Kṛṣṇa told the messenger that he was leaving for Kāśī. The king of Kāśī was Pauṇḍraka's friend. Pauṇḍraka came to Kāśī with a huge army and Kṛṣṇa came on Garuda and in the war that ensued that he killed both Pauṇḍraka and the King of Kāśī. The king of Kāśī had a son who prayed to Mahādeva to create a demon to kill Kṛṣna and Mahādeva agreed. That demon arrived at Dvāraka and flame was coming out of his mouth. Kṛṣṇa used his Sudarśan Cakra and the demon ran all over to escape from the Sudarśan cakra. Finally the demon ran to Kāśī and burnt up the entire city.

Bh. Skanda 10.

Sāmba

Sāmba was Krsna's son, by his wife Jāmabavatī. Hearing about the *svayamvara* of Lakṣaṇā, daughter of Duryodhana, Sāmba went to Hastināpura and took her by force from among the various kings who were present there. Duryodhana captured him. This news reached Dvārakā through Nārada. Hearing this Yādavas went for a war, but Balarām restrained them and he went himself. He went to Hastināpur but did not enter the city. Duryodhana and others came to pay him respect and Balarām said that King Ugrasena desired that Sāmba be released. But Kauravas got angry as it appeared as an order. Balarām got angry. He pulled out the foundation of Hastināpura and about to throw away in the river Bhāgīrathī and this brought Kauravas to their knees. Sāmba and his wife were handed over to Balarām.

Bh. Skanda.10.

The end of Yādavas

Once in the pilgrimage place of Piṇḍāraka a few yādava youths met sage Kaṇva, Viśvāmitra and Nārada. The yādavas dressed Sāmba in the dress of a pregnant lady and asked the sages whether she would deliver a boy or girl. Angered by the insult, the sages said that the person would give birth to a club, which will destroy the clan. Shortly a club came out of Sāmba's body. Learning about the curse king Ugrasena ground the club into small particles and scattered it in the ocean. A small portion could not be ground and hence was thrown away into the ocean. The particles became sharp reeds in around the ocean. The small piece was swallowed by a fish and the fish was caught by a fisherman. The small piece was acquired by a hunter named Jara. All the yādavas went to a pilgrimage place known as Prabhāsa except Uddhava. The yādavas began to drink, became uncontrollable, started fighting and killed each other with the reeds that were grown on the shores. Ultimately Kṛṣna and Dāruka, Kṛṣṇa's charioteer alone were left out. While wandering in the forest Kṛṣṇa and Dāruka found Balarām sitting, a huge snake came out of his mouth and fell into the ocean, indicating Balarām was dead. Kṛṣṇa instructed Dāruka to inform Ugrasena about all the happenings, also that Dvārakā will be swallowed by sea and Kṛṣna himself would die soon. Kṛṣṇa sat down to meditate and the hunter Jara arrived, who had made an arrow out of the small piece from the club. Seeing Kṛṣṇa's feet, he thought it to be a part of a deer and shot the arrow. Jara begged pardon and Kṛṣṇa comforted him and then left the body. He was hundred years old. Arjuna found the bodies and performed Śrāddha. *MB. Mau.*

Kali Era

Account of Kali Yuga was given on the request of Maitreya. There will not be distinction of *Varṇa and āśrama*. Wife will not obey husband. Money will be everything. Dharma will lose its power. Humans will be short in height and as well as the tenure. Selfishness will be the rule and flourish. Duration of tapas of ten years of

Satya Yuga will be equal to one day of Kali Yuga, and will be the only advantage.

Destruction, their Nature – in Stages

Three types of destructions have been explained. *Naimittika Pralaya* takes place after a *kalpa,* that is after one day of Brahmā, *Prākṛta pralaya*, when prakṛtī becomes one with Paramātman and the third type of destruction is *Adyātika pralaya* when disappearance due to three types of distress, that is due to ailments, external distress like cold etc and distress due to ghosts, snakes etc.

Bhāgavata Purāṇa

This Purāṇa is also called Srimad Bhāgavata, an authoritative text dealing with Sri Krsna's life and His doings. It also deals extensively with the topics of other incarnations of Viṣṇu and is in the form of narration by sage Śuka to King Parīkṣit. This Purāṇa is prominently marked for the glories of Lord Kṛṣṇa. It also deals with King Parīkṣit, cosmic form of the Lord, creation of the world, curse incurred by Jaya and Vijaya, Hiraṇyakaśipu, Prahlāda, Kapila, Dhruva, Ganges, Tripura, Uddhava Gitā, and sketch of Kali yuga. This Purāṇa sheds its brilliance through 18,000 verses, and belongs to 600 A.D. There are twenty four incarnations of Viṣṇu, but Purāṇa could account only for twenty two and they are:

- A celibate Brāhmaṇa to declare the duties of a Brāhmaṇa
- Varāha – a wild boar to rescue the world.
- Nārada – to instruct men on devotion to Viṣṇu.
- Nara and Nārāyaṇa – to perform difficult meditation.

- Kapila – Sāmkhya philosophy.
- Dattātreya – instructed the path of true knowledge.
- Yajna – held the title of Indra.
- Ṛṣabha – to instruct on the best form of meditation.
- Pṛthu – to milk the cow, the earth.
- Matsya – as a fish to save Vaivavasta Manu.
- Kūrma – to churn the ocean.
- Dhanvantari – medical knowledge.
- Mohinī – to prevent asuras from getting *amṛta.*
- Narasimha – to kill Hiraṇyakaśipu.
- Vāmana – to contain Bali.
- Paraśurāma – to contain the Kṣatriyas.
- Veda Vyāsa- to make Vedas more understandable.
- Rāma – to annihilate the demons.
- Balarām – as brother of Kṛṣṇa.
- Kṛṣna – to establish dharma.
- Buddha – originator of Buddhism.
- Kalki – yet to come.

Vedavyāsa and Nārada

Vedavyāsa was the architect to divide the Vedas into four and taught the four Vedas to his four disciples and Purāna, which is the fifth Veda taught to his disciple Romaharṣaṇa. But he was still not satisfied and was feeling that there was something missing. One day when he was pondering over this, Nārada happened to come there and Vedavyāsa revealed his feeling of incompleteness to the sage. Nārada suggested that he may write the exploits of Sri Kṛṣṇa and thus came Bhāgavata Purāṇa.

Parīkṣit

Parīkṣit was a good king. He had four sons and out of them Janamejaya was most important. One day, he heard that the demon Kali was invading the land after Kṛṣṇa gave up his body. So he set out to conquer the world and Kali. In the course of his sojourn, he overheard the conversation between the 'earth' in the form of a cow and 'dharma' in the form of a bull about the evil which has befallen the earth. A Śūdra was seen beating the cow and the bull. Parīkṣit took out his sword to kill the man, who was none other than Kali and he started begging for mercy. Then Parīkṣit told him to get out of his country, but his kingdom was very vast so Kali was allowed to stay where gambling and drinking took place, also in gold and women etc.

Once Parīkṣit went for hunting and he became thirsty. He saw a hermitage in which a sage was meditating. Parīkṣit asked the sage for some water but the sage did not hear him. The king felt insulted and there was a dead snake which he took and put it around the neck of the sage. Gavijāta, the son of the sage, when came to know about this, cursed that Parīkṣit would die of snake bite within seven days. The sage whose name was Śamīka felt very remorse about the curse as he knew that the king was a good man. Parīkṣit also took the curse in the right spirit. He decided that his end would come in the banks of Gañga and the seven days he would spend in contemplation on Kṛṣṇa. He handed over his kingdom to his son Janamejaya and started fasting and contemplation. Almost all the sages assembled there and Śukadeva, son of Vyāsa also arrived there. The king worshipped Śukadeva and asked him what should one, who was about to die, hear and Śukadeva narrated about

Viṣṇu. Śukadeva talked about the exploits of Kṛṣṇa for six days. Having heard the Bhāgavata Purāṇa Parīkṣit told Śukadeva that he was no more afraid of death as he had understood the nature of Ātmā. When Śukadeva left, the king sat and meditated on the various forms of Viṣṇu.

De. Bh. Skanda 12.

Takṣaka, the snake, in the guise of a Brāhmin inspected the place and there was no way to step into the place. Takṣaka asked his relatives to go to the king in the guise of Brāhmins carrying flowers and fruits as presents. Takṣaka crept inside a beautiful fruit in the shape of a worm. The servants of the king took the fruits brought by the Brāhmins to the king and the king struck by the beauty and size of the fruit took it and cut it open. He saw a worm inside, red in color with two black spots as eyes. The king took it in his hands and at that instant it changed into Takṣaka and bit the king. After that it rose up into the air and disappeared. Pariksit's son Janmejaya was furious and performed a sacrifice in which all the snakes came and fell into the fire. Takṣaka went and hid himself at Indra's place. Janamejaya finally stopped the sacrifice on the intervention of Bṛhaspati. *De. Bh. Skanda 12.*

Kardama and Devāhūtī

Devāhūtī was the daughter of Svayambhuva Manu and married sage Kardama. The sage performed a very strenuous *tapasyā* on the banks of Sarasvaṭi. Viṣṇu was so pleased that he granted a boon that he would be born as his son. For a hundred years Devāhūtī and Kardama lived in an aerial vehicle and she gave birth to nine daughters and then Viṣṇu was born as Kapila. After the birth of Kapila, Kardama went away on pilgrimage and Devāhūtī brought up Kapila. Once Devāhūtī told her son that she was tired of the illusions of the world and wanted to know that, which is imperishable. Kapila taught her the Sāmkya philosophy, the knowledge about the union of Jīvātma with Paramātma. He taught her the Kapila Śāstra and after the teachings, Devāhūtī performed a Yajna on the banks of river Sarsavatī and performed extreme austerities. She became blind to all external objects and was immersed in meditation. In course of time she attained liberation. *De.Bh. Skanda 8.*

Priyavrata and Descendants

Priyavrata was among Pṛthu's descendants and was not interested in becoming a king, but on persuasion from Brahmā and Nārada became king. He did not like night befalling after sunset. He decided that one night he would travel on his flaming chariot around the world, to keep the night away. His chariot was looking like a second sun, but while traveling the wheels of his chariot gouged at seven places and they became oceans. These seven oceans surround the seven *dvīpas.*

Citraketu

As an answer to a question by king Parīkṣit as to how a demon can become a devotee of Viṣṇu Śukadeva narrated the following story. There was a king named Citraketu ruling over Mathurā. Though he had many wives, he had no son and he was sad. Sage Aṅgiras suggested performing a yajna and the rice pudding which came out of the sacrificial fire was given to his eldest wife named Kṛtadyuti and a son was born. The other queens felt jealous and fed poison to the child and the child died. Citraketu and Kṛtadyuti were heart broken. Nārada and the sage Aṅgiras came to comfort them. Nārada tried to console them by telling that body alone dies and not Ātmā and who was related to whom? Then Nārada used his powers and asked the Ātmā of the boy to enter the body again. But the Ātmā replied "I have lived in many bodies. Which body I should enter?" This had convinced the grief stricken parents; finally Citraketu did penance and had got to see Viṣṇu's form. He spread the knowledge of Viṣṇu. But once Citraketu happened to insult Śiva and was cursed by Pārvatī that he would be born as a demon. He was born as Vṛtra but continued to be a devotee of Viṣṇu. *Skanda 8.*

Ambarīṣa

King Ambarīṣa ruled over the entire world and he had everything, what one may desire in this world. But his mind was always devoted to Viṣṇu. He and his wife performed a special sacrifice at the end of which, they had to fast three nights and should eat at the end of third night. At the end of the function, when the time had come to eat, sage Durvāsā arrived. After paying obeisance to the sage Ambarīṣa asked the sage to partake the food and the sage agreed, but he wanted to take bath. Time passed, the sage did not return back and for Ambarīṣa it was necessary to take food otherwise the whole sacrifice would become waste. So the king took water as a compromise. When Durvāsā returned he knew that the king had taken water. The sage became furious, pulled out a hair and threw it down out of which a demon appeared and wanted to kill Ambarīṣa. But the king was a devotee of Viṣṇu and immediately the Sudarśan Cakra emerged from Ambarīṣa's forehead, destroyed the demon and went behind Durvāsas. Durvāsas ran for his life and went to Viṣṇu loka but Viṣṇu asked him to go to Ambarīṣa. Durvāsas went to Ambarīṣa and he was forgiven. *Skanda 9.*

Duṣyanta and Śakuntalā

Duṣyanta was one of Parīkṣit's ancestors. Once he went on a hunt, wandered and came to the hermitage of sage Kaṇva. There he met Śakuntalā, daughter of Viśvāmitra and Menakā, whom sage Kaṇva had brought up. He fell in love with her and sage Kaṇva was away at Cakratīrtha. He married her according to *gandharvas'* rules and lived with her at the *āśrama* for a few days. Meanwhile Śakuntalā became pregnant but emissaries from the kingdom came and the king returned with them. He left the *āśrama* after making promise that he would come back. He gave her the signet ring. Sad over the separation from Duṣyanta and immersed in thought about him, Śakuntalā was sitting in the *āśrama* when sage Durvāsā came there. She did not see the sage and so did not welcome him respectfully. He got angry at this and cursed her that she be forgotten by him, about whom she was so intensely thinking. Śakuntala did not hear the curse also, but her companions who heard the curse begged pardon and prayed for absolution from the curse. Then the sage said that if Śakuntalā showed any signs of their relationship, the king would remember her. The sage Kaṇva welcomed the marriage between Śakuntalā and Duṣyanta. Days and months passed by, yet Duṣyanta did not return and Kaṇva sent Śakuntalā in whom the signs of pregnancy became prominent, to the palace along with her friend and his disciple. Her companion Anasūyā by name particularly reminded her to take the signet ring. On the way to the palace they bathed at the river Somavāratīrtha and nobody noticed Śakuntalā losing her ring. They reached the king's palace, but nobody paid any attention to them. Duṣyanta did not even remember seeing her and the signet ring was missing. After leaving Śakuntalā at the palace, her companions returned to the *āśrama*. Menakā, her mother could not tolerate the wailing of her daughter, took her and left her at the *āśram* of Kaśyapa. The signet ring, which was lost by Śakuntalā, was swallowed by a fish and the fish was caught by a fisherman. He found the ring in its stomach. He wanted to sell it in the market place, when the king's sentries picked him up and took him to the palace. At the sight of the ring, the king remembered the past and felt very sad. Śakuntalā delivered a boy in the *āśrama* and the boy was named Sarvadamana. Sage Kaśyap taught him everything and the boy was very courageous. Duṣyanta while returning from the war between gods and demons came to the *āśram* of Kaśyap, where he found Sarvadamana counting the teeth of a lion, he had caught. The king went inside the *āśrama* and found Śakuntalā. He brought Śakuntalā and the boy to the palace with the permission of the sage. This boy became the famous emperor of India, known as Bharata. *Skanda 8.*

Kucela

Sudāmā, better known as Kucela was a Brāhmin and class mate of Sri Kṛṣṇa at the *āśram* of sage Sāndīpani. One day Sāndīpani's wife deputed Kucela and Kṛṣṇa to collect firewood from the forest and they had to stay in the forest the whole night, due to thunder and heavy rain. After their education was over they separated, Kṛṣṇa became the Lord of Dvārakā, and Kucela a house holder with many children. Due to poverty, the family used to starve. One day at the instance of his wife, Kucela started off for Dvārakā to visit Kṛṣṇa with a small bundle of pounded rice as a gift to Kṛṣṇa. Kṛṣṇa welcomed his friend whole heartedly and asked him what he had brought for him. Kucela could not tell him and Kṛṣṇa took the bundle out himself. He took and ate one handful of pounded rice. Rukminī, who was present there, prevented him from taking a second handful. After some time Kucela started homeward without asking any help from Kṛṣṇa. By the time Kucela reached home, his old dilapidated house had become beautiful mansion. His wife and children were very happy. It was Kṛṣṇa's blessings that converted the poor Kucela into a very rich person. *[Bh.10th Skanda.]*

Śiva's Problem

Śiva, Brahmā and Viṣṇu have the powers to grant boons and also curses. An *asura* named Vṛka resolved to please Śiva and he cut each of his organs and offered it in the fire as an oblation. At last when Vṛka was about to cut his head, Śiva appeared and granted him a boon that on whomsoever head he put his hand that person would die. The demon wanted to try the boon, on the giver himself, as he wanted to marry Pārvatī. Śiva was running and the demon followed him wherever he went. Then Viṣṇu came to his rescue. Viṣṇu told him that whatever boons were bestowed by Śiva would be useless as he had no such powers. He induced the demon to try out the boon on his own head. The demon put his hand on his own head and died. *Skanda 10.*

Best among Trimūrtis

Once, when a yajna was being performed, all the *Maharṣīs* had assembled and a dispute arose as to who was supreme among the trinity of Gods- Brahmā, Śiva and Viṣṇu and they sent sage Bhṛgu to ascertain. Bhṛgu was Brahmā's son. He went to Brahmā first and did not bow down to Brahmā, but sat down. Brahmā was very angry but controlled his temper because he was his son. Then he went to Śiva. Śiva embraced him, but Bhṛgu started shouting at Śiva. Śiva was furious and took out his trident but Mother Pārvatī prevented him. Bhṛgu then went to Vaikuṇta and Viṣṇu was sleeping at that time. The sage kicked Viṣṇu on his chest. Viṣṇu woke up and begged pardon of the sage. He declared that he would carry Bhṛgu's foot print permanently on his chest as a sign of his repentance for having shown disrespect to the Maharṣi. The foot print still remains on Viṣṇu's chest, by the name "Srīvatsa". It was concluded that Viṣṇu is supreme. *Skanda 10.*

Guru

Yadu, ancestor of Yādavas met a learned young man and asked him from which guru he had got the wisdom. The young man replied that one can learn from nature and surroundings itself. From the earth one can learn perseverance as the earth is being stamped and hurt but it forgives everybody. The air fills everybody's lungs but does not get attached to anybody. Just as sky does not get stirred up by clouds one can learn not to get stirred up by sense organs. From water one can learn purification. From fire one can learn that though the Ātmā appears as many but in fact it is one only.

Nārada Purāṇa

This Purāṇa is in the form of a narration by Nārada to Sanatkumāra. Nārada teaches the dharmas of *Bṛhatkalpa*. This is in two parts, the first part is known as *Bṛhan-nāradīya purāṇa* and the second one contains independent treatises. The subjects touched upon are varied and they include:

1. Essence of the eighteen *Purāṇas*.
2. Sacred knowledge.
3. History – accounts.

4. Secret spiritual practices.
5. Aspects of *Dharma and Bhakti.*
6. Divisions of the *Vedas – the Samhitā, Brāhmaṇa, Āraṇyaka, Vedānta.*
7. Six *aṅgas of the Vedas – śikṣa* – phonetics, *kalpam* – code of rituals, *vyākaraṇam* – grammar, *niruktam* – etymology, *chandas* – metre, and *jyothiṣam* – astrology.
8. Particular days of the month and performance of related spiritual practices, such as 12th day, bright fortnight, fourth day, *aṣtami,* full moon day, 11th day, solar eclipse, lunar eclipse, when sun is midway, when sun is in auspicious position, *Rohiṇī, Aśvini,* Saturday, Wednesday and many other days depending upon the placement of stars and their conjunction.

Another remarkable feature of this Purāṇa is that it deals with various *mantras* and the methods of repeating them. The *Lalita sahasranāma* in the 89th chapter is entirely different from what is being practiced now, which is part of Brahmāṇda Purāṇa. There are 25.000 slokas and supposed to have been composed somewhere between 900- 1600 A.D.

In a forest, known as *naimīṣāraṇya* many sages were meditating, all of whom had controlled their sense organs and they were trying to achieve the four goals of life – *dharma, artha, Kāma and mokṣa.* – Righteousness, that which gives meaning to life, fulfilling the desires of life and liberation. While they were discussing the ways and means to achieve this, sage Śaunaka suggested that they might go to sage Sūta, who was Vedavyāsa's disciple, well versed in Purāṇas and hear Purāṇas from him.

Everyone present was very happy at this suggestion and they all went to the hermitage of Sūta. At that time Sūta was engaged in performing *agniṣtoma yajna* and after that was over, all sages requested him to recite the wisdom of Purāṇas. Sūta said that this was recited by Nārada to Sanatkumāra and hence known as Nārada Purāṇa.

The Gańgā

The confluence of Gańgā and Yamunā is the most holy tīrtha. Even gods are fond of the waters at this confluence. The Gańgā is so sacred that even if one thinks of Gańgā, all miseries are relieved and sins are pardoned. There are some other rivers, in which Gańgā is present and they are: Godāvari, Sarasvatī, Kālindī, Kāverī, Kṛṣṇā, Reva, Vahūda, Tuńgabhadra, Bhīmarati, Vetravatī, Tamraparaṇi, and Śatdri. Prayāg is the *tīrtha,* where Brahmā himself had performed a yajna.

Aditi's *tapasyā*

Aditi was the daughter of Dakṣa and was married to sage Kaśyap. Indra and other gods were her children. The demons were the sons of the other wife of Kaśyap named Diti. Frequently the demons had driven away the gods from their place and Aditi was very much depressed to see her sons being deprived from their positions, especially by king Bali. In order to banish the demons and to restore Indra's position she decided to do *tapasyā.* She meditated on Lord Viṣṇu in the standing posture and also standing on one leg. Bali wanted to disturb her meditation and sent some demons, who in the form of gods tried to persuade her but when that was in vain, from the anger of demons flames appeared, but due to the strength of her *tapsayā* the flame could not go near her, but in turn burnt the demons. Finally Viṣṇu appeared and gave her a boon that he would be born as her son and deliver her sons from the miseries. And that was the *Vāmana avatār* of the Lord. *Ch. 8.*

Performing of Religious Rites

A summary of some important rituals are given here. *Ekādaśī* is the eleventh day of the lunar fortnight. That day the *Śalagrāma* is given *abhiśekam* with milk, and offerings are made to Viṣṇu and Lakṣmī. One should fast on that day and *Brāhmaṇas* are to be fed. Another *Vrata* is *Pourṇamāsya vrata* which is performed on the full moon day. This *vrata* can be performed by anybody and the prayer is to Viṣṇu and Lakṣhmī. The *vrata* known as *dvajārohaṇa* is that, in which a flag is hoisted on the top of Viṣṇu temple. The flag is hoisted on an *ekādaśī* day of *śukla pakśa* and it is said that, when the flag flutters by the wind, the sins of the hoister are forgiven.

Sumati

Sumati was a king in the *Satya Yuga*, who was very righteous and his wife was also like husband. They performed *dvajārohaṇa vrata* regularly. One day a sage came to his place and was received with great honor. The sage wanted to know why they were performing *dvajārohaṇa vrata* and why the queen was dancing in the temple. Sumati recounted the following: The king and queen being *jatismara,* they knew about their previous lives. The king in his earlier life was a *Śūdra* who did all sinful acts. His name was Marūli. Once while wandering he came to a dilapidated Viṣṇu temple and started living there. He did some repair work to the temple. After some years a woman named Kokilini came there who was also a sinner. Marūli married Kokilini and they used to drink and dance in the temple and on one such occasion they died. Having danced in the temple and having erected a flag in the Viṣṇu temple, they went to *Viṣṇuloka*. Being a *jatismara* they knew the past and therefore they were continuing *dvajārohaṇa* and dancing.

Bhadraśīla

Sage Gālava had a righteous son, named Bhadraśīla and he was a *jatismara*. On being questioned by his father about his previous birth, he recounted his earlier life. He was a king named Dharmakīrti of lunar dynasty and though he was righteous in the beginning, later on committed only sins and had bad company. One day he went on a hunt and was very tired. So he took bath in the river Reva but there was no food. That being *ekādaśī* day some pilgrims also arrived and they were doing the *vrata*. The king had to fast on that day and next day he died due to starvation. Because of his fasting on *ekadasi* he became entitled to heaven and so in the next birth he became very pious.

Atonement

Some details about performing atonement for different sins are available. A killer of a Brāhmin inadvertently has to retire to forest after begging pardon from the dead and should have only fruits as food and that too only once. This has to be done for twelve years. Drinking of wine is a sin and the penance is drinking of clarified butter and cow's urine. Like this there are atonements prescribed for various sins like stealing gold etc.

Path of Action and Knowledge

King Khāṇḍikya and Keśidhvaja were learned. The latter was the paternal uncle of the former. Both were well aware of the ways of union with the divine life. Khāṇdikya had become an expert in the path of action for becoming one with the divine whereas Keśidvaja tried to achieve oneness with divine by *Jñānayoga* – the path of self knowledge. Each desired to subdue the other. Consequently Khāṇdikya lost his kingdom and had to live in a forest with his priest and minister. Keśidhvaja who tried the path of knowledge to attain Absolution performed several sacrifices for that purpose and cut himself asunder from the bonds of action. Once, while he was performing a sacrifice, a tiger came to the place of sacrifice and killed the sacrificial cow. Then Keśidhvaja asked the priests who were conducting the sacrifice, what the atonement was for the death of the sacrificial cow. The priests sent the king to the hermit Kaśeru, who sent the king to Bhṛgu. Hermit Bhṛgu in his turn sent the king to the hermit Śaunaka. But the matter did not end there. The hermit Śaunaka could not dictate the atonement for the death of the sacrificial cow. So he sent the king to Khāṇḍikya who was living in the forest. The moment Khāṇḍikya saw Keśidhvaja he stood ready to kill him. But Keśidhvaja revealed everything to Khāṇḍikya. When he understood the situation Khāṇḍikya told him with sincerity the rites given in the Śāstras to atone the death of the sacrificial cow. Keśidvaja returned and completed the sacrifice. The one item of *guru dakṣiṇā* remained. So Keśidvaja came to the forest again. Khāṇḍikya raised the sword to cut him. Keśidhvaja told him that he had come to give *gurudakṣṇā* to the teacher. Khāṇḍikya repented his rashness and requested Keśidhvaja to tell him the ways of cutting himself asunder from the bonds of sorrow and grief. Keśidhvaja advised him the ways to obtain eternal bliss. *Ch. 11.*

Devamāli and his Sons

A *brāhmaṇa* named Devamāli was learned but as he was poor and had to take care of the family, he did trading on all such things, which a *brāhmaṇa* was not supposed to do. In this process he became very rich. One day he happened to count his coins and found that he had million coins. At the same time he also started feeling that as much as one earned, the thirst for earning only increased. So he divided his wealth in four parts, one part each he gave away to his sons Yajñamāli and Sumāli and the balance he spent on good deeds like building temples, digging ponds, construction of hermitage etc. He also joined the sages in their meditation and got good advice from them. Thus he was freed of all his illusions. His elder son Yajñamāli was religious and pious, so he gave away half the wealth to his brother, but his brother was evil personified. He spent all his money in evil ways. When his brother advised him to mend his ways, he took a sword and went to kill him and was arrested but later on let off due to the good offices of his brother. Yajñamāli ultimately spent all his wealth in noble causes and retired to a temple to worship the Lord. By fate, both the brothers died on the same day and Yajñamāli was taken to heaven whereas Sumāli went to hell. Yajñamāli wanted to save his brother and asked how he could save his brother. He was told that he could give part of his *puṇya* and could retrieve him. Yajñamāli did that and saved his brother too. After some time his brother had to be reborn.

Holy Water

Devotion to the Lord does not come automatically. Only meritorious deeds can give the mental inclination for devotion to the Lord. Gulika was a hunter and the sins he had committed were countless including killing of

Brahmins and cows. One day he saw a temple in the city of Sauvīra. He saw lots of gold pots on the top of the temple and he decided to steal them. But a sage named Uttaṅka was sleeping there. Gulika decided to kill him. So he raised his sword to kill Uttaṅka, when the sage told him that he would have to suffer the results of sin during many rebirths, if he committed a sin. This admonition of Uttaṅka so touched the heart of the hunter that he fell dead on the spot with a repentant heart. Uttaṅka sprinkled Gaṅgā water, used for *abhiśekam* of the Lord's idol, on the corpse of the hunter, who attained Vaikuṇṭha. *Ch. 11.*

Yajñadvaja

Yajñadvaja was a king and a great devotee of Viṣṇu. In his kingdom he ensured that the temples were cleaned daily and lamps were lit in the night. There was a Viṣṇu temple on the banks of the river Reva and he maintained that temple also in the same way. One of his priests named Vitahotra asked him why was he so particular about the cleaning and lighting of the lamps. The king, being a *jatismara*, recounted the following. There was a *brāhmaṇa* named Raivata. Though he was very learned, still he was acting as priest to people, whom he should not. He was very greedy and traded in goods, which a *brāhmaṇa* should not. Due to all these, all his friends deserted him. He was wandering here and there and became very sick and died. His wife, named Bandhumati too was evil and gave birth to a son named Daṇdaketu. He too turned out to be a sinner. He drank, stole and committed all types of sins. One day it so happened, that he had to sleep in a temple of Viṣṇu, so before lying down he cleaned the place with his cloth and lit a lamp for better visibility. But then the king's sentries picked him up thinking that he was a thief and killed him. Even inadvertently cleaning the temple and lighting the lamp gave so much of *puṇya* that he attained heaven. The king then said that even for doing these acts unintentionally brought so much of good. The king then said he was Daṇḍaketu. *Ch. 11.*

The Garuda Purāṇa

Among the scholarly groups, there is a difference of opinion about this Purāṇa as some feel that this is a Vaiśṇavite work composed in the tenth century, but still it is held in high esteem. Its recitation during the performance of death ceremony and after death ceremony is considered auspicious as this Purāṇa deals with the eschatology in great detail. The number of verses also seems to be varying from 8,000 to 19,000. This Purāṇa is supposed to have been taught by Lord Viṣṇu to his mount Garuda. First part of this Purāṇa is encyclopedic in nature as it deals with several topics such as contents of Ramāyaṇa, Mahābhārata, cosmography etc. The second part deals with *pretakalpa,* which deals in great detail with death, journey of the *Jīva,* various rites etc.

Rules for doing Prayer

The Garuda Purāna deals elaborately on the prayers offered to various deities like Sūrya, Lakṣmī, Viṣṇu etc and it also gives the thousand names of Viṣṇu. It also talks elaborately on the *Sālagrāmas* and the varieties of *Sālagrāmas,* its names and its properties. These prayer *mantras* should be learnt from a *guru* only to make it effective.

Snake Bites

There is a *mantra* which can be chanted for snake bites. It says that if the snake bite occurs in cremation ground, termite hill or a mountain and if the bite has three lines, the person can not survive. Otherwise in other cases there is a *mantra* named *prāṇesvara mantra,* which should be written on each petal of an eight petal lotus flower, drawn on a cloth is wrapped on the body of the victim and bathed, when the poison would be nullified.

Jyotiṣa

It is the science about the stars and heavenly bodies. From the very ancient days men believed that these planets and stars in the sky played an important part in controlling the growth and acitivities of all the living and non-living things in the world. Astronomy has two sides, the doctrinal side [*Pramāṇa bhāga*] and the result-side [*Phala bhāga*]. Prediction and casting horoscope of living beings is the *Phala bhāga.*

In the chapter of *Jyotisa* there is a detailed explanation of the twenty seven stars, auspiciousness of the various stars, auspicious time for starting various works and about the twelve Zodiac signs. Different positions of the planets, its effect, how to match the horoscopes of bride and bride groom are discussed. For example a bride of Leo sign can marry a groom with Capricorn etc.

Physical Features

Linking the physical features to the physical characteristics is an art. [*Sāmudrikā lakṣaṇa*]. For example a man with a soft foot, without sweating, invisible veins and round thighs would be a king. Rough toe nail indicates poverty. From the lines on the forehead the longevity can be decided. A woman with a round face would bring prosperity whereas a woman with round eyes would become a widow. Few lines on the palm of a woman show poverty and the sign of a wheel indicates that she would become a wife or mother of a king.

Precious Stones

There is a story as how precious stones are found in the earth. Once a demon named Balāsura defeated the gods and he had become unconquerable. It was a matter of worry for the gods. The gods arranged for a sacrifice and requested Balāsura to offer his body and he agreed. When the gods were taking his body in a *vimāna* in the sky, the body fell down and became bits and pieces. Wherever his part of the bodies fell, different precious stones were found. There are many precious stones like diamond, ruby, pearls, emeralds, sapphire, corals etc. Diamonds formed from his bones. From his teeth which fell into the ocean and entered the oysters, became pearls. His skin which fell on the Himālayas became Topaz. *Uk. Ch 6.*

Wedlock

Inter marriage between different *varṇas* are permitted on a selective basis. For example a brāhmaṇa can marry a woman from either a *Kṣatriya or Vaiśya* but a brāhmaṇa girl should not marry from other *varṇas.* Marriages are of many types. Brahmā marriage is one in which the groom is invited and handed over the girl with many jewels. When the daughter is given away in a *yajña* to the priest is known as *daivi* marriage. *Ārya* marriage is where two cows are accepted as the price of a bride. When the daughter is handed over to maintain *dharma* is known as *Prajāpati* marriage. A love marriage is called *gandharva* marriage. When the bride is kidnapped with her consent it is called *rākśasa* marriage.

Transmigration

According to the *karma* of an individual, the *Jīva* acquires a new body. For sins committed one has to remain in hell for some period. The sin of killing a Brāhmaṇa gives a birth as dog, frog, and then an owl. A liar is reborn as a dumb. Steal a fruit and be born as a monkey. The point to note down here is that one has to account even for a small sin and there is no escape from that.

Āyurveda

Dhanvantari was the father of *Āyurveda.* This science was originally taught to sage Suśruta and it is dealt elaborately in the *Garuda Purāṇa.* In Āyurveda three factors are taken for consideration of any illness. They are *vāta, pitta and kapha.* Diagnoses are based on the above three only. There are five steps in any treatment and they are – *nidāna* – diagnosis before the appearance of symptoms, *pūrva rūpa* – where the symptoms start manifesting, *rūpa* – where full symptoms are visible, *upāsaya* – beginning of treatment and *samprāpti* – cure of the disease. The entire Āyurveda uses only herbs and no chemical things are added. This system has got medicines even for severe snake poison.*Talisman* is prescribed for both physical as well as for protection from unwanted quarters. This system of medicines is available even for treating horses, elephants etc. Ailments are of four types: *Śārīrika* refers to fever, skin diseases etc; *Mānasika* refers to those arising out of anger etc; *Āgantuka* refers to cuts, wounds, injuries and *Sahaja* refers to hunger, thirst, old age etc.

Consideration to Less Fortunates

Helping the 'have nots' is of great importance in the Purāṇas. Donating to the right person is considered as the best form of worship as well as *dharma. Dānas* are of four types. *Nitya dāna* is giving, without expectations. *Naimittika dāna* is the one which is made for penance or to take care of ill omens. *Kāmya dāna* is that in which there are some expectations like getting a child etc. *Vimala dāna* is one which is done to please the gods.

True Knowledge

This Purāṇa gives a cursory glance on True knowledge, which is the union of *Jīvātma with Paramātma.* The *Jīvātma* is without beginning. *Paramātma* is beyond the experience of time and space. That which is not seen by the eyes, but that by which the eyes are able to see – that alone is Brahmān and not that which people worship here. Towards this goal it mentions about the yoga to achieve this.

What is After Death

Garuda Purāṇa deals elaborately with the funeral *mantras* and also funeral ceremonies. These ceremonies are meant to release the *preta,* and enable it to join the ancestors. On the subject of travel after death, it is in the form of discussion between Lord Viṣṇu and Garuda, where the Lord replies to the questions put by Garuda. The Lord says that a man who has no son goes to a hell called *punnama naraka.* After leaving the body the *Jīvātma* travels according to the merits, in its store. It has to go to hell to pay for all the evil deeds before obtaining another body according to its merits / demerits. There are many hells and some of them are *raurava. Mahāraurava, attiṣta, nikṛnatana* etc. There is a ten days period in which various rituals are to be performed to the dead. But the dead are not offered *piṇḍa or tarpaṇa,* if the death is due to poison, snake bites, fire, cholera etc. For such deaths there are special ceremony known as *nārāyanāvali.* The first ten days invariably *piṇḍa* is offered to the dead. It is said that out of the *piṇḍa* offered, one fourth goes to *yama dūts,* one fourth for the *preta* to survive and the remaining is used to form a body for the soul to undertake the journey. On the eleventh day a *śrāddha* is performed, which is the first for the dead, in which a bull is donated, known as *vṛṣṭosarga.* For one year every month *śrāddha* is performed till first ritual is performed after completion of one year. It is said that it takes one year for the *preta* to reach Yama's abode. During the period it lives only on the *piṇḍas* offered. After the one year period only, it remains no more a *preta* but joins the ancestors. Lord Viṣṇu continued to tell Garuda. *Sapiṇḍaka* indicates those who are entitled to perform the funeral rites for the dead and they are the sons, grand sons, brothers etc. If there are no *sapiṇḍakas* the wife can perform the ceremonies and in the absence of anybody, one can perform for himself before death. A story is said to emphasise the point. Babhruvāhana was a righteous king and one day he went to the forest for hunting. He killed many deer but one deer, which was hit by his arrow, ran away. The king followed that deer and was lost in the forest. He became so tired that he slept under a tree. He woke up to noises around him and found that many ghosts were fighting among them to eat him up. The king asked the ghost in front as why he became ghost. In reply the ghost said that many of them did not have anybody to perform the *śrāddha* ceremony or died of unnatural causes. The ghost also requested the king to perform the *śrāddha* and release them. The king has the right to perform the *śrāddha* for those who did not have anybody to perform the rituals. The ghost said that though he was a righteous *Vaiśya,* he became ghost because he did not have sons to perform the rituals.

Garuda had a doubt. He asked the Lord as how the *piṇḍas* offered go to the ancestors. Lord said that every *śrāddha* ceremony, the brhāmaṇas are invited and the ancestors enter the bodies of brāhmaṇas and partake at the offerings. In this context the story of Rāma and Sītā was quoted. Rāma was performing the *śrāddha* ceremony for Daśaratha. Sītā cooked the food as several sages had been invited, but at the time of serving Sītā was not to be found and Rāma did the serving. Sītā appeared when the guests had left. Rāma enquired as where she had been and the reply was that she was hiding because she felt ashamed. She said that she saw Rāma's father, grandfather etc sitting with the guests and was ashamed to give them such poor food to eat. This shows that the ancestors partake of the food. On a question from Garuda about donations, Viṣṇu said the important things to be given at the time of *śrāddha* are umbrella, which is for the travel to Yama's abode, a pair of sandals and a seat. By donating a seat, the *preta* gets food and then a water pot. It is said that *Varuṇa* takes all these offerings, passes on to Sūrya devata, who in turn takes these to the *preta.* At the conclusion Viṣṇu told Garuda about the life of human beings, and about the human body and its functions.

Padma Purāṇa

This is a voluminous work, in five sections *Sṛṣṭi* [creation], *Bhūmi* [earth], *Svarga* [heaven], *Pātāla* [netherland], and *Uttara kāṇḍa* [end section]. This is supposed to have been composed in 800 A.D. and there are about 51,000 verses. It is a scripture of Vaiṣṇavites in two distinct recensions – the Bengali and south Indian, and the later one is only available in print. Various topics have been covered and to mention few are stories, legends, sacrifices, worlds of goblins, gandharvas, and heaven etc. it also contains worship of Śiva, Viṣṇu and *sahasranāmas* of Viṣṇu and Rāma.

Various sages wanted to hear about this Purāṇa and Lomaharṣaṇa narrated them.

Sons' Devotion

Śivaśarmā lived in Dvārakā and was well versed in scriptures. His five sons were Yajñaśarmā, Vedaśarmā, Dharmaśarmā, Viṣṇuśarmā and Somaśarmā. They were very much devoted to their father and in this story Śivaśarma verifies their integrity and devotion to him by the power of illusion. [Magical]. First son obeyed the order of cutting the body of his dead mother and throwing the pieces away. He asked his second son to convince a woman to marry him on any condition. The woman had put a condition that she would marry his father only when he cuts his head and he fulfilled the condition. The severed head of the second son was given to the third son and he started to pray. His prayers were answered by the god and he got two boons, one his elder brother was restored back to life and also that he would always be devoted to his father. The fourth son was asked to get amṛt from Indra so that he could become young and marry the woman he wanted. Indra gave him amṛt only after testing his devotion to father, by offering woman and disturbing him with demons etc. Finally Indra gave him what he wanted and the fourth son gave the amṛt to the father. Having ensured that all the four sons were devoted to the father, he resurrected his wife and told his sons that he was pleased with their devotion to father and sent all of them to *Viṣṇu loka* by the power of his *tapasyā.* So four sons went to *Vaikuṇtha* and the fifth son alone was left. In order to test the fifth son he told him that he and his mother were going on a pilgrimage and asked him to protect the amṛt. After a while when the parents returned, the father made himself and his wife lepers and asked him to look after them. The son took care of his parents pretty well. The father one day, through his power made the amṛt to disappear. Then he asked his son to get the nectar. But when Somaśarma looked into the pot it was empty. He carried the pot to his father saying to himself "Let there be nectar in it, if I am truthful, if I have served my elders well and if I have observed pure penance". The pot was filled with nectar. The father was satisfied. Then Somaśarmā started practicing most severe penance. When the time for his death came, *asuras* approached him. Fear about *asuras* gripped him, while in deep meditation and as he breathed his last thinking about *asuras* he was born in his next life as Prahlāda, son of Hiraṇyakaśipu [Bhūmī Kāṇḍa]

Indra

Gods requested Lord Viṣṇu for a ruler and the Lord said that their mother Aditi would have a son, who would be known as Indra, and would be their King. Aditi, wife of sage Kaśyap, who was the mother of all the gods, did penance for one hundred years, and a son was born to her. The child had four arms with brilliant radiance and became to be known as Indra, ruler of the gods.

Steadfast Devotion

A poor *Brāhmaṇa* by name Somaśarmā was living with his wife on the banks of the river Reva and the couple had no sons at all. Somaśarmā went to sage Vasiṣṭha and asked the sage why he was poor and also had no sons? Vasiṣṭha told him that he was poor because of his actions of previous birth in which he was a rich *Śūdra* and accumulated a lot of wealth but would not make any charity. Because once he welcomed a *Brāhmaṇa* as an honored guest and performed *Edkādaśi* vratam along with the guest, he was born as a *Brāhmaṇa.* He was asked to meditate upon Viṣnu. In spite of lots of obstacles like snakes, ghosts, wild animals etc; he meditated upon the Lord and got the boon for a son and also comfortable life.

An ardent devotee of Viṣṇu, named Dharmāñgada was born as Suvrata, as son of the Brāhmaṇa. He was so much devoted to the Lord that he used to call all his friends by the name of the Lord only. He used to be so much immersed in meditation that he would forget even thirst and hunger. By his extreme devotion, not only he attained heaven but also liberated his parents. *Ch. 21.*

Bala

Among the wives of sage Kaśyap, Aditi was the mother of gods, whereas Diti was the mother of daityas / demons. Lord Viṣṇu was the cause, behind the killing of many of her sons. Diti went and requested sage Kaśyap to get her a son who would be strong. As per the advice of the sage, Diti meditated for hundred years and gave birth to a child who was named Bala, meaning strength. Sage Kaśyap taught Bala *Śāstras* and various other things. His mother told him that Viṣṇu had killed many of her children and that he should kill Viṣṇu. Accordingly, to accomplish some special powers he started to do penance. In the meantime Aditi told Indra that in order to prevent Bala becoming powerful, he should be killed. Indra went and killed Bala with his *Vajrāyudha*, while he was doing penance. *Ch. 65.*

Vṛtra

Having heard about the fate of Bala, sage Kaśyapa plucked a hair from his head and flung it down, from which a fierce son was created, who was named as Vṛtra and Kaśyapa ordered him to kill Indra. Accordingly Vṛtra started practicing warfare. Indra got frightened and sent the Saptaṛṣīs for mediation. The Saptaṛṣīs offered Vṛtra half the Indraloka and he agreed. One day while Vṛtra was wandering in a beautiful garden named *nandankānana* Indra sent an *apsarā* named Rambhā to entice Vṛtra. As soon as he saw her he fell in love with her. Rambhā made him to drink wine and when Vṛtra fell unconscious Indra killed him with his *vajra.*

Bhūmi Khāṇḍa – ch 23.

Sunītā

Sunītā was the mental daughter of Yama – lord of death-*Mṛtyu* and was famous for her beauty.Once while going into the forest with her friends she happened to come across the hermitage iṅ which a *gandharva* by the name Suśaṅka was meditating. Sunītā tried to disturb his meditation, but being a woman, he did not curse her but asked her to go away. Being the daughter of Yama she was proud and slapped him. Enraged by this, he cursed her that the son born to her would be extremely evil. Aṅga was the son of Kuru and once he happened to go to the garden of Indra. There he witnessed the gods serving Indra and wished to have a son as powerful as Indra. On the advice of his father he performed penance in Mount Sumeru. To test him Viṣṇu created many hurdles but Aṅga was not perturbed. So Viṣṇu appeared and offered a boon. Aṅga got a boon from Viṣṇu, that he woould have a righteous son. In the meantime Sunītā performed some *tapasyā* so that the effect of the curse could be mitigated.

Because of the curse nobody wanted to marry her. Sunītā charmed Aṅga and they were married. Their son was Vena. *Vā -47.*

Vena

Vena learned Śāstras etc and was very righteous. His mother too always emphasized to him about righteous living, remembering the curse and Vena became the king after the death of Aṅga. But unfortunately he came in contact with a religious teacher of Jainism and adopted that religion. He deviated from the path of righteousness and banished Vedas from his kingdom. He would not take the advice of either his father or even the Saptarṣīs. As the pleadings of the *ṛṣīs* did not have any effect on Vena, all the sages gathered together and recited spells and struck him with *Kuśa* grass and killed him. As without king there was a spell of chaos, the hermits joined together and churned the left hand of Vena, from which a man of short stature came out, to whom the hermits said 'Niṣīda' [sit], and he came to be known as Niṣāda. Then the hermits churned his right hand and a person as huge as mountain with divine signs came out. *Va. Ch 47.*

Pṛthu

As Pṛthu appeared after the evils from the body of Vena had been taken out he was very righteous king and served his subjects well. Brahmā performed a yajna after Pṛthu was born. From the yajna was born a very wise and intelligent demon named Sūta and a scholarly Māgadha was born. They were commanded to praise Pṛthu. But the people were hungry as during the period of Vena, the goddess of earth had drawn all vegetations inside. Pṛthu followed the goddess of earth with his bow and arrow. The goddess said that she would allow him to milk the earth but wanted a calf. Therefore Pṛthu made Svāyambhuva Manu as calf and milked the earth. And so goddess of earth got the name Pṛthvī. *Ch. 47.*

Sukalā

In Vārāṇasi there lived a Vaiśya named Kṛkala, who had very dutiful, pious and highly religious wife named Sukalā. He had learnt that *'tīrtha yātra'* is very good; he decided to go on the pilgrimage. But his wife would not allow him to go alone and wished to accompany him because, as far as she was concerned, her husband was everything to her. So one day when she had gone to temple, Kṛkala left without telling her. When she came to know of her husband's departure she felt very miserable and said that she would do penance for having been deserted by the husband. When the friends tried to console her she narrated the story of Sudeva to them.

King Ikṣvāku was a very righteous king, who ruled Ayodhyā. At that time Kāśī was ruled by King Devarāta, who had a daughter named Sudeva and she was the wife of Ikṣvāku. Ikṣvāku and Sudeva are said to be the incarnations of Viṣṇu and Lakṣmī. Once when Ikṣvāku went for a hunt, Sudeva also accompanied. In the course of the hunt the king killed many animals. At that time there lived a family of wild pigs. The male pig told the female pig to take care of the family as he was going to be hunted. In spite of an a request from the female pig to run away, the male pig gave a good fight to the king and ultimately died. Seeing that the husband had been killed the female pig advised the children to run away and the eldest son and the female pig took up the fight. Ikṣvāku killed the eldest son but did not kill the female pig, in spite of the fact that the female pig wounded many of the soldiers. When questioned by the queen, he said that he did not want to kill the female, but one of the king's fighters struck the female pig and it fell down unconscious. Sudeva could not bear the suffering of the pig and she poured some water and wiped the blood. The female pig said that because of her touch her sins had been cleansed. Surprised to hear the pig talking, the queen asked about their stories. The female pig narrated the story of the male pig.

The male pig was a *gandharva* with good voice named Raṅkavidyādhara. Once he started singing near the hermitage of sage Pulastya. The sage asked him to go elsewhere and sing but he would not listen. Instead he advised the sage that he could go elsewhere to meditate. The sage went away. The gandharva wanted to play a trick, so he changed his form to a pig and started goring the sage. Initially the sage ignored the disturbance but subsequently the sage realized that the same *gandharva* had come in the form of a pig. He cursed him to be born as a pig. Alarmed by the turn of events, the *gandharva* fled to Indra for help, but Indra was unable to help him except saying that when he was killed by Ikṣvāku he would become *gandharva* again. When queen Sudeva asked to tell the story of the female pig, it continued.

A Brāhmaṇa named Vasudatta had a daughter Sudevā [different from the queen]. He loved his daughter so much that he refused to marry her and was looking for a son-in-law who would stay with him. Ultimately he found a groom for his daughter, a well learned but a poor Brāhmaṇa named Śivaśarmā and Sudevā was married to him. Unfortunately Sudevā was a spoilt child and she did not give any respect to her husband. She showed contempt at every opportunity. When it became unbearable Śivaśarmā left the house. Vasudatta was unable to bear this and wanted to throw her daughter out of the house. Then his wife narrated the story of Ugrasena and asked him to banish his daughter. The parents banished Sudevā. Sudevā traveled from place to place and started begging. One day, while begging she came across a palatial house and thought she might get some alms. The house holder came out, saw Sudevā and told his wife to give some food. The house wife gave her lots of food but Sudevā could recognize the house holder as none other than her husband. Śivaśarma too recognized her and told his wife that she was the daughter of Vasudatta, his wife. Both the husband and wife treated Sudevā well but unable to bear her past misdeeds she died. Subsequently Sudevā took many births as various creatures and now was the female pig. The female pig then begged queen Sudevā to do something to mitigate her suffering.The queen granted whatever *puṇya* she had earned in the past one year and the female pig was changed into a divine woman.

This story was narrated by the female pig, during its conversation with queen Sudevā. Ugrasena was the ruler of Mathurā and was comparatively poor to his wife Padmāvatī's father, Satyaketu. Though Ugrasena was devoted to his wife, she did not reciprocate his love, as he was not as prosperous as her father. After a few years Satyaketu asked Ugrasena to send his daughter for a short while and he sent his wife. As she was more comfortable there, she never bothered to return to her husband's place. One day she happened to visit the place of Kubera, the lord of wealth and Kubera's companion Godila fell in love with her. As he could not marry her, he adopted the form of Ugrasena and Padmāvatī, taking him to be her husband started living with him and subsequently only she realized that it was not Ugrasena.

When asked why he deceived her, the reply was that had she loved her husband she would not have left him. After that he left her. She went back to Ugrasena and he gladly welcomed her. After some time, she gave birth to a terrible son, which was not Ugrasena's but of Govila and he was Kamsa who was killed by Kṛṣṇa. *Ch. 42.*

When Sukala completed the story, every body was aghast with wonder. Her fame spread even among gods. Indra wanted to test her. He sent a messenger to Sukala who told her that she was wasting her time. That her husband had not gone on pilgrimage but had deserted her. He suggested that it would be better she married his master. Sukala asked the messenger to bring his master and Indra appeared. Indra tried to convince her but Sukala would not budge. In the meantime when Kṛkala was returning home, a celestial voice told him that his pilgrimage was waste and his ancestors would not be released as any pilgrimage without the devoted wife was waste. Kṛkala hurried back home and delighted his wife. They performed a ritual for the ancestors in which Indra was also present and blessed them that they would be always righteous. *Bhumikhāṇḍa – ch 42.*

Power of Devotion to Parents

Kuṇḍala, a Brāhmin residing in Kurukṣetra, had a son named Sukarmā. Sukarmā's parents were old and Sukarmā spent most of his time, looking after his sickly parents. Kuṇḍala taught his son all the Vedas and Śāstras. At that time in the *gotra* of Kaśyap was born a Brāhmin named Pipplāda. Controlling his senses and abandoning all passions he did severe penance in a forest called Daśāraṇya. The greatness of his penance made animals of the forest leave their mutual enmity and live in perfect peace. Even the *devas* were astonished at the power of penance. Pippalāda did penance sitting as majestic and motionless as a mountain for a thousand years. Ants had made over him mole hills. He sat inside without any motion. Black cobras circled around him but made no difference. Three thousand years went like this. Brahmā appeared and gave him the boon 'sarvakāmasiddhi' and by the blessings of Brahmā he became very knowledgable also. Pippalāda became arrogant with the boon. One day while he was sitting on a river bank, a swan appeared before him and said in clear tone: "Pippalāda, why are you so proud of your greatness? I do not think you have that power of universal attraction. This art is *arvācīna* [modern]. You do not know *prācīna* because you are illiterate. Do you know Sukarmā, the wise son of Kuṇḍala? He is the man who has acquired this power of attraction. There is no *mahājñānī* like him in this world. Even though he is a child, you do not possess knowledge like him". Sage Pippalāda came in search of Sukarmā one day. By seeing Pippalāda Sukarmā said, "I know you have spent thousands of years in penance and gods granted you the boon to control all objects in the universe, but the swan had told you that you know nothing". Pippalāda asked who the swan was. The reply was that it was Brahmān. Pippalāda questioned whether he could also subjugate all the objects. To demonstrate Sukarmā called all the gods. Indra and all others appeared immediately and asked what they could do for him. Sukarmā explained that he performed no penance but all the powers were because of his devotion to his parents. *Ch. 60 - 62.*

Yayāti

In the Lunar dynasty Nahuṣa was a righteous king and had six sons and they were Yati, yayāti, Samyāti, Āyāti,

Ayati and Dhruva. Yayāti was also a good king. He had two wives and four sons. He ruled for eighty-one thousand years and his fame spread all over. Seeing the rigorous observance of Yayāti's virtuous life, Indra began to be alarmed. He sent his charioteer Mātali to bring Yayāti to Indraloka. But Yayāti refused saying that he would go to heaven with his physical body. Yayāti also instructed his subjects to be righteous and so there was no old age and death. Yama complained to Indra that he had no work. Indra sent some *gandharvas* to enact the drama of *Vāmanāvatāra* before Yayāti. Enchanted by the charm of Rati on the stage, the king became fascinated. Yayāti started losing some of his clean habits and old age entered his body. Once he went to the forest for hunting, where he found a beautiful woman sitting on a large lotus. On enquiry he was informed that she was Aśrubiṇdumatī, daughter of Rati. Yayāti wanted to marry her but she refused telling that she would marry him only if he becomes young. On his return to the palace, he called all his four sons and requested them to exchange their youth. His last son, Puru alone fulfilled his father's desire and all others refused. He exchanged the youth of his son and married Aśrubindumatī but with so many conditions like he would not treat his other wives like wives. Ultimately having enjoyed the life thoroughly, returned the youth to his son and ascended to the heaven.*Ch – 84 -85.*

Cyavana

In the lineage of sage Bhṛgu, there was a sage named Cyavana. He wanted to get true knowledge, but thought that he would get knowledge by visiting *thirthas,* and accordingly he visited the places on the banks of the rivers Narmadā, Sarasvatī and Godāvarī and came to a place called Amarakaṇṭaka. Cyavana was tired of traveling and he sat down under a banyan tree, in which a parrot was living with its wife and four sons. Daily the sons would go out to find food and bring home something for their parents too. That day the sons had just returned back. After food the father parrot enquired his sons about the place they visited for food. The eldest son said that they visited Plakṣadvīpa and narrated a story. A king named Divodāsa wanted to marry his daughter Divyādevi and whenever a groom was fixed up he would die before the marriage and this happened for twenty one times. Finally when the king decided that he would conduct svayamvara, all the princes who had come for the svayamvara fought among themselves and died. Divyā renounced and went to forest. Moved by pity, a sage taught her ***'Aśūnyaśayana' vrata***. She practiced with devotion and Mahāviṣṇu appeared and took her to Viṣṇuloka. The son parrot asked father why such things happened with Divyā? The father parrot gave the reply.

Bhumikhāṇḍa Ch.85 to 88.

In the city of Vārāṇasi lived a Vaiśya named Sudhira and had a wife named Citrā. He was devoted to his wife. But his wife was an evil character and never obeyed her husband; on the contrary she would talk ill of him with her neighbors. As Sudhira could not stand such behavior of his wife, he married again. Citrā left her husband and started having contacts with thieves and robbers. When she died she had to undergo a lot of sufferings and finally was born as Divyādevi. As she was responsible for destroying many families she would not have her own family. The son parrot, named Ujjvala asked that if she was so bad how was it that she was born as the daughter of a king? The reply was that once she happened to wash the feet of a mendicant and because of that she got a higher birth.

Then the father parrot asked his next son Samujjvala about his experience. Samujjvala recounted his experience. He went to Himalayas and visited Mānasarovar. There he saw several swans, white ones with black leg and beaks, some were black, some were pure white and some were blue. Then four fierce looking women appeared. The black swans started bathing and other swans circumambulated the lake and the women were laughing. Then a huge swan emerged from Mānasarovar, followed by three other swans and all of them flew away. Then a good looking hunter arrived there followed by his wife. The wife did not recognize her husband but the husband recognized the wife and asked for food. When she denied that he was her husband he said that when he took bath in the *Narmada saṅgam,* his appearance got transformed and he took her to that tirtha. The swans and the four women also followed. The hunter's wife became divine in appearance after bathing, the black swans became white, but the four women fell down and died. Samujjvala said that he did not understand anything. The father parrot gave the explanation. Once Indra asked Nārada which was the most sacred tīrtha but Nārada could not reply, so Indra summoned all the tīrthas and asked them who were superior to all of them? They replied that most sacred are Prayāg, Puṣkara, Arghyatīrtha and Vārāṇasi and there is a story about it. A Kṣhatriya named Vidura lived in Pañcāla. Bcause of penury he killed a Brāhmin. After that Vidura discarded his lock of hair and holy thread, went to every house and started begging, saying "I am a slayer of a Brāhmin. Please give alms." But there was no remission for his sin. Once he was sitting under a tree, grieving. At that time Candraśarmā, a Brāhmin came. He had killed his teacher. He visited several *tīrthas* for atonement, but futile. Vidura and Candraśarmā traveled together. On the way they met another Brāhmaṇa named Vedaśarmā, who had committed the sin of marrying some one he should not have and all the three started traveling together. The group met Vallāla, a Vaiśya who was a drunkard and killer of cows. Eventually, the four met a sage and asked him for a way out of their sins. The sage advised them to take a dip in Prāyaga, Puṣkara, Sarvatīrtha and Vārāṇasī. But instead of getting rid of their sins the tīrthas got contaminated. The four contaminated tīrthas took the form of the black swans and followed the sinners. Wherever they bathed that *tīrtha* got contaminated and took the form of black swan, where they did not bathe, the *tīrtha* took the form of white swans and followed them. There were now sixty four in the group and when the sinners took a dip in Mānasarovar, it got contaminated and became gigantic black swan. Finally when the group made the trip to the confluence of Narmadā and Reva and bathed there, their sins were pardoned. The four women were the personification of sins and since the sins were washed off, they died. And this tīrtha is known as Kubjatīrtha.

The narration of the third son Vijvala was this: He went to Mount Sumeru, where there was a beautiful garden and lake with plenty of swans and lotuses. While waiting he saw a *vimāna* descending and a well dressed, good looking man and woman descended. They took bath in the lake. After the bath they picked up a sword and just then saw the dead body of a man and woman, looking exactly like them. The female started slicing the female body and eating it and the male sliced the male body. At that time two beautiful looking women arrived and started laughing at them. Two fierce looking women also arrived and started begging for a share. When they ate they drank water from the lake and left and the corpses were replenished. Every day he witnessed the same and asked the meaning of it. Kañjala, the father bird recounted the following story.

Subāhu, the king of Chola kingdom, was very handsome and righteous. His wife was Tārkṣyi. He performed many sacrifices, but his priest was not satisfied and advised to give alms but the king was interested in living in the abode of Lord Viṣṇu. He started performing difficult penance with his wife. When they died they were taken to Viṣṇuloka. But though Viṣṇuloka was beautiful, the couple felt hungry and thirsty and no food or drink could be found. They came across the sage Vāmadeva and explained to him their difficulties. The sage said it was because they had never given any alms and suggested remedy that since their dead body had not decomposed, they eat that flesh daily till they hear the hymns on Viṣṇu. The two women laughing at them were 'knowledge' and 'śraddhā' – faith. For their salvation Kuñjala taught the sacred hymn to Vijvala. Vijvala recited the hymns and the couple attained salvation.

The fourth son, named Kapinjala narrated the following story. He was in the habit of going to mount Kailāś. The mount was full of lakes and there was one gigantic lake. Adjacent to the lake was a big boulder on which he found a woman seated and kept on crying. The drops of tears, which fell on the water turned into beautiful lotuses. Nearby there was a Śiva temple in which a sage worshipped Śiva, who lived only on dried leaves. The lotuses which emerged from the tear drops of the woman was plucked by the sage and offered to Śiva. Then he would sing in praise of the Lord, dance and finally start weeping. The son wanted to know what the mystery was. The father parrot explained:

Śiva and Pārvatī lived in Mount Kailāś, where there was a beautiful garden known as *nandanavana*. One day Śiva took Pārvatī to the garden and there was one tree which appeared to be superior to others.The Lord said that it was *Kalpavṛkṣa*, which would give whatever one wished. To test, Pārvatī wished that it may produce a beautiful woman and a woman emerged, whose beauty could not be described. The woman asked mother Pārvatī, what her orders were? Pārvatī said "your name will be Aśokasundarī and King Nahuṣa will marry you". And the woman started living in the garden.

There was a demon named Viprachitti who had a son named Huṇḍa. He happened to go to *nandanavana* and met Aśhokasundarī. He wanted to marry her but she refused. Huṇḍa through his māyā power adopted the form of a woman and appeared before her. When enquired who she was, the woman said that her husband had been killed by Huṇḍa and she was performing *tapasyā* to kill Huṇḍa. She invited her to her hermitage. Aśokasundarī accompanied her and as soon as they reached the so called hermitage, Huṇḍa came to his original form and tried to abduct her. Aśokasundarī repulsed his attempt and started doing penance so that king Nahuṣa may kill him. While all this was happening Nahuṣa was not even born. King Āyus who did not have a son obtained a boon for a powerful and righteous son after performing penance to Sage Dattātreya for hundred years. Huṇḍa knew that Āyus's son would kill him. Indumatī, wife of Āyus gave birth to a son and when the maid left the room, Huṇḍa entered the body of the maid, took the child and ran to his palace at Kāñcanapura. He gave the child to his wife Vipula and asked her to make sauce of the child for him. Vipula gave the child to the cook. The cook hid the child, made sauce out of some other flesh and took the child to sage Vasiśṭḥa. Vasiśṭḥa named the boy Nahuṣa - meaning 'fearless' and brought him up. The sage taught him, all the warfares and told him about his antecedents. He told him to kill Huṇḍa and marry Aśokasundarī, who was waiting for him. All the gods offered weapons to Nahuṣa. Nahuṣa killed the demon after a fierce battle, married Aśokasundarī and was reunited with his parents.

Ch – 102 -117.

Demon Huṇḍa had a son by the name Vihuṇḍa. Having known about the fate of his father, he decided to do penance to kill Nahuṣa and destroy the gods. The *tapasyā* was so terrible that the gods went to Viṣṇu. Viṣṇu adopted the form of a beautiful woman and went to *nandana.* When Vihuṇḍa saw her, he wanted to marry her. The lady agreed and said "There is one condition. You should worship Śiva with seven crores of *kāmoda* flowers, make a garland of these flowers and put it on my neck." As nobody knew anything about *kāmoda* flower, Vihuṇḍa approached Śukrācārya. The ācārya said "Kāmoda flowers fall from the laughter of a lady named Kāmoda and these are offered to Śiva, but when she cries a red odorless flower comes which should not be touched." The gods asked the help of Nārada. Nārada convinced Vihuṇḍa that he need not go to collect the flowers but he could pick them up when they came floating in Gaṅgā. Then Nārada made Kāmoda to cry by telling her that the hermit Bhṛgu had cursed Viṣṇu and changed him into a man. On hearing this Kāmoda started crying. Red flowers fell from her lips. Vihuṇḍa gathered them and went to the place of Śiva. Pārvatī saw the red flowers and did not like red flowers being offered. It angered Pārvatī so much that she killed Vihuṇḍa.

Ch. 119 -130.

The sage Cyavana overheard the entire conversation. He asked Kañjala how he was so much learned. Kañjala narrated his own story. A brāhmaṇa named Vidyādhara had three sons, Vasuśarmā, Nāmaśarmā and Dharmaśarmā. The first two sons followed the footsteps of the father but Dharmaśarmā was not interested in it and people started avoiding him. One day when Dharmaśarmā was sitting repentant in a temple, a siddha came to the temple. When Dharmaśarmā saw him go and sit for meditation, he went and stood in front of him very respectfully. After some time when the siddha opened his eyes, he saw Dhramśarmā and enquired. Dhramaśarmā requested him for instructions to acquire the supreme knowledge. The siddha obliged and soon Dharmaśarmā himself became a siddha. While on a pilgrimage, Dhramaśarmā got a parrot. He took very much care of the Parrot like his son. One day when Dhramaśarmā was away a cat caught and ate the parrot. Dharmaśarmā was grief-stricken and died after some time. Since his last thought before death was parrot, he was born as a parrot, which was Kañjala. As the *Jñānopadeśa* was still lingeing in his mind at the time of death, it was not lost. *Ch - 122.*

Gandharvas are by class singers in the heaven. Five *gandharvas* had one daughter each, they were pretty, and good friends. Their names were Pramohinī, Suśīlā, Susvarā, Candrikā and Sutārā. For the worship of Pārvatī in the month of Vaiśākha, they went to the forest to collect flowers. There was a beautiful lake in the forest. All the friends bathed in the lake and collected lotus flowers. While the five were worshipping Devī, the eldest son of sage Vedanidhi came to bathe in Acchoda pond. He was very charming and looked like another Kāmadeva. All the five daughters of *gandharvas* fell in love with him. They asked him to marry them, but he refused telling that he was performing difficult penance. But still, when the girls continued, he fled from that place. The next day, again the girls ran to the pond. The boy too came and the girls once again approached him and encircled him, one caught the leg, the other hand and so on. He used his power of *māyā* and disappeared. Disappointed they returned home and the next day again went to the forest. Tīrthaparavara, the Brāhmaṇa again happened to be there. When they again raised the topic he lost his temper and cursed them to turn into female demons. The daughters of the *gandharvas* in turn cursed him to become a demon. So there were six demons wandering in the lake for food. After long, sage Lomāśa happened to visit that place and all the six wanted to eat him, but they could not even go near him. They prostrated the sage and asked for a way to redeem their original form. Lomāśa was greatly moved and he took them to the banks of river Narmadā. At that time a wind blew and drops of water from the river changed them into their original forms. On advice from Lomaśā Tīrthaparavara married all the five of them. *Ch-22.*

Vikuṇḍala

Hemakuṇḍala was a very pious and religious Vaiśya, who had earned lots of money and in his old age one sixth of the wealth he spent on various works for social betterment. He had two sons, namely Srikuṇḍala and Vikuṇḍala. Hemakuṇḍala divided his wealth between the two sons and retired to forest. Being young and having got money without having to do labor, both the sons got into all sorts of vices and ultimately became poor. To make a lively hood they turned out to be hunters. In the forest, the elder one was killed by a tiger and other by a snake bite. In the Yamaloka Srikuṇḍala was sent to severe hell whereas Vikuṇḍala was sent to heaven. When questioned that both of them were together and did the same actions and how can there be different punishments the *Yamadhūtas* recounted the following to Vikuṇḍala: "There was a Brāhmin, who was well versed in all branches of scripture. He was the son of Harimitra and had his hermitage on the southern bank of Yamunā. You and Harimitra had become friends in the forest. Because of the friendship, you were able to take bath in two Māgha months in the holy river of Kālindī, which is capable of washing away the sins. So you became eligible for the attainment of heaven". Vikuṇḍala wanted to know whether his brother could be saved and he was told that by transferring some of his *puṇyas* which was accumulated by his service to sages by giving them *bikṣā some* eight lives ago, his brother could be redeemed. Vikuṇḍala gladly saved his brother. *Ādikāṇḍa Ch. 30.*

Eighteen Purāṇas

They are assigned to the various limbs of *Virāt Puruṣa.*

Daṇḍaka

Daṇḍaka was a thief, who made the world to tremble. There was not one sin he left uncommitted including killing of Brāhamaṇas and cows. One day Daṇḍa went to a Vaiṣṇavite temple to commit robbery. When he reached the steps of the temple, he wiped his feet on the ground as it was wet and by this a small depression in the temple got levelled. He broke the lock with an iron rod and entered the temple. Inside he saw a beautiful idol of Śri

Kṛṣṇa with Rādhā and he bowed down to Rādhā. Impelled by his evil nature, he took away the yellow silk robe of Kṛṣṇa He bundled whatever he could take and ran but he was bitten by a snake and died. This simple act of leveling a pit by the mud in his leg and bowing down to Rādhā led him to heaven. *Ch - 1.*

Varatanu

A king named Śridhara of Kuru dynasty had a wife named Prabhāvatī. Though they were rich and prosperous, did not have a son. Once Vyāsa came to his palace and the king asked him the reason of being childless. The sage replied that in his previous birth, he was a Brāhmin named Varatanu and his wife was Śaṅkarī. One day, when both of them were going some where, they saw a child drowning but did not do anything to save the child and the child was drowned. That was the reason they did not have any child in this birth. Following the advice of Vyāsa they donated gold, clothes, oxen etc and performed the rite named *Bāla vrata* and got a lovable son. *Ch - 6*

Śuklāṣtamīvrata

In Kṛtayuga there was a beautifu lady named Līlāvatī, but a prostitute. She had to leave her own place to another place for better prospects. On the way, she saw a big assembly of people in a temple. They were observing *Rādhāṣtamī* and worshipping their deity. When she went and enquired, she was told that they were observing the birth day of Rādhā Devī, which falls on the *Śuklāṣtamī* of the month *Proṣṭhapada*. On hearing that, Līlāvatī decided to observe the *Vrata*. She joined the devotees and observed the *Vrata* with great devotion. But soon she died of snake bite. Though as a prostitute, she committed lot of sins, because of the power of the *Vrata* she was absolved of all the sins and the *Pārsadas of Viṣṇu* came to take her to heaven. *Bh.K – Ch 7.*

Lakṣmīvrata

King Bhadraśravā was the ruler of Saurāṣṭra and his queen was Suraticandrikā. They had seven sons and a daughter –Śyāmabāla. When Śyāmabāla had been away for playing Śrī Lakṣmī arrived in the form of an old Brāhmaṇa woman to tender advice to the queen and about her merits of her previous birth. In her previous birth the queen was a Vaiśya woman and performed Lakṣmī vrata. But the queen did not receive her advice and sent her away. While going back, Śyāmabāla happened to meet the old lady and enquired as to why she was weeping. The old lady told about the *vrata,* which Śyāmabāla decided to do herself. When she left her parents after marriage the king and the queen became poor and even the wealth given by Śyāmabāla was turned into charcoal. Once when the mother visited the daughter, Śyāmabāla made her mother to perform Lakṣmī vrata and they regained all their wealth. *Ch - 11.*

Visvāmitra against Human Sacrifice

A king named Dīnanātha did not have a son and he was advised by the sage Gālava to perform a Yajna and offer a perfect and handsome human being as sacrifice. The king sent his men to fetch a handsome and young man. They went around all the places, came to a village and found a Brāhmaṇa having three sons, who were strong and handsome too. They asked the parents of the boys to spare one. When refused, they abducted the second son and took him away, leaving some gold coins as compensation. On the way they happened to encounter

Sage Viśvāmitra. The sage after learning the purpose for which the boy was being taken, he offered himself for the sacrifice. But the king's men thought him to be too old for sacrifice and refused. The sage volunteered himself and accompanied the sentries. Viśvāmitra convinced the king Dīnānātha that the yajna could be performed without human sacrifice and he guaranteed the result. Viśvāmitra took the boy to the parents himself. The king performed the yajna and a son was born to him. *Ch - 12.*

Aṣṭamīrohiṇī Vrata

Citrasena, a Mahārājā was a great sinner, having committed such sins as stealing things belonging to Brāhmaṇa, drinking and causing injury to living beings. On a Kṛṣṇāṣṭamī day - the day of Kṛṣṇa's birth, he happened to go for a hunt. Chasing a tiger, he felt completely exhausted at dusk and came to the banks of river Yamunā, where many maidens were observing the *vrata* of *Aṣṭamīrohiṇī.* There were a lot of offerings to Lord Kṛṣṇa and the king begged something to eat and drink. But the maidens said that it would be a sin to eat, when they were observing the *Vrata.* Hearing this there was a change in the king's mind and he felt that he himself should observe the *vrata.* Because of this, though the king was a great sinner, he attained heaven after his death. This story was told by sage Vasiṣṭha to Dilīpa to impress him about the vrata. *Ch - 13*

Service to a Brāhmin

A low caste man, named Bhīma, who engaged himself in the profession of a Vaiśya. An outcast from practices pertaining to a Śūdra, he enjoyed the company of a Vaiśya woman. He had killed many Brāhmins, molested many and he was a robber too. Once he went to a

Brāhmaṇa's house, with the intention of stealing his property, but pretended to be a beggar and asked for food. The Brāhmaṇa said that as there was nobody in the house to cook food, but told him to help himself with some rice and cook it. Bhima said that as he too had no one and offered to stay with him to help him. The Brāhmin agreed and Bhīma thought that he could stay with him and steal at a proper time. But by living with the Brāhmin, he used to pour on his head the water, which was used by the Brāhmin, washed off his sins. Once when a thief came into the house, Bhīma prevented him and was killed. As the water with which the feet of the Brāhmin was washed, fell on his head, his sins were washed off and he attained a better loka. *Ch- 15.*

Āṣāḍhakṛṣṇaikādasī

Hemamālī used to supply flowers to Vaiśravaṇa. He had a beautiful wife named Viśālākṣī. Once when he returned with flowers from *Mānasaras,* he felt an onrush of love and spent time at home with his wife. Kubera went to the temple for worshipping Śiva at noon and though he waited there till evening for Hemamālī to bring the flowers, the latter did not come. Kubera got angry and sent for Hemamālī and Hemamālī came trembling. Kubera cursed him and the curse turned him into a leper, afflicted with eighteen types of leprosy, separated from his wife and fell from Alkāpurī. Hemamālī came to Hemādri and happened to meet sage Mārkaṇḍeya to whom he narrated his unfortunate story. The sage advised him to observe Āṣāḍakṛṣṇaīkādasī. Hemamāli observed the *vrata,* got cured of the disease and returned to Devaloka. *Ch- Ut. K- Ch - 54.*

Ekādaśī

Vallabhā's wife Hemaprabhā was not at all accommodative and was always quarrelling with her husband. One day Vallabhā gave her good thrashing. Hemaprabhā was so angry that she fasted that day and did not take even water. That day happened to be the *Ekādaśī* [eleventh day of the lunar fortnight]. When she died, due to this *vrata* all her sins were washed off and had a place in *Viṣṇuloka.*

There are more instances to demonstrate the efficacy of *vratas.*

Varāha Purāṇa

The text of Varāha Purāṇa has only 10,000 verses, whereas it is mentioned in other Purāṇas like Matsya Purāṇa as 24,000 verses. Probably it might have been in two parts and only one of them could be recovered. Lord Viṣṇu, in his incarnation as *varāha* – boar is said to have given these teachings to *Bhūdevī* – the mother earth at her request. The recensions are two, namely *Gaudīya* and *Dākṣiṇātya* and in some places they differ with each other. This Purāṇa deals with general topics mostly and the two episodes – *Madhurākhyāna* and *Nāciketopākhyāna* are very popular.

The goddess *pṛthvī* – the earth went to Viṣṇu and appealed: "O Lord, at the end of every *kalpa,* as some or other incarnation you deliver me from the miseries and re-establish me, but still I do not know your powers, your identity. I request you to reveal yourself to me." Viṣṇu was then in the Varāha incarnation in which *pṛthvī* saw the entire cosmos in the stomach of the boar and she started praying to the Lord. And the Lord started to explain.

Nārada

Priyavrata was the son of *Svāyambhuva Manu* and once Nārada went to meet him. The king had many questions and after obtaining the answers for them, requested Nārada to tell about some wonderful events. Nārada recounted an incident. Once Nārada went to a lake in Śvetadvīpa, which had a lot of fully bloomed lotus flowers and a beautiful woman was standing silently besides the flowers. Nārada asked her who she was, but did not get any reply. Three luminous entities issued forth from her body and vanished. He again put the question. The woman replied "I am Sāvitrī, the mother of all the Vedas. You refused to recognize me. So I am taking away alll your knowledge about Vedas."

Nārada asked "How am I to get back all the knowledge I have lost?"

Mother Sāvitrī asked Nārada to bathe in the lake and then he would not only gain the lost knowledge but also about his previous births. After the bath he regained his knowledge and also about his previous births. Now the king wanted to know about Nārada's previous births. Nārada told the following: In his earlier birth, his name was Sarasvata and led a peaceful life. One day while he was sitting quietly, he realized that the world is transitory and he should concentrate on meditation. Accordingly he started meditating on Nārāyaṇa and the Lord was pleased. Sarasvata asked that he may get dissolved into the Lord. The Lord advised him that he has got still more time to live and said that henceforth he would be known as Nārada – water giver. Sarasvata again spent his time on meditation. When he died, he spent some time in Brahmā loka, then was born as a son of Brahmā and was called Nārada. Nārada taught Priyavrata a beautiful hymn on Nārāyaṇa. *Ch.15.*

Aśvaśiras

Now the mother earth asked whether Nārāyaṇa and Brahmān are one and the same and the boar replied in affirmative. The boar said that Brahmā, Śiva and Nārāyaṇa are all one and the same. He narrated the following story. Once Aśvaśiras, a king asked sage Kapila as to how to worship Nārāyaṇa. The reply was that there were two Nārāyaṇas and he can worship anyone. [Kapila meant that he himself was the manifestation of Nārāyaṇa] The king asked "how can you be Nārāyaṇa as he has four hands and conch and disc in the hand?" Kapila showed him the form of Nārayaṇa, to the utter surprise of the king. The king asked why Nārāyaṇa could not be seen always. Kapila said that Nārāyaṇa is manifest in everything and is also unmanifest and that is the supreme knowledge.

MB. Ch. 65.

Devotion

A. King Vasu handed over his kingdom to his son, went to Puṣkara and performed a *yajna.* He dedicated it to Viṣṇu. From the *Yajna* fire emerged a figure and asked for orders. When enquired about his antecedents the figure told the story. In an earlier life Vasu was the king of Kaśmīra. Once while hunting, he killed a deer which was in fact a sage who was in the form of a deer. As a penance he gave a lot in charity etc, but he died of stomach pain and while dying he called Nārāyaṇa. Actually the figure which emerged from the fire was a demon. When Vasu killed the sage, the demon entered into his body, for having killed a brāhmaṇa and also gave him the stomach pain. As Vasu happened to remember

Nārāyaṇa at the time of death, he went to heaven and the attendants of Viṣṇu drove away the ghost after severe beating. Before long Vasu was again born as king of Kaśmīra, the ghost again entered his body. But when he performed the *Yajna* the demon had to go out but then it got purified. Vasu gave a boon that the demon would be born as a hunter, but a righteous one.

B. Sage Raibhya went to Gayā, performed rituals for ancestors and then started meditating. One day a sage arrived at the hermitage of Raibhya and congratulated him. The sage bloated himself to gigantic proportions. Raibhya asked for his identity and the sage said he was Sanatkumāra. He congratulated him as he gave oblations to ancestors. In emphasizing the importance of offering oblations to the ancestors Sanatkumāra recounted a story. Viśālā was a prosperous king but unhappy as he had no sons. His well wishers advised him to go to Gayā and offer oblations to the dead ancestors. As soon as the king offered oblations three figures appeared. One figure was white, one red and one black. The white one was Viśālā's father as he had committed no sins. Red and black were his grand father and great grand father and as they had committed sins and so were suffering. Once the oblations were offered, they were released from the bondage. Raibhya continued his penance after Sanatkumāra left and finally Nārāyaṇa appeared and granted him a boon that he would go to the abode of *Sanatkumāra.* *MB. Ch. 38.*

Vaiṣṇodevī

Goddess Vaiṣṇodevī decided that she would not marry, went to mount Mandāra and began to meditate. One day her concentration was slightly disturbed and from this disturbance, appeared millions of women. Vaiṣṇodevī constructed a palace for all these small goddesses and ruled over them. Nārada happened to pass by, on his way to Brahmā and he was awestruck by the beauty of Vaiṣṇodevī and other goddesses. Nārada immediately hatched a plan to humble a demon named Mahiśāsura. Nārada went to Mahiśāsura and talked about the beauty of Vaiṣṇodevī. Mahiśāsura decided that Vaiṣṇodevī would be his wife and sent a messenger along with a huge army. Gods came to protect Vaịṇodevī but they were defeated. Ultimately Vaiṣṇodevī fought for a long time and killed Mahiśāsura. [This is a different version of Mahiśāsura than what is seen in Devi Māhātmyam]

Satyatapas

The Varāha continued telling the goddess *Pṛthvī.* Sage Satyatapas was meditating in the Himalayas. While chopping the wood, once, he cut one of his fingers and instead of blood, ashes came out. When he tried to place the finger in position the finger got attached to the hand. A *kinnara* [a set of Devas, holding *Vīṇās* in their hands] who was watching this, told about the incident to Indra. Viṣṇu and Indra wanted to test the power of the sage. Viṣṇu adopted the form of a boar, with an arrow pierced in its stomach and Indra, a hunter. Indra came to the hermitage of Satyatapas and asked whether he had seen a boar with an arrow in its body, as he had hit it. Satyatapas thought about it. The eyes had seen it but it can not speak. Mouth can speak but had not seen it. So he kept silent. Then Indra and Viṣṇu revealed themselves and blessed the sage.

Śveta

Śveta was a king of Ilavṛtavarṣa, who performed a lot of sacrifices and charities. Vasiṣṭha was his priest and advised him to give some rice also but the king did not take it seriously. Śveta attained *Mokṣa* by performing auster *tapas.* But since he failed to earn god's grace by giving food to the hungry, even in heaven, he was tormented by hunger and thirst. His craving for food grew to phenomenal heights that he came to *bhūloka,* went to the place where his body had been cremated and started licking at the ashes. Sage Vasiṣṭha happened to see this and mentioned that it was a consequence of his not having given food at any time. At last as suggested by Brahmā, he was born again on the earth and after a visit to sage Agastya re-entered the heaven again.

The boar mentioned that it had recounted till now, the *Varāha samhitā* of *Varāha Purāṇa.* This was expounded first by Brahmān and then Brahmā -> Pulastya -> Paraśurām -> Ugra -> Manu. This Purāṇa was later composed by Vedavyāsa.

How earth [*pṛthvi*] was rescued

Once sage Sanatkumāra asked the goddess *Pṛthvī* how was she retrieved. The earth sank into the underworld and she appealed to Viṣṇu to save her and she sang a hymn named *Keśava stutī.* Accepting the appeal, Viṣṇu incarnated himself as a huge boar and entered the ocean. The entry of the boar into the water caused such uproar that many mountains got dislodged. The boar lifted up the earth with its tusks and held it up till the next creation. The boar told the goddess of earth that to please him, elaborate rituals were not necessary but genuine devotion was enough. Viṣṇu likes white flowers and the twelfth lunar day is important.

Mārkaṇḍeya's Discussion with Varāha

Once sage Mārkaṇḍeya discussed with Varāha about giving respects to one's dead ancestors. Seven generations are considered as ancestors. *Śrāddha* can be performed at the time of lunar eclipses and solstices [*Uttarāyaṇa and Dakṣṇāyana*]. If a *śrāddha* is performed on the eighth lunar day, it is said to be satisfying the *pitṛs* for thousand years. The benefit of performing *śrāddha* is that one remembers his earlier life and an example is Gaurmukha. He had forgotten that he was the sage Bhṛgu. Mārkaṇḍeya advised him to perform *śrāddha* for twelve years and chant the hymn on ten *avatāras*. After doing so Gaurmukha could remember his early life.

Worship of Viṣṇu

The boar told goddess earth that in worshipping Viṣṇu only genuine devotion is needed. One should wear white clothes and offer white flowers. It is more efficacious if worshipped on *dvādaśī.* Those who are calm, vegetarian, and free from jealousy, hatred, pride and ego, the Lord favours such devotees. The following are to be avoided for the worship of Viṣṇu: Eating unclean things, worshipping without taking bath, when dressed in blue, red or black, in anger, after eating fish or duck, eating without offering, after drinking wine or asafetida, eating or selling pork, going to pond with footwear etc.

Durjaya

Durjaya was the son of Supratika and he had a boon from sage Durvāsā, that he would have the power to become invincible, but at the same time he had also acquired his curse that he would be unsympathetic. Once when two brothers, namely Hetri and Suhetri, sons of Svāyambhuva Manu attacked gods and tried to deprive them of their kingdom, Viṣṇu made their army to run hither thither. The two brothers ran away to mount Sumeru. Durjaya happened to go to Sumeru and met Sukeśī and Miśrakeśī, the daughters of Hetri and Suhetri. Durjaya fell in love with them and married them. Because of the boon from Durvāsā he could conquer the three worlds and drove out the gods from their kingdom. With a big battalion of army once he went on a hunt and visited the hermitage of sage Gauramukha. The sage had a wonderful gem, named *Ciṅtāmaṇi,* which was obtained from Lord Nārāyaṇa. The jewel was wish yielding one and with that, the sage could feed the huge army, Durjaya had taken with him. Durjaya wanted to have the jewel and he sent his minister Virocana to the sage to get the jewel, but the sage refused to part with it. So Durjaya sent an army to get it but Gauramukha asked *Cintāmaṇi* to protect him. An army issued forth and defeated Durjaya's army. Hetri and Suhetri sent their army. The sage Gaurmukha appealed to Viṣṇu and the entire army was destroyed by Visnu's *Sudarśan cakra* in no time. As the operation was completed within the time of the winking of the eyes, the place where, this incident happened is known as *naimiśāraṇya. Naimiś* means minute in Sanskṛt. Durjaya's father Supratika was grieved *over* his son's death but took it as the god's will. Viṣṇu was pleased with his attitude, appeared before him and blessed him. *Ch - 17.*

Tithis

By the grace of Viṣṇu, the soldiers who came out of Cintāmaṇi became kings and among them one was Suprabha. He once went to meet a sage named Mahātapas and the sage enlightened the king about the *tithis* – lunar days.

Pratipādā is the first lunar day and is suitable for worshipping *Agni* as on this day only Brahmā created fire out of his anger.

Dvitīyā is the second day and is important to worship the *Aśvini kumarās* – the twin gods, physicians of the gods. *Aśvini kumāras* are the two sons born to Sūrya and Samjna when they were in the form of horses and hence the name.

Tṛtīyā is the third day and is associated with Rudra. It is said that Brahmā created Rudra and asked him to perform creation, but Rudra could not create. Brahmā asked him to meditate under the water to get the power of creating and after this Rudra got a luminous body. The wedding of Śiva and Pārvatī took place on *tṛtīyā,* so Rudra should be worshipped on that day.

Caturthī is associated with the worship of Ganeś. Since Ganeś's birth took place on a caturthī it is important to worship Ganeś.

Pañcamī is suitable for snake worship as on this day only Brahmā sent the snakes to the under world, as they were causing havoc among human beings.

Ṣaṣthī is the sixth lunar day, which is very important for worshipping Kārtikeya and prayers made on this day fulfills all the desires. It was on that day Brahmā appointed Kārtikeya as the general of the gods' army. Tārakāsura could be killed only by Kārtikeya.

Saptamī, the seventh day is associated with the Sun god. On this day the gods appealed to Sūrya to reduce his brilliance.

Aṣṭamī is connected with the destruction of the demon *Andhaka*. [Some Purāṇas link *aṣṭamī* with the birth of Kṛṣṇa and so is the importance.]

Navamī was the day when Vetrāsura was killed by Gāyatrī. Vetrāsura's father was killed by Indra with foam as he could not be killed by any other method. In his next birth he could remember what had happened to him, in his earlier birth and did penance to obtain a son to kill Indra. The river Vetrāvati came in the form of a woman and married him and Vetrāsura was born. He conquered the entire world soon and drove out the gods. The gods went to Śiva, but Śiva knew the invincibility of the demon and all of them went to Brahmā, who was meditating on the banks of Gaṅgā on Gāyatrī and so he was oblivious of the arrival of Śiva and the gods. But goddess Gāyatrī appeared with lots of weapons, fought with the demons for long and killed Vetrāsura.

Daśami, the tenth day is good for worshipping the gods who were created by Brahmā on that day and they are ten in numbers and they are the gods of the quarters.

Ekādaśī is the day of Kubera's birth, from the dust storm which arose from the mouth of Brahmā.

Dvādaśī was the day, when Nārāyaṇa adopted the form of Viṣṇu, on the request of the wind god, *Vāyu.* Also this was the day when Lakṣmī was married to Nārāyaṇa and worship of Lakṣmī Nārāyaṇa is good.

Trayodaśī was the day, when Brahmā appeased the god of Dharma. He had four feet, three horns and was in the form of a bull. The god of Dharma would lose one leg in each Yuga as evils increase and in Kali Yuga he would have only one leg. Once when Candra had forcibly taken away the wife of Bṛhaspatī, Dharma got disgusted and went away. Lawlessness prevailed. On Trayodaśī Brahmā appeased Dharma.

Caturdaśī is important for Rudra.

Amāvasya is the day for *pitṛs. Tanmātras* were created by Brahmā from his body and Brahmā had asked them to be the ancestors of living beings. Therefore on *amāvasya* day offerings are made in the form of water and sesame seeds, which is known as *tarpaṇa* – means satisfying.

Purṇamāsya is the full moon day. This is associated with the Candra. *Ch. 18.*

Vratas

Now the boar explained about the religious rites to be performed. The important ones are: *Dvādaśa vrata* was the one performed by the goddess earth, when the earth sunk into the ocean, with which Nārāyaṇa was pleased to take the incarnation of boar. This *vrata* was taught by the sage Durvāsā to a hunter, named Satyatapa, who was very righteous and he attained realization. Another one is known as *Varāha dvādaśī* which is also very efficacious. *Avigna vrata* was performed by Lord Śiva before killing Tṛpurāsura, which removes all the hurdles and it should be performed on *caturthī. Śānti vrata* when performed on *pañcami,* bestows peace in the family.

Why Kali Yuga?

Lord Śiva himself had declared that Nārāyaṇa is the foremost, who has the right for oblations. The curse of sage Gautama has made Kali Yuga different. The sage Gautama had obtained a boon from Nārāyaṇa that he would have plenty of food and fruits. During drought he had used this boon to feed many sages. When the situation improved, the sages left the hermitage, not only without even telling sage Gautama but they made to appear that they were leaving because of a sin committed by Gautama. The sages created a cow by their powers and left it in the hermitage of Gautama. As soon as the sage saw the cow, he gave it some water, but the cow immediately died. Then the sages accused him of committing the sin of killing a cow. To do penance Gautama left for Himalayas and Lord Śiva was pleased and gave him a strand of his matted hair, by which Godāvarī Gaṅgā started flowing. By the touch of the water the dead cow became alive and now the sage Gautama realized that it was a trick played by the other sages. That time the Saptarṣīs had also come to greet Gautama for having created a new river and in front of them Sage Gautama cursed the sages that they would no longer be regarded as brāhmaṇas and they would not be permitted to do religious sacrifices. The sages begged that the curse was too severe, but Gautama expressed his helplessness and asked them to go to Śiva. It was modified by Śiva that they would be born as liars and cheats in Kali Yuga. To make it lighter Śiva gave them *Śiva samhitā* and said that not all of them would be born as evil men. *Ch. 18.*

Nārāyaṇa is Supreme

Viṣṇu is the manifestation of Satva alone. While doing meditation under the water, Śiva saw the form of Nārāyaṇa of the size of the thumb, but Śiva ignored and continued the meditation. Then eleven fiery forms appeared and disappeared. Then a self effulgent figure appeared and Śiva asked who he was and the reply was that he was Nārāyaṇa. The eleven forms were of Ādityas.

Viṣṇu told Śiva that he had granted him divine vision and said that without his grace he could not see Viṣṇu. Then he assumed a miniature form of the size of a thumb and then assumed a gigantic form, the head of which could not be seen. It was then Śiva declared that Nārāyaṇa is supreme.

How to do Atonement

The goddess earth asked the boar how to do atonement for the sins. The boar explained the various forms of penance. It also pointed out how to avoid the rebirth as an animal. If one dies at a holy place named *kokāmukha,* one can avoid taking birth as a bird or animal and also can remember the earlier birth. The story goes like this: Once a hawk swooped down and took away a fish, caught by a fisherman. But unable to bear the weight of the fish, it fell down and died. The fish also died. In the next birth the hawk was born as a prince and the fish as princess and married each other. After some time the prince started having headache and they went to *kokāmukha* and prayed to Viṣṇu. By His grace they remembered their early birth and knew that the headache was because, while falling down the hawk had hit against the ground. And their prayer to Viṣṇu gave them liberation. Some of the sins are: praying to Viṣṇu without washing the mouth for which one has to sleep direct under sky without a cover. Touching of Viṣṇu's image without following the prescribed rituals is a sin. Not taking bath after returning from the cremation ground is a sin.

Māyā

The boar also dealt about *māyā* – illusion. Everything other than Viṣṇu is said to be Māyā. It tried to make the point with a story: A Brāhmana named Somaśarmā was an ardent devotee of Viṣṇu and pleased with him Viṣṇu appeared before him. In spite of the Lord's persuasion not to ask, Somaśarmā wanted to know about Māyā. Viṣṇu asked him to bathe in the river, which was flowing nearby. Somaśarmā dived into the river and became the daughter of a fisherman, married to another fisherman and became mother of three sons and four daughters. The woman spent fifty years and one day again Viṣṇu came and asked the woman to bathe in the river and she dived into it. When came out she became Somaśarmā. All his neighbor sages asked him why he was so late. But Somaśarmā remembered his life as a fisherwoman; the evil deeds committed then and was brooding over his miseries. The husband of the fisherwoman came in search of his wife to the river and seeing her clothes he started moaning for her. Somaśarmā tried to console him by telling the truth but by then the village and everything vanished. Then Viṣṇu appeared and told him that he had been deluded by māyā. Having understood, Somaśarmā dedicated his life to meditation.

Tīrthas

Now a small brief about the tīrthas is given. Kubjāmraka is the place where Viṣṇu appeared in the form of a mango tree. Kubjāmraka means mango tree, bent with weight. A visit to this place is as good as offering a gift of a thousand cows. Other places are Mānasa, Māyā, Sarvakalika and Varāha kṣhetra. It was the place where the Varāha rescued the earth. Vaivaśvata is the place where the Sun god meditated for thousand years.

Mathurā

Varāha Purāṇa glorifies Mathurā as a favorite place of Viṣṇu. As it is the place of incarnation of Kṛṣṇa, his living presence is always there. A hunter took bath in Yamunā at Mathurā and was drowned, but he was born as a king of Yakśamadhanu. One day his wife noted him moaning in the dream. When asked for the reason for it, the king put a condition that he would tell, only when he was allowed to hand over the kingdom to his son and go to Mathurā. After reaching Mathurā they devoted their time in prayers and the king told that for very long he was longing to come to Mathurā.

Naciketā

This Purāṇa makes a detailed account of Naciketā, in the Nāciketopākhyāna which is the basis for Kaṭhopaniṣad. It also has detailed description of heaven and hell. Nāciketā was the son of Uddālaka, who gave away lots of gifts after performing a Yajna. Finding that his father was giving away cows, which had become old and of no use, he was asking his father persistently as to whom he was going to give him away. In a mood of anger the sage said he was going to give him away to Yama. Taking his father's words seriously, Naciketā set out to Yama loka. There he had to wait for three days to have an audience with the Yama and as a penance for having made a brāhmaṇa to wait, Yama offered him three boons. Out of which one boon was the teaching of Ātma vidyā – Self knowledge, which Naciketā acquired from Yama.

Section III

Purāṇas Dealing with the Exploits of Śiva

Vāyu Purāṇa

This Purāṇa was told by the *Vāyu devatā* himself, to the sages gathered for performing Yajna, which lasted for a very long time. This Purāṇa is a Śaiva – Pāśupata work and it has got four sections, designated as *Pādas* and they are *Prakriyāpāda, Anuṣaṅgapāda, Upodghātapāda* and *Upasamharapāda.* The scholars agree that the core content of this Purāṇa is ancient, but many verses are found in the other Purāṇas also. The topics dealt are geographical description, manvantaras, place of pilgrimage, details of *śrāddha* ceremonies etc. This has got 24,000 verses and belongs to A.D. 200.

In the *naimiṣāraṇya* forest, many sages organized a great Yajña in which the chief priest was Bṛhasapati himself.

Elimination of the Demon Dundubhi

King Bṛhadaśva belonged to the solar dynasty and he had twenty one thousand sons, eldest being Kuvalayaśva. The king wanted to hand over the kingdom and go to forest, but before he could go, sage Utaṅka arrived and told him that a demon named Dundubhi was very much disturbing his spiritual activities. The demon when exhaled his breath once a while a big cloud storm was created, followed by earth quake and no body was able to conquer him. The king told the sage that his son Kuvalayaśva would take care of him. The prince left with all his brothers and started digging up the shores in search of the demon. When the demon knew about the impending attack he unleashed a terrible storm, in which fire also broke out and all the brothers except three were killed. But the storm did not affect Kuvalayśva and he killed the demon. Because of this his name became *Dundhumāra.* *Ch. 58.*

Creation of Loka by Sage Viśvāmitra

King Trayyāruṇa had a son named Satyavrata, who was very strong, but at the same time he was very greedy for riches and in the process he committed many sins. The king, unable to bear the behavior of his son decided to abandon him and the proposal was approved by the royal sage Vasiṣṭha. The king told his son to go and live with *caṇḍālas.* The prince started living with the outcasts and the king left for the forest, leaving the kingdom without a king. Anarchy and drought prevailed in the kingdom. At that time sage Visvāmitra left his family and went for a long meditation on the shores. Unable to bear the poverty, his wife decided to sell one of her sons and buy some cattle. The man, who bought the sage's son, tied a rope around his neck and dragged him away. Having understood what had happened, Satyavrata rescued the boy and started tending the family of Viśvāmitra, by hunting. On one occasion he could not get any animal so he stole the cow of Vasiṣṭha and fed the family. When the sage Vasiṣṭha came to know about this, he cursed Satyavrata for three sins of taking away somebody else's property, displeasing his father and killing the cow. The curse was that henceforth he would be known as

Triśańku - meaning three sins. Sage Viśvāmitra returned after the drought was over and was more than overwhelmed to learn that Triśańku had taken care of his family. Despite Vasiṣṭha, he installed Triśańku as the king. Triśańku had a desire to go to heaven with the mortal body and Viśvāmitra arranged for it through his powers. [When gods refused to accept and pushed Triśañku down, Viśvāmitra created another intermediary world and it was named as '*Trisanku svarga*'].

MB Adi parva Ch12.

Burning Up of all Material Objects

Kārtavīryārjuna was a powerful king and he performed a very strenuous penance. He acquired four boons from Lord Dattātreya. The boons were that he would have thousand wonderful arms, power of persuasion to bring people to righteous path, he would conquer the entire earth and that he would be killed only by one who would be superior to him by all means. With these wonderful boons, he ruled over the earth and performed several *Yajnas.* It is said that he ruled the earth for eighty seven thousand years. Once *Agni* {fire god] came to him in the form of a brāhmaṇa and asked for alms as he was hungry. Kārtavīrya allowed him to feed upon mountains and trees, anywhere from his kingdom. *Agni* began to devour everything and in the process it burnt the hermitage of sage Āpava. Having come to know that Kārtavīrya was responsible for the havoc, he pronounced a curse that he would be killed by Paraśurāma. *Ch. 58.*

Lińga Purāṇa

This Purāṇa mainly describes the worship of Śiva through Śivalińga known as Phallus. Though a number of subjects are dealt with, it deals mainly with the manifestation of five aspects of Śiva, i.e, *Sadyojāta, Vāmadeva, Tatpuruṣa, Aghora and Īśāna;* Śiva appearing as a huge pillar of fire to Viṣṇu and Brahmā; Vyāsa and his disciples; stories of Dadhīci and Śilāda; creation; four Yugas; Nandi and his worship; dynasties; Vratas; Śiva pańcākṣarī mantra; pilgrimage; Śiva as *astamurtis* etc. This Purāṇa contains 11,000 verses.

Nārada after wandering around the world came to *naimiṣāraṇya* forest, where many sages had assembled. They welcomed Nārada and at that time Lomaharṣaṇa too arrived there whose arrival sparked great happiness. They requested him to recite that Purāṇa which speaks about the glory of Śiva-lińga. Lomaharṣaṇa first talked about creation and then talked about *Pāsupata yoga.* It was said that Śiva takes *avtatāra* in every Kali Yuga and there had been twenty eight Kali Yugas in the present Kalpa. The twenty eight names are: Śveta, Sutāra, Madana, Suhotra, Kāńcana, Lokākśi, Jaigisavya, Dadivāhana, Ṛsaba, Muni, Ugra, Atri, Bali, Gautama, Vedaśirsa, Gokarṇa, Guahavāsi, Sikandabṛt, Jatamāli, Attahāsa, Dāruka, Lāńgali, Mahākāya, Śūli, Muṇdīśvara, Sahiṣṇu, Somaśarmā and Jagadguru. In every Kali Yuga Śiva also incarnates as Vedavyāsa and the names are: Kratu, Satya, Bhārgava, Angīrā, Mṛtyu, Satakratu, Vasista, Sarasvata, Tridhāma, Trivṛta, Nārāyaṇa, Tārākṣu, Āruṇi, Deva, Kṛtańjaya, Ṛtańjaya, Bhāradvāja, Gautama, Vācaśrava, Suśmayni, Tṛṇabindu, Rakṣa, Śaktri, Dhimana, Satateja, Pārāśara, Jātukarṇa, and the latest Vedavyāsa is Kṛṣṇa Dvaipāyana.

Why the form of Lińga?

During *Pralaya* it was total dark and everywhere only water was there. Nārāyaṇa was sleeping. Without recognizing Viṣṇu, Brahmā asked him who he was. Viṣṇu woke up and asked Brahmā "how are you son?" Brahmā was very angry and said "I am the creator and how can you call me son?" Viṣṇu reminded him that he was Viṣṇu, but Brahmā did not agree and a dispute started. At that time a glittering Liṅga appeared and it seemed it had no beginning or end. Viṣṇu asked Brahmā what was that pillar of fire? To find out what it was, Brahmā went up in the form of a swan and Viṣṇu went down in the form of a boar. But they could not discover the beginning or end. They realized that they were in front of a power which is beyond them. When they started to pray to Liṅga, Śiva appeared from within the LIṅga and he was known as Vedanāma. He explained them that the Liṅga was the origin of universe from which the primordial egg appeared. He also taught them the sacred Gāyatrī *mantra*. Since then Śiva is worshipped, in the form of Liṅga.

Brahmā and Viṣṇu

This is from *Padma kalpa.* At the time of *Pralaya,* Viṣṇu was sleeping and he created a lotus from his naval. There Brahmā appeared and asked Viṣṇu, who he was? Viṣṇu said that he was the lord of everything. Brahmā said that he was the creator of everything, suggested to Viṣṇu to enter his stomach and see for himself. Viṣṇu entered Brahmā's stomach and found the fourteen worlds. In turn Brahmā too entered Viṣṇu's stomach and could not find the end. In the meantime Viṣṇu had closed all the exit points and Brahmā had to come through the lotus. Viṣṇu suggested that as a token of friendship Brahmā would be known as his son. At that time Śiva approached them and he was praised by both Viṣṇu and Brahmā. Śiva offered boons. Viṣṇu wished that he might always be devoted to him and Brahmā wanted that Śiva would be born as his son. In the initial creation Brahmā was not happy and in that sorrowful condition, the eleven Rudras, manifestations of Śiva, were born. [In some other Purāṇas it is mentioned that Rudra was created by Śiva].

Devadāru Araṇya

In a forest full of Deavadāru trees, many sages lived there with their families and they were very much devoted to Lord Śiva with their penance. Śiva was pleased but wanted to test them. So he appeared in the form of an uncouth man with ugly form. The sages despised him but their wives began to follow around him. Hearing the harsh words from the sages, Śiva disappeared. The sages reported this to Brahmā, who scolded them and told them that it was none other than Śiva. He rebuked them that they had failed in their *dharma* of honoring the guest and told the story of Sudarśana. Sudarśana was a great sage and he had instructed his wife to be very gracious with the guests. Once the god of *dharma* wanted to test them and he arrived when Sudarśana was not at home. But his wife honored the guest very much and the god of *dharma* was very much pleased. He blessed them that they would go to heaven. Brahmā continued. Sage Śveta was a devotee of Śiva. Whole of his life he prayed to Śiva and the time of his death came. Unperturbed he was going on praying to Śiva. Yama said that there was no use, praying to Śiva. When Yama prepared to take away the soul of Śveta, Śiva appeared with his *gaṇas* and Pārvati. At the mere sight of Śiva, Yama fell dead. After hearing these two stories, the sages returned back and contemplated on Śiva ardently. Śiva appeared with ashes all over his body, but this time the sages and their wives prayed to him with flowers and the Lord was pleased. *M.B. Ch. 28*

Dadhīci

[In some Purāṇas Dadhīci had been described as having sacrificed his body to make weapons for devas.] Sage Dadhīci had King Kṣupa as his friend. One day an argument started as to whether brāhamaṇa is superior or Kṣatriya and each insisted that their *Varṇa* was superior. King Kṣupa happened to have the weapon *vajra* given to him by Indra to fight the demons. In the argument Dadhīci gave a punch to Kṣupa and the king in turn used *the vajra* and sliced Dadhīci into two. Dadhīci died but before dying he called Śukrācārya, the guru of demons, who had the capacity to bring back the dead to life and Dadhīci was brought back to life. Śukrācārya advised Dadhīci to pray to Śva so Dadhīci began a difficult *tapasyā* and Śiva was pleased. Dadhīci obtained three boons. 1. His bones would be as hard as *vajra.* 2. Make Dadhīci prosperous. 3. He could be never killed. Armed with these boons Dadhīci went to Kṣupa and kicked him on his head. In turn Kṣupa picked up the *vajra* and hit Dadici but it had no effect. Amazed by this, Kṣupa prayed to Viṣṇu to have better powers. He appealed to Viṣṇu to enable him to defeat Dadhīci, but Viṣṇu said that as Dadhīci had been blessed by Śiva it would be difficult. Viṣṇu appeared in front of Dadhīci in the form of a brāhmaṇa but Dadhīci recognized Viṣṇu and asked the Lord what he wanted. Viṣṇu suggested that he would bring Kṣupa to his place and Dadhīci may say that he was scared of Kṣupa. But when Kṣupa came Dadhīci said that as a devotee of Śiva, how can he be scared of anybody? Viṣṇu got angry and used *Sudarśan cakra* but it was of no avail. Viṣṇu hurled *Brahmāstra* but even that could not hurt Dadhīci. Dadhīci picked up few straws and flung at the gods, who had come to help Viṣṇu and these had become flaming weapons and gods started running helter skelter. Then

Viṣṇu adopted the *Visva rūpa*, but Dadhīci was not scared. Then Brahmā intervened and settled the matter and Kṣupa acknowledged the superiority of brāhmaṇas.

MB. Ch. 100

Nandī

Śilāda, a great sage did penance to get an immortal son and Indra appeared before him but said that granting of an immortal son was not in his power. He was asked to pray to Śiva. Śilāda did a very difficult penance for very long and his whole flesh had been eaten away by termites. Virtually there was nothing left out in his body. Finally Śiva appeared and said that he himself would be born as his son. He also brought him to normal health by his touch. Śilāda performed a *Yajna,* out of which came a *puruṣa* with three eyes and four arms and he was named Nandi. When Śilāda returned home, the boy became a normal one and within eight years he had learnt the whole Vedas. One day Mitra and Varuṇa came to the hermitage, saw the boy and declared that the boy would die at eighth year. The father was grief stricken. Nandi consoled his father and started to pray to Śiva and Śiva blessed him that he would always be with him and was made leader of the *gaṇas.*

Liṅgas in Vārāṇasi

In Vārāṇasi Śiva always is predominantly manifested. Brahmā established a *liṅga* known as Saṅgameśvara. Other *liṅgas* in Vārāṇasi are Śaileśa, Svarṇileśa, Madhyameśvara, Hiraṇyagarbheśvara, Goprekṣaka and Jambukeśvara.

Narasimha

Viṣṇu adopted the form of half lion and half man and after the death of Hiraṇyakaśipu, nobody was able to pacify the Narasimha. Gods led by Brahmā fled to Śiva for protection and Śiva assured them protection. He created Vīrabhadra from his body and asked him either to pacify or kill Narasimha. Vīrabhadra went to Narasimha and appealed to him to give up the form as he was Viṣṇu himself, but Narasimha would not listen. He reminded him that Śiva was superior but of no avail. So Vīrabhadra adopted the form of half deer and half bird, grasped Narasimha and rose up and flung him on the ground and killed Narasimha but Viṣṇu did not die. He realized and prayed to Śiva. He repeated the one hundred and eight names of Śiva. *Ch. 101.*

Jalandhara

There was a demon named Jalandhara, who was so powerful that he defeated all the gods. Then he challenged Viṣṇu for a dual and there too he found success. After this he took all his companions and went to Kailāś. Śiva asked them the purpose for which they had come. Jalandhara said that they had come to fight with him. Śiva dipped his tow into the ocean and churned it from which *Sudarśan cakra* appeared. Śiva told Jalandhara that if he could raise the cakra with his big toe then only he would fight with him. With great difficulty Jalandhara lifted it and placed it on his shoulder. As soon as he placed it, the cakra slit his head and everywhere there was blood and flesh. Śiva sent all these to Yama, who created a hell, called *mahārourava.* *PP. Ch 3 – 5.*

One Thousand Names of Śiva

In a fierce battle between gods and demons, the gods were defeated and they ran to Viṣṇu and requested him to obtain the *Sudarśan cakra.* And to obtain that *Sudarśan cakra* Viṣṇu and all other gods prayed to Śiva with his one thousand and eight names.

Skanda Purāṇa

The Skanda Purāṇa is the biggest among Purāṇas with 81,000 verses. It is found in two forms, one is divided into *khaṇḍas* and the other into *samhitās*. It has seven *khaṇḍas* and six *samhitās.* The seven *khaṇḍas are: Māheśvara khaṇḍa, Vaiṣṇava khaṇḍa, Brahmā khaṇḍa, Kāśī khaṇḍa, Avantya khaṇḍa, Nagara khaṇḍa, and Prabhāsa khaṇḍa.* The verses are spread over in 1671 chapters. The six *samhitās are: Sanatkumārasamhitā, Sūtasamhitā, Śaṅkarasamhitā, Vaiṣṇava samhitā, Brahmā samhitā and Saurasamhitā.*

Now only the first three *samhitās* are available, but all the seven *khaṇḍas* are available. This Purāṇa has been taught by Śiva to Pārvatī, Pārvatī to Skanda, Skanda to Nandi, Nandi to Atri and Atri to Vyāsa. This Purana has dealt with numerous subjects. The *Satyanārayaṇa vrata* has got a prominent place.

As in other Purāṇas, in this Purāṇa also Lomaharṣaṇa agreed to the request made by sages in the *Naimiṣaraṇya* forest.

Indrasena

Indrasena was a king, a manifestation of evil and always only two words were in his mouth – *ahara and prahara* meaning 'gather' and 'punish'. But astonishingly when he died, he was taken to heaven as the words he was always uttering had 'hara' indicating Śiva – though unintentionally.

Nandi

This story about Nandi is different from other Purāṇas. Nandi was a *vaiśya* living in Avanti. There was a temple of Śiva, where Nandi used to go daily and offer worship with rich offerings. A hunter also used to worship the same Liṅga. One day the hunter found the offerings made by Nandi. He threw them away and made his own offerings of *bilva* leaves and some deer meat. When Nandi saw that his offerings have been thrown away he took away the liṅga to his house. When the hunter found that the liṅga had gone, he was angry. He shouted at Śiva to reveal him self but when there was no response he took out his intestines and filled the gap and offered some *bilva*. Pleased with his devotion, Śiva appeared and made him the chief of his attendants. Nandi was watching this, hiding and he was surprised. He told the hunter to tell Śiva about him also. The hunter too made a plea to Śiva persistently and Śiva made Nandi also his attendant along with the hunter.

Devotion

True devotion to Śiva takes one to Śiva loka. An insect flew into a Śiva temple to eat the offerings and while flying the wings removed some dust from the temple so the insect could go to heaven and take rebirth as a princess. That princess every day used to go to Śiva temple and clean the floor with her own hands. For a question by the sage Uddālaka that she could get it done through her servants, she replied that she wanted to do it herself, as there is no other way of serving Śiva. Many demons were the devotees of Śiva.

Churning of Ocean

The Ocean was churned to obtain *amṛta* and one of the things that appeared was poison, which started burning Brahmā loka etc. Lord Gaṇeś appealed to Śiva to save the world. Śiva drank the terrible poison and by this his throat had become blue, as the poison was held up in the throat. So he is called *Nīlakhaṇṭha.*

Glory of Śiva Lińga

Once Nandi explained to sage Agastya about the glory of Śiva lińga. At the time of *pralaya* – when the whole creation gets resolved, they get resolved into the Lińga along with the three *guṇas* – the Śiva Lińga is without any *guṇas – nirguṇa.*

Skanda

This Purāṇa deals elaborately on the birth of Skanda / Kumāra. Śiva, after Dākṣāyaṇi sacrificed herself in the sacrificial fire and the chaos committed by the demons, went on meditation. When Śiva married Pārvatī, daughter of Himavān, the gods had high hopes. The demon Tārakā had driven out the gods from their places as he had become powerful due to Brhamā's boon that he could not be defeated by anybody except a child. Brahmā and Viṣṇu sent Agni god to see what was happening in Kailāś. Agni entered without the knowledge of Nandi, who was keeping vigil, but Pārvatī saw *Agni. Agni devatā* begged for alms. Pārvatī gave part of Śiva's energy as alms. Because Agni is the carrier of all oblations to gods, the energy, which was given as alms also, had to be shared by the gods and this became a big problem. With the advice from Visṇu all gods prayed to Śiva and they were advised to vomit the energy. For Agni, the Lord told to give it to somebody, who would be shivering due to cold. Next morning Agni was waiting near the lake, saw the wives of *Saptarṣīs* coming shivering and they wanted to warm themselves but Arundhatī was not willing. Agni transferred the energy to six of them. For this, the six wives were cursed by their husbands that they would become *nakṣatra* and they were known as *kṛttikas.* These six wives of the sages gave away the energy to Himalaya and there the energy became one, flowed down and from it was distributed to reeds. And from that a boy with six heads was born. The child was named *Kārtikeya.* Pārvatī knew it through her powers and Nārada also confirmed about the boy. All including Lord Śiva went to see the child and as per the request from the gods Kārtikeya was appointed as the general of the army of gods. At that time Sena, the daughter of yama, who had done penance, on Brahmā's advice, to marry Kārtikeya, arrived there. Kārtikeya married Sena. Now there was difference of opinion among Pārvatī, Kṛttikas and Gaṅgā about who would be the mother of Kārtikeya and on the advice of Nārada, it was agreed that Pārvatī would be the mother, but Kṛttikas would have a place in the sky. Skanda immediately after his birth started using arrows and spears. All the gods made great presents to the newly born. Now the war started between demons and the gods. Skanda rode a chariot and Candra was holding a shield, and all the gods joined the battle. Fiery battle commenced and the gods fought valiantly but they could not stand Tārakāsura and now Skanda came to the fore. Skanda and Tārakā hurled various weapons and finally Skanda killed Tārakā. *Va. 57 – 61.*

Killing of other Demons

Skanda also killed other demons like Pralamba and Vāṇa. Pralamba was a cruel demon, who ran away from the battle of Tārakāsura and hid himself in the underworld. From there he started killing the snakes. When Skanda heard of the news he hurled a spear, which flew to Pātālaloka and killed Pralamba. Another demon named Vāṇa, fled due to fear of Skanda. When he was in mount Krouṇca, Skanda hurled a spear and killed Vāṇa and his army.

Śiva and Pārvatī in Dice Game

Once in the presence of Nārada, Śiva and Pārvatī played a dice game and first time Śiva won but the second time Pāravatī won. She told the Lord that she had defeated him. Śiva pointed out that no one could defeat him. There was an argument and Pārvatī snatched away the moon, snake etc, as that was the bet she had won. Śiva opened his third eye but nothing happened and Pārvatī embarrassed him saying that she was not Yama or Madana. Śiva went away to meditate. After some time, Pārvatī's companion Vijaya persuaded her to do something. Pārvatī adopted the form of a beautiful woman and attracted Śiva and Śiva wanted to marry her. Without revealing her identity, she told Śiva to ask permission from her father Himālaya. When Śiva approached Himālaya, he reminded him that he was already his son-in-law. Embarrassed Śiva went to *gandhamādana* to meditate. Finally all the inhabitants of Kailāś including Pārvaīi met Śiva and brought him back.

Tīrthas

Skanda Purāṇa gives elaborate details about creation and holy places. Sage Nārada once explained the geography to Arjuna. In that, mention was made about the five *tīrthas* avoided by sages and holy persons. Arjuna once happened to visit the holy *tīrthas,* which were known as Kumareśa, Sthambheśa, Varkareśvara, Mahākāla and Siddheśa. Arjuna asked the sages why these *tirthas* were being avoided and the reply was that there were crocodiles. Arjuna took bath in Sthambheśa. As soon as he got in, a crocodile caught him, but valiant as he was, he fought with the crocodile and came to the shore. As soon as the crocodile came to the shore, it became a beautiful *apsarā.* The *apsarā* recounted the story that five of them tried to disturb the penance of a handsome *brāhmaṇa* and were cursed. Arjuna rescued the other four too. Nārada also told Arjuna about *mahi-sagara-sangama* which was considered very holy. Once Narada asked sage Bhṛgu about holy land, the sage mentioned about ***mahīsāgarasaṅgama*** and told the story. Once sage Bhṛgu went to that place for bath and found a sage, named Devaśarmā grieving there. When the sage asked about the reason for his remorse he replied that he used to give oblations to his ancestors at the confluence of Gaṅgā but he found that the ancestors of another sage Subhadrā were happier because he offered oblations at ***mahīsāgarasaṅgama***. He too wanted to do the same but his wife would not agree. At that time sage Subhadra happened to come there and it was agreed that Subhadra would do oblations to the ancestors of Devaśarmā and in return Devaśarma would transfer one fourth of the *puṇya* he had acquired through meditations. Nārada further stated that as a penance for killing of Tārakāsura and as per the advice of Viṣṇu, Skanda established three liṅgas in the *Mahi – sagara – saṅgama.* These Liṅgas were constructed by Viśvakarmā and they are known as *Pratijneśvara,* where Skanda decided to kill the demon, the second one *Kapāleśvara,* where his spear pierced the demon and the third one where he died is called *kumareśvara.* Skanda also established a pillar, known as *stambheśa.* Nārada continued to recount the virtues of the *tīrtha.* A princess was born to the king of Sinhala, with the face of a she-goat. The girl grew up and remembered her previous birth, in which she was a she goat. The stretch from *mahī-sāgara-saṅgama* to *Stambheśa* was full of bushy thorn and the goat got caught in the thorns and died. Its body fell on the confluence whereas the head got stuck up. She requested her father to go to the confluence and it was arranged. She found the head still got stuck up. The head was cremated and the ashes were immersed into the confluence. Her face became that of a beautiful woman. In spite of many offers for marriage she decided to take up meditation on Lord.

Nandi told Mārkaṇdeya about the glory of Aruṇācala Mountain. It is situated in the south. King Vajrāṅgada, who was the ruler of Pāṇdya kingdom, went for hunting around Aruṇācala. He went behind a musk deer and was totally exhausted. The king then saw that both his horse and the deer which he was chasing became *vidyādharas* [singer of the heaven] and rose towards the sky. The *Vidyādhras* told the king that once they disturbed the meditation of *Durvāsā* and he cursed them to become a horse and a deer. He also said that the curse would end when they circumambulate the *Aruṇācala* and now they had done the circumambulation. It was said that by circumambulating this mountain only Gaṇeś got the fruit from Śiva whereas Skanda went around the whole world in his peacock and so circumambulating *Aruṇācala* is as good as circumambulating the Lord as his living presence is there. Hearing this, king Vajrāṅgada gave up his kingdom and started meditating. The Lord appeared before him and said that he was *Indra* and was cursed for having been disrespectful towards the Lord.

Sage Bhāradvāj told Arjuna that in the *Veṅkateśvara* hill Viṣṇu always lives. *Añjana* mother of Hanumān climbed over this peak and mediated when Lord of Vāyu appeared before her and said that he would be born as her son.

Badrikāśram, another holy place was explained by Śiva himself to Skanda. There is a tree named Badari from which life saving liquid oozes and hence the name. It is also supposed to be a place where Śiva is always present. Vedavyāsa told Yudhiṣṭhira about Dharmāraṇya, which was a thickly wooded forest. Once Yama, the god of death did an extremely difficult penance. Indra got perturbed and sent an *apsarā* named Vardhani to disturb him, but she told Yama, her purpose of visit and Yama was pleased for having told the truth. Yama continued his *tapasyā* and it was so long that birds had started building nests on him. Gripped by fear, all the gods approached Śiva and Yama was offered a boon by Śiva. Yama wanted the *araṇya* to become a hallowed one and named after him. Śiva agreed and established a *liṅga* there and the forest was named as Dhramāraṇya – as Yama is called *Dharmarāj*. *MB. VP. Ch. 82.*

Lord Viṣṇu was also associated with this *araṇya.* This was told by Śiva to Skanda and also by Vedavyāsa. The gods performed a *yajna* and wanted to invite Viṣṇu but the Lord was in meditation with a bow in the hand. The gods put a wasp on the string so that when the string was cut, the Lord would be disturbed, but when the string was cut, the bow gave a hit to Viṣṇu's head and the head was cut off and the severed head went above. The reason was that, in a heated argument as to who was supreme,

Brahmā cursed Viṣṇu. Viśvakarmā wanted to fix the head but the head could not be found and so the head of one of the horses of Sūrya was sliced off and fitted on to the torso. Thus Viṣṇu was known as *Hayagrīva.*

The *kāśīkāṇḍa* of Skanda Purāṇa deals elaborately about *Kāśī.* There is a story as how *Kāśī* was created. After marrying Pārvatī, she lived with her parents and Śiva also started living there. They were quiet content. But her mother once taunted Pārvatī that having married after long penance; her husband seemed to be of no worth. Wounded by this remark Pārvatī asked Śiva whether there is any place on the earth for them to live. Śiva at once asked Viśvakarmā to create a city. A wonderful city was created and Śiva and Pārvatī started living there, which is *Kāśī.* It is said that before leaving, Śiva created one crore liṅgams there.

Prabhāsa Kāṇḍa of Skanda Purāṇa, the last kāṇḍa deals with the holy place named Prabhāsa, meaning luminous one. In *Tretā Yuga* two brāhmaṇas named Ujjayanta and Praleya decided to live in Prabhāsa. While traveling to Prabhāsa they were famished with hunger and thirst so could walk no more therefore started rolling on the ground. Moved by their plight Śiva created two *liṅgas* in front of them and the *liṅgas* were very powerful. A divine voice was heard telling them that they could stay there only and there was no need to proceed further. But both the brāhmaṇas were determined to go to Prabhāsa. Seeing their determination Śiva made their bodies healthier and they reached Prabhāsa safely. This is the glory of Prabhāsa.

Agni Purāṇa

Agni, the god of fire, is said to have communicated this Purāṇa to sage Vasiṣṭha. Though it is essentially a Śaivite work, the incarnations of Rāma and Kṛṣṇa are dealt in this. Distinct from other Purāṇas, this deals with arts and science, astrology and architecture. This Purāṇa contains twelve thousand verses and is supposed to have been composed during A.D. 800.

In the forest, known as *Naimiṣāraṇya* sage Śaunaka and other sages were performing a great *Yajna,* to Lord Viṣṇu and sage Sūta also arrived there. The sages requested Sūta to enlighten them about the most sacred thing in the world. In reply Sūta said that he had learnt from Vyāsācārya that Agni Purāṇa is the most sacred as recounted by Vasiṣṭha himself. The sage recounted the ten incarnations, which are: *Matsya, Kūrma, Varāha, Narasimha, Vāmana, Paraśurāma, Rāma, Kṛṣṇa, Buddha and Kalki.*

Rāma

Viṣṇu incarnated in the solar dynasty as Rāma, the son of Daśaratha and Bharat, Lakṣmaṇ and Śatrugan were his three brothers. Sage Viśvāmitra came and requested king Daśaratha to send Rāma to protect his *yajnas.* Rāma annihilated the demons and pleased with this, Viśvāmitra taught Rāma the use of all divine weapons. Viśvāmitra took Rāma to king of Videha, where his daughter Sītā chose Rāma as her husband after he broke the bow of Lord Śiva. Daśaratha wanted Rāma to be anointed as the king, but his second wife, on the strength of two boons she received earlier, wanted Rāma to go to forest for fourteen years and Bharatha to become the king. In order that his father could keep up his promises, Rāma went to the forest, alongwith Sīta and Lakṣmaṇa. After meeting sage Bharadvāja and others, they finally put up their hermitage at Citrakūta, on the banks of the river Mandākini. At Ayodhyā king Daśaratha could not bear the separation from Rāma and gave up his life. Bharata, who was away at his grandfather's house went to Citrakūt to convince and bring back Rāma but was not successful, so took Rāma's sandals and returned. From Citrakūta Rāma moved to Daṇḍakāraṇya, on the banks of Godāvarī. There was a demon woman named Śūrpaṇakā, who wanted to marry Rāma and to achieve this she wanted to eat up Sītā. So Lakṣmaṇa cut off her nose. She fled to her brother Khara and Dūṣaṇa, who came with a big army. But they were quickly annihilated. Śūrpaṇakā then went to her brother Rāvaṇa and said that she wanted him to abduct Sītā for himself. Rāvaṇa sent a demon named Marīch, who adopted the form of a golden deer and went in front of Rāma's hermitage. Sītā was very much attracted by the golden deer and wanted Rāma to capture it. Leaving Lakṣmaṇa to be with Sītā, Rāma followed went behind the deer. Rāma Killed the deer, but the deer, while dying took the name of Lakṣmaṇa and Sītā loudly and fearing some harm to Rāma, Sītā sent Lakṣmaṇa against his will to look for Rāma. Rāvaṇa then abducted Sītā in his aerial chariot and Jatāyu, the king of the birds was injured while trying to protect Sītā. Finding Sītā missing from the hermitage both the brothers were very upset and they went in search of her. They got the friendship of Hanumān, a monkey and helped Sugrīva, the king of monkeys by making him king after killing his brother, Vāli. Sugrīva sent monkeys on all the directions to look for Sītā and south bound monkeys especially Hanumān found Sītā to be in Laṅkā. Rāma and Lakṣmaṇa came to the shores of the sea and built a bridge to go over to Laṅkā.

In the terrible war that ensued, Rāma killed Kumbhakarṇa and Lakṣmaṇa killed Rāvaṇā's son Indrajīt. Rāma finally killed Rāvaṇa with a powerful divine weapon. By this time fourteen years were over and Rāma returned to Ayodhyā. Rāma was then anointed as the king.

Mahābhārata

One of the Kuru's descendants was King Śantanu, who married Gaṅgā and Bhīṣma was the eighth son out of this marriage. In order to enable his father to marry Satyavatī, Bhīṣma pledged that he would remain celibate and protect the kingdom. They had two sons Citrāṅgada and Vicitravīrya. Chitrāṅgada died young and Vicitravīrya was married to Amba and Ambālikā. Vicitravīrya too died without any child and by the blessings of Vyāsācārya, Amba gave birth to Dhṛtarāṣṭra and Ambālikā gave birth to Pāṇdu. Dhṛtarāṣṭṛa was blind by birth and was married to Gāndhāri and Pāṇdu had two wives namely Kuntī and Mādrī. Gāndhārī had hundred sons, the eldest being Duryodhana, Kuntī had three sons, namely Yudhiṣṭhira, Bhīma and Arjuna, while Mādri had two sons Nakula and Sahadeva. Yudhiṣṭhira was born by the energy of Dharma, Bhīma by the energy of Vāyu devatā and Arjuna by the energy of Indra himself. Kuntī had a son through Sun god, whom she had to abandon as the boy was born before the marriage and he was known as Karṇa. Pāṇdu died early due to a curse by a sage. As Duryodhana had an unquenchable thirst for power he tried to kill Paṇḍavas by somehow or other with the help of his uncle Śakuni. He had put them in a house of lac and set fire to it but they escaped and went to a place known as Ekacakra. In a *Svayamvara,* they won the hands of Draupadī the daughter of Drupad and all five of them married her, due to the commandment of their mother. Under pressure from Bhīṣma, half the kingdom was handed over to Pāṇḍavas and they built a new city by burning Khāṇḍava. In the process Arjuna got divine weapons from *Agnideva.* Yudhiṣṭhira had become a popular king and performed *aśvamedhayajna.* This kindled the jealousy of Duryodhana more. He invited them for a dice game between Yudhiṣṭhira and Duryodhana but Śakuni played on behalf of Duryodhana. In an unfair game Yudhiṣṭhira lost everything including his wife and brothers. As a penalty Pāṇḍavas had to go to forest for twelve years and live one year without being detected. After the twelve years, Pāṇḍavas came to the kingdom of king Virāta, Yudhiṣṭhira in the disguise of a Brāhmaṇa, Bhīma as a cook, Arjuna as a dance teacher, Nakula and Sahadeva in the horse stables and Draupadī as a maid to the queen. The queen's brother Kīcaka tried to molest Draupadī and was killed.This aroused the suspicion of Duryodhana, as nobody except Bhīma could kill him. He attacked Virāt and robbed the cattles. But Arjuna defeated them and saved the cattle. Now fortunately the one year had come to a close, when their identity was known. King Virāt's daughter Uttarā was married to Arjuana's son Abhimanyu, Lord Kṛṣṇa's nephew. A war became imminent as Duryodhana refused to part with any portion of the kingdom. Lord Kṛṣṇa went as an emissary for peace and said that even if they were to get five villages the war could be avoided but Duryodhana was admant. He was not willing to give even an inch. Now the army had assembled for the war, but seeing all his relatives and teachers in the battle field Arjuna refused to fight. In order to make him to understand his duties he was taught by Lord Kṛṣṇa, the *Ātma Vidya,* that the Self is immortal, which is popular as Bhagavad Gītā. Arjuna made Śikhaṇḍl as his charioteer and wounded Bhīṣma. After that Droṇācārya took over as the general and he gave up weapons after hearing the rumors that his son Aśvatthāmā had been killed, but not before killing Virāta, Drupada and many other kings. Droṇācārya was killed by Dhṛṣṭadhyumna and after that Karṇa became the general. He was killed by Arjuna. The final war was fought between Bhīma and Duryodhana and Duryodhana was killed by breaking his thighs. The turn of events made Aśvatthāma to kill the five sons of Draupadī when they were sleeping. On the demand of revenge by Draupadī both Arjuna and Aśvatthāma were to release their most powerful divine weapon *Brahmāstra,* but on persuasion, Arjuna could withdraw his weapon while Aśvatthāma could not. He released the weapon and destroyed the baby in the womb of Uttarā, who was brought to life by Sri Kṛṣṇa. After the war, those that were left out were Kṛtavarma, Kṛpācārya and Aśvattāma on the Kaurava side and the five Pāṇdavas on the Pāṇdava's side. Bhīṣma gave up his body after teaching the duty of the kings to Yudhiṣṭhira and the glory of Viṣṇu / Kṛṣṇa. Lord Kṛṣṇa used the Pāṇḍavas only as a tool to rid the earth of unrighteous elements.

Prayers, Building of Temples and Making of Idols

Several chapters of Agni Purāṇa deal with the subjects of conducting prayers, building of temples etc, and also with special *mantras* to please different gods. It describes the benefit of building of a temple, temple images etc, with specifications for various points, which are to be taken care of while chiseling the idols. For example, though idols of *Matsya and Kūrma* may have the shape of fish and turtle, but the idol of *varāha* should have four arms like human beings, with mace, a lotus, a conch shell and discus in the hands. It also specifies what should be in the different hands of various idols. *Śiva liṅga* may be made out of earth, wood, iron, jewels, copper, gold, silver, bronze or mercury.

Places of Pilgrimage

Pilgrimage has got as much merit as performing yajnas. Puṣkara is the best place of pilgrimage and there itself there are two places, namely *Jambumarga and Taṇdulikāsrama.* Kurukṣetra is considered to be very holy, as it has the living presence of Viṣṇu and other gods. River Sarasvatī flows there, which is very sacred. Wherever Gaṅgā flows that place becomes holy. *Prayāg* is very holy because of the confluence of Gaṅgā and Yamunā. Lord Śiva had told Pārvatī that *Vārāṇasī* is very holy and the Lord never leaves the place. Because the rivers Vāraṇa and Asī flow there it is called as Vārāṇasī. Gayā is the holiest of the place. Gayāsura, a demon started performing penance and it was so great that gods ran to Viṣṇu. Visnu appeared before him and offered a boon. He wanted that he should become the most sacred *tīrtha* and the moment it was granted Gayāsura disappeared. But the gods felt that earth was looking lack of luster. Viṣṇu told Brahmā to perform a sacrifice and also to get the body of Gayāsura. Gayāsura agreed and as soon as he agreed his head fell off from the body. Brahmā then proceeded to perform sacrifice on the head less body but the body started shaking. As sacrifice can not be performed on a shaking body, the solution was that, all gods should enter into a stone and that stone be kept on that body. Viṣṇu also entered the stone. As Viṣṇu and all gods are present in that stone, Gayā is holy. There is also a story behind the stone. Once sage Marīci, son of Brahmā was tired after coming back from collection of wood and flowers. So he told his wife Dharmavrata to wash his feet. When she was washing the feet, Brahmā happened to come there. At this, she was wondering whether she should attend her husband or Brahmā and she decided that she should attend to Brahmā. At this Marīci got angry and pronounced a curse that she would become a stone. Dharmavrata was greatly distressed by this and did *tapasyā* for many years. Viṣṇu and other gods were pleased. Dharmavrata wanted that the curse be waived. Viṣṇu told her that, it was not possible as Marīci was a powerful sage, but he would make her a holy stone. And all the gods promised to be always inside that stone. That was the stone which was put on the body of Gayāsura. And Gayāsura got a boon that Gayā will be the most sacred *tīrtha*. *Ch. 144.*

Yoga

It is Jnāna that reveals Brahmān. Yoga shows the way to concentration to realize that goal. Yoga is the perfect union of Jīvātma and Paramātma. Yoga is activity with the body as its basis. Maharṣīs assert that there is an inseparable connection between matter and soul. Matter and soul are merely the two phases of the single '*astitva*'. The object of the yoga is to achieve union with *ParaBrahmān*. Recitation of *mantras* is important in many disciplines connected with the pratice of Yoga. There are two broad divisions of *Yoga - Haṭḥa Yoga* and *Rāja Yoga*. *Haṭha yoga* is mainly concerned with the disciplining of the body by various kinds of exercises. *Rāja yoga* aims at arousing *Prajnā* by control of the senses. *Rāja yoga* involves practice of eight disciplines. They are:- *Yama, Niyama, Āsana, Prāṇāyāma, Pratyāhāra, Dhāraṇā, dhyāna and Samādhi.*

Yama

Yama demands the practice of:

1. *Ahimsā* – Non violence or not killing any creature.
2. *Satya* – Truth ; Practicing truth in thoughts, words and deeds.
3. *Asteya* – Not stealing.
4. *Brahmācarya* – Celibacy.
5. *Aparigraha* – not coveting wealth or pleasures, which are not absolutely necessay.

Niyama

While Yama is a negative discipline, Niyama is positive one. It requires the practice of virtuous courses. Niyama includes five things:

1. *Śauca* - cleanliness both external and internal.
2. *Santoṣa* - cotentment.
3. *Tapas* – Penance and austerities.
4. *Svādhyāya* – study of the Scriptures and incantations.
5. *Īśvarapraṇidhāna* – dedicating all actions unto the Lord.

Āsana

The way of sitting or posture. Different postures have been prescribed for different actions.

Prāṇāyāma

This is regulation of breathing. Inhale air through left nostril, retain the air in the lungs for few seconds and then exhale it through the right nostril. Then the process is reversed. This is the first step in *Prāṇāyāma.* The object is to awaken *Kuṇḍalinī.*

Pratyāhāra

This is the process of withdrawing the five senses from the outer world. A man who practices this becomes oblivious to the external world. This helps the concentration of the mind on Ātman.

Dhāraṇā

Withdrawing the mind from the outer objects and concentrating on the self.

Dhyāna

Meditaion, concentrating the mind on several places like Bhrūmadhya and Nābhīcakra. Repeating the sacred syllable ***OM*** is very useful in dhyāna.

Samādhi

In samādhi the soul and mind unite, the mind merging into the soul. It is defined as 'when the mind and soul unite just as salt and water unite, that state is called *Samādhi'.*

Ch. 372.

Sins and Atonements

When a sin is committed atonement for it should be done, which is known as *prāyaścitta.* Otherwise it was the duty of the king to punish. The worst possible sins are drinking of wine, killing of a Brāhmaṇa and theft. Other sins are criticizing *Vedas*, false witness, lying, forsaking parents, killing a cow, murder, selling of ponds etc. A killer of Brāhmaṇa had to live in a forest for twelve years, after giving away all his wealth to another Brāhmaṇa. If a Brāhmaṇa steals gold he has to report it to the king, who will hit him with a club.

Vratas

Depending on the day, star position and the month various rituals are performed which are known as *Vratas*. Some of them are:

Lunar day	Month	God to be worshipped	Pakṣa
First	Kārthik, Aśvina & Caitra	Brahmā	Both
Second	All months	Two Aśvin kumars	Both
Second	Kārtika	Yama	Śukla
Third	Caitra	Śiva and Pārvatī	Śukla
Fourth	Māgha	Gaṇa devatas	Śukla
Fifth	Śravaṇa, Bhādra Aśvina & Kārtika	Common to all gods	Śukla
Sixth	Kārtika and Bhādra	Lord Kumāra	Both
Seventh	All	Sun god	Both
Eighth	if it is Wednesday	General	Both
Eighth	Bhādra	Kṛṣṇa	Krsna
Ninth	Aśvina	Devī	Śukla
Tenth	All months	General	Both
Eleventh	All months	Viṣṇu	Both
Twelfth	All months	Viṣṇu	Śukla
Thirteenth	All months	God of love	Both
Fourteenth	Kārtika	Śiva	Kṛṣṇa

Giving Alms

Giving alms is known as *Dāna* and it is most important duty of a householder. Alms should be given to the deserving and at proper time. In the place of pilgrimage and temples alms are given. The donor should face the east and the receiver should face the north. Best objects of *dānam* are cows, gold, daughters, trees, houses etc. if one promises and fails to give, he is sure to be destroyed. The object of giving away is lost if one expects gratitude. In *Satya Yuga* the donor went in search of a recipient. In *Tretā Yuga* the recipient had to come to the giver's house. In *Dvāpara Yuga* the donor never gave anything unless asked for. In *Kali yuga* one gives only to those who are servile to him.

Gāyatrī Mantra

This mantra is the most powerful *mantra*. Before doing *japa* of any other *mantra* it is imperative that *Gāyatrī* be chanted, if it has to be efficacious. Gāyatarī represents the four *Vedas* and it is also a metre, having twenty four words. It is also compulsory that this *mantra* is chanted daily and the Purāṇa elaborately gives the various benefits of chanting. It is said that at the time of *Tripura dahana* Lord Śiva hung Gāyatrī mantra as a string on top of his chariot.

The Duties of a King and Rāma's Advice to Lakṣmaṇa

This Purāṇa deals elaborately with the duties of a king, like punishing the enemies, protecting the citizens, maintaining dharma etc. It also deals elaborately as to the procedures to be adopted before the coronation of a new king. Who should be appointed to what posts and how should be the behavior of such people, who were appointed are also specified. Criteria for selection of places for building a fort, temples have also been dealt with. The king is entitled to one sixth of all the *puṇyas* of his citizens, but he is also credited with one sixth of all the sins committed in his kingdom. The mode of taxing and distribution of the same, punishment to be given have been elaborated. It deals even with minor points like protecting the property of a minor orphan and how the stolen property should be recouped. Paying attention to the prince, his education, assigning body guards etc are talked about. Seven techniques in ruling the kingdom, i.e. *Sāma, Dāma, daṇḍa, bheda, māyā, upekṣa and indrajāla* have been explained. On the same line Rāma advised Lakṣmaṇa about the duty of a king. He mentioned that a king has to earn money, increase it, protect it and then donate it for the welfare of the people. He had enumerated few important points such as politeness, humility, non-violence, truthfulness, clean habits and forgiving. He had elaborately dealt with the seven components of kingdom such as king, the ministers, the friends, the treasury, the army, the fort and the state itself.

Dreams

Some dreams are stated to be good and some are bad and *prāyaścitta* has been prescribed. Some of the bad dreams are: seeing as grass or tree growing in one's own body, shaven head, shabby clothes, killing of snakes, drinking oil or eating bird meat etc. Some of the good dreams are: dreams involving palaces, mountains, snakes etc, riding a horse, having many arms or heads, eating rice pudding, eating wet meat, milking a cow or buffalo with one's own mouth etc. Dreams come true if certain conditions are met.

Omens and Signs

Before going out one should take care of bad omens and they are: cotton, dried grass, cow dung, leather, hair, a lunatic, dead body etc and if one comes across such things one should pray to Viṣṇu. Good omens are: white flowers, full vessels, meat, distant noises, old goat, cow, horse, elephant, fire, gold, silver, umbrella, conch shell etc. Various sounds made by the animals too have good and bad effect.

Battle

Under this topic everything connected with the battles such as preparation, method of proceeding, the direction they should face, position of the king, lokas attained by those who die and those who run away, who should fight whom etc are dealt with.

Dhanurveda

Another important topic dealt in this Purāṇa is Dhanurveda that is about the arms and weapons. It talks about five categories of weapons and they are:

- The one which are released by machines. – *Yantramuka.* A launcher or bow.
- Weapons which are flung by hand – *Paṇīmukta.* Spears and stones.
- Weapons which can be flung and withdrawn. *Paṇi*
- Weapons which are never released from hand. – Sword etc.
- The last category is known as '*amukta'.* – Brute force and strength.

Āyurveda

The physician of the gods, known as Dhanvantari taught this system of medicines to sage Suśruta and it contains not only the treatment of human beings but also talks about trees plants, gardens, treatment of animals, and the mantra for snake poison.

Yama Gīta

Agni Purāṇa talks about Kaṭhopaniṣad in which Lord Yama teaches, Nāciketas, a small boy Ātma vidyā, whom his father had said that he was giving him to Yama. Yama was pleased with the boy that in spite of his offering of many beautiful things of this world, the boy refused to take any thing except the knowledge of Self.

Matsya Purāṇa

This Purāṇa is said to have been taught by Lord Viṣṇu himself in his incarnation as *Matsya,* [fish] to Manu Satyavrata. This Purāṇa, though contains ancient material, it appears that many portions have been taken from various Purāṇas like Vāyu, Viṣṇudharmottara Purāṇas etc. Apart from dealing with the normal topics, this Purāṇa also contributes to other areas of knowledge. There is also beautiful summary of all the topics in chapter 290, without omitting any subject. This has got 14,000 verses and the period of composition may be A.D. 300.

Matsya Avatāra

Once while Brahmā was chanting the *Vedas*, an *asura* stole the *Vedas* from his side and went under the water with the Vedas. Lord Viṣṇu decided to take the form of a fish and recover the *Vedas.* Vaivasvata Manu was once doing penance in Badari. He went for a bath in the river Kṛtamālā, when a small fish appeared and told him not to forsake it as it was afraid of big fishes. Manu put the fish in his *kamaṇḍalu* and brought it to his hermitage. In few days the fish grew bigger than the pot, he put it in a pond. The fish grew beyond and was shifted to the river Gaṅgā at the request of the fish. After few days the river itself became too small. The fish told Manu that in seven days there would be a great flood and instructed him to arrange a big boat, take *Saptaṛṣīs* with him and promised to help him. Manu got ready with a big boat and torrential rain started. Everything was under flood. Then a horn sprouted from the head of the fish and Manu tied his boat to the horn, as per the instructions from the fish. The fish reached the peak of Himalayas and tied the boat to the peak. The peak to which the boat was tied is known as '*naubandhana śṛñga'*. When the rain stopped, it was seen that everything had been destroyed except the boat. Then Manu asked several questions to Viṣṇu which were answered by the Lord.

Dharma is Superior to *Artha* and *Kāma*

King Purūravā was righteous and had performed many Yajnas. In life there are four goals *dharma – artha – Kāma – moksa,* Righteousness, wealth, Fulfillment of desire and liberation. Once the gods of *Dharma, Artha and Kāma* wanted to assess king Purūravā, to know, among them to whom did he give preference. They went to him in the form of human beings. Purūravā treated them most reverentially but he gave more importance to *Dharma*, which angered the other two. Artha cursed Purūravā that he would be destroyed by his greed and Kāma cursed him that he would be mad by being separated from Urvaśī. Dharma blessed him that he would never deviate from the path of righteousness and that his descendents would rule for ever. Some time later, when Purūravā was driving through a forest, he found a demon carrying away Urvaśī and Citaralekhā. He fought with the demon, released them and took them to Indra. Indra was pleased with him. Indra decided to celebrate the occasion with a dance programme, but Urvaśī was watching Purūravā and missed her steps. Nārada who was present there cursed her that she would live as a creeper, separated from Purūravā for sixty years. On earth Urvaśī married Purūravā and had eight sons. *Ch.12.*

Attempt to Resurrect Dead Asuras to Life

There used to be always war between the gods and the *asuras.* The *asuras* always got the beatings and were defeated. Śukrācārya was the preceptor of the demons and they went and wept in front of Śukrācārya. Śukrācārya consoled them and said that he would do a difficult penance to please Śiva and get the mantra for bringing back to life the dead. He instructed them not to have any fight with the gods, in his absence and asked them to be with his father, sage Bhṛgu. Śukrācārya performed the difficult *tapasyā* and when Lord Śiva appeared he told him that he wanted the mantra of *mṛtasañjīvanī.* Śiva told him that he would have to do penance for one thousand years, surviving only on smoke and Śukrācārya agreed. Having come to known that the demons had given up the arms, gods attacked the demons, in spite of their plea that it was wrong to fight when they had given up their arms but gods would not listen. The demons fled to Śukrācārya's mother, and she assured them protection. When Indra appeared she made him immobile, like a statue and the gods started running. Then Viṣṇu came to their rescue and told Indra to enter his body. But Śukrācārya's mother threatened that she would burn both of them and Viṣṇu sliced her head off with the *Sudarśan cakra.* When the sage Bhṛgu came to know about this he cursed Viṣṇu that he would have to take several times birth on the earth. That was the several incarnations of the Lord. Sage Bhṛgu resurrected his wife with his power. As Indra was not successful in his attempt he plotted another way. He had a daughter named

Jayantī and he told her to go and disturb the penance of Śukrācārya. Jayantī served sincerely Śukrācārya throughout the period and when the period was over Śiva appeared and taught him the mantra. Śukrācārya noticed Jayantī and said that he was pleased with her and said he would grant her a boon. She expressed the desire that he should be her husband for ten years. Śukrācārya was thus attracted by her and stayed with her for ten years. Now Indra asked Bṛhaspati to adopt the form of Śukrācārya and go to the camp of the demons. The demons accepted and revered him. After ten years Śukrācārya went to the demons, found Bṛhaspati and there was argument between them but the demons thought that the man who lived with them for ten years was real Śukrācārya and the real Śukrācārya was driven out. He cursed the demons that they would be destroyed. Then Bṛhaspati took his original form and the demons realized their mistake but it was too late. *Bhag. Skanda 4.*

Second Prayer from Diti

It has already been discussed that sage Kaśyapa's wife, Diti made an unsuccessful attempt to get a son to kill Indra. She made another request to her husband for a son, who can kill Indra. Sage Kaśyapa said that her wish could be fulfilled if she did *tapasyā* for ten thousand years, then her son would have as hard a body as the weapon *vajra* of Indra. Diti followed her husband's advice and gave birth to a son, who was named as Vajrāṅga. At suitable time Diti told him that Indra had killed many of his brothers and that he should kill Indra. Vajrāṅga went to heaven and very easily tied up Indra and brought him to his mother. But killing of Indra would bring catastrophe and so Brahmā and Kaśyapa rushed to Vajrāṅga and told him not to kill Indra as his defeat itself was as good as death to Indra. Vajrāṅga agreed to it on condition that he should be granted a boon to do great *tapasyā.* The boon was granted and also Brahmā created a beautiful woman, named Varāṅgī and was married to Vajrāṅga. Vajrāṅga went to the forest to meditate. He meditated for long, standing on one leg, then standing up side down and then he went to meditate inside the water. When he went inside the water, his wife was patiently waiting on the shore and she was also meditating. But Indra did not keep quite. He troubled her by creating storm, torrential rain, adopted the form of a monkey and uprooted all the trees in her hermitage. He became a sheep and ate up all the grass. He became a snake and tried to bite her. When Vajrāṅga came out and underestood how Indra troubled his wife, he again went for meditation to have a son who would give sleep less nights to the gods. Varāṅgī bore the baby for a long time and when the boy was born, there were tidal waves. That was Tārakā. This Tārakāsura obtained a boon from Brahmā that he would be killed by a six year old boy and was killed by Skanda. *Ch. 29.*

Varāha Avatār

This Purāṇa gives different version about *Varāhāvatāra.* Due to the presence of huge mountains during the creation, the earth sunk into the water and on the request of *Pṛthvī Devī* Viṣṇu adopted the form of a boar and rescued the earth.

Architecture

This Purāṇa speaks elaborately on architecture. The architects of the Vedic periods were the sages Bhṛgu, Atri, Vasiṣṭha, Viśvakarmā, Maya, Nārada, Nagnajit, Viśalākṣa, Purandara, Brahmā, Kārtikeya, Nandīśvara, Śaunaka, Garga, Vāsudeva, Aniruddha, Śukra, and

Bṛhaspati. It specifies right from the selection of site to choosing of woods, selecting the auspicious days to start the work. Minute details regarding building of palaces, temples, making of idols etc, have been provided. It also specifies on what sort of site buildings can be made and where. Various types of woods and which type of wood can be used for what type of work is also specified.

Kūrma Purāṇa

This Purāṇa was taught by Lord Viṣṇu himself to the sages like Nārada in his incarnation as *Kūrma* or tortoise. This Purāṇa is in two parts. The first section is called *Brāhmīsamhitā* which is a bigger work, consisting of four samhitās namely – *Brāhmī, Bhāgavatī, Saurī and Vaiṣṇavī* and among them the last three have been lost. It was later recast by the *Pāśupatas* during the eighth century A.D. it consists of many topics, generally found in other Purāṇas such as *Varṇas, āśramas, Manus,* genealogies of *ṛṣīs* etc. The *Brāhmīsamhita* also includes *Īsvaragīta and Vyāsagīta.* This has got 18,000 verses.

This Purāṇa was narrated to many sages by the sage Romaharṣaṇa in the *Naimiṣāraṇya* forest.

Thousand names of Mother Pārvatī

King Himalaya and his wife Menā wanted Mother Pārvatī to be born as their daughter and for this the king used to chant the thousand names of the Mother and Kūrma Purāṇa gives the thousand names.

Teaching of real knowledge

King Indradyumna, after his death was reborn as *Brāhmaṇa* and he prayed to Lakṣmī. When the goddess appeared he requested her to tell him about her true nature and what is considered as true knowledge. Lakṣmī told him that she is the *māyā* and not different from Viṣṇu but regarding true knowledge he should ask Viṣṇu only. The *Brāhmaṇa* continued to meditate on Viṣṇu and the Lord instructed the *Brāhmaṇa* on the path of true knowledge. When the other gods and the sages wanted to know what was taught, Lord Viṣṇu repeated the teachings in the form of *Kūrma.*

Kṛṣṇa's Desire for a Son

Lord Kṛṣṇa wanted to have a son. So he went to the sage Upamanyu. The hermitage was situated in a breath taking surrounding, with constant chanting of *Vedas* and Gaṅgā flowing nearby. Kṛṣṇa entered the hermitage and the sages worshipped him. Sage Upamanyu was very happy to receive the Lord and enquired about the purpose of his visit. Kṛṣṇa wanted to know the way to have *darśan* of Śiva. Sage Upamanyu suggested difficult *tapasyā* and Kṛṣṇa decided to perform *Pāśupata vratam* which was very difficult. He put on barks in place of clothes and continuously chanted Śiva's name. Śiva and Pārvatī appeared and asked Kṛṣṇa about the necessity of penance to Him, who was the Lord of the universe. Kṛṣṇa expressed the desire to have a son like Śiva himself and who would be devoted to Śiva. The boon was granted and he had a son, named Sāmba through his wife Jāmabavatī. *Bha. Skanda 10.*

Incarnations of Śiva

Normally Purāṇas speak about the incarnations of Viṣṇu but never heard about the incarnations of Śiva. The Kūrma Purāṇa lists out the incarnations of Śiva and they are: Śveta, Sutāra, Madana, Suhotra, Kankana, Lokākṣi, Jaigisavya, Dadivaha, Ṛsabha, Bhṛgu, Ugra, Atri, Bali, Gautama, Vedaśiras, Gokarṇa, Śikaṇdaka, Jatamāli,

Attahāsa, Dāruka, Laṅgali, Mahāyama, Muni, Śūli, Piṇdamunīsśvara, Sahiṣṇu, Somaśarmā and Nakulīśvara.

Īsvara Gīta

When the Kūrma Purāṇa was being explained by Lomaharṣaṇa to the sages, Vedavyāsa arrived there. As Vedavyāsa was the author of Scriptural works, all the sages were eager to know the path of true knowledge. What Vedavyāsa had told them is known as *Īśvara Gīta. Paramātma* is the only Truth and all other things, including the universe are nothing but illusion. The goal of human birth is to understand that 'that *Paramātma* is none other than this Jīvātma'. *Yoga* is an aid which leads to the path of Knowledge. *Yoga* consists of eight basic steps and they are *Yama, niyama, āsanas, prāṇāyāma, pratyāhāra, dhyāna dhāraṇa and Samādhi.*

Rituals

Gāyatri japa is to be done compulsorily, three times a day. *Vedas* should not be read at the following occasions: eclipse time, funeral ceremony, lying down, after eating meat, at the time of storm and on the night of the new moon.

Real and Illusory Sītā

It is known that in Rāmāyaṇa, Rāvaṇa abducted Sītā and took her away to Laṅka. But Kūrma Purāṇa says that Rāvaṇa abducted only the illusory Sītā. When Rāvaṇa approached Sītā, Sītā had the intuition of what was going to happen and she prayed to *Agni devatā. Agnideva* absorbed the original Sītā into Agni and left an illusory Sītā for Rāvaṇa to take away. After the war when Sītā entered *Agni* to prove her purity, the original Sītā came out and the illusory one was absorbed into the *Agni.*

De. Bh. Skanda 9.

CHAPTER IV

Upa Purāṇa

Śiva Purāṇa

The Śiva Purāṇa contains:

Tārakāsura

He got a boon, from Brahmā for his penance that none created should be as strong as him and the second boon was that he should be killed only by a child. At that time Śiva had no sons. Sati had died and the marriage with Pārvatī had not taken place. Armed with this boon, Tārakāsura employed the gods as his personal servants.

Burning of Kāmadeva

The gods were desperate and approached Brahmā. Brahmā said that unless Śiva had a son, Tārakāsura could not be killed. Indra called Kandarpa, the god of love to make Śiva, who was meditating, somehow to fall in love with Pārvatī. Kāmadeva went to the place where Śiva was meditating. There suddenly spring bloomed and Pārvatī also arrived at that place. Though Śiva liked Pārvatī, he felt that something was wrong as spring could not bloom at that time and his eyes fell on Kāmadeva, who was hiding there. Śiva got angry and in that anger, he opened his third eye and burnt down Kāmadeva. Kāmadeva's wife was Ratī. She, along with all the gods went and prayed to Śiva that it was not at all the fault of Kāmadeva as it was to find an end to Tārakāsura. Śiva said, whatever had happened could not be remedied and

Ratī had to wait till Kāmadeva takes birth as Kṛṣṇa's son Pradyumna.

Pārvatī's Tapasyā

Pārvatī wanted to marry Śiva and Nārada advised her to do penance. With the permission of her parents she started doing extremely difficult penance, during monsoon sitting on the floor and in winter under the water. All the gods and sages were witnessing the penance. Śiva adopted the form of a brāhmaṇa, and Pārvatī welcomed him with flowers and fruits. He enquired Pārvatī, the reason for her tapasyā and she said that it was to attain Śiva as her husband. The brāhmaṇa ridiculed her for her decision. Pārvatī got angry and was about to leave the place when Śiva appeared in his form. Śiva agreed to marry her and Pārvatī returned home.

The Marriage

The Saptaṛṣīs were sent as emissaries on behalf of Lord Śiva to Himavān and he gladly accepted the proposal. Gandharvas, apsarās and all the gods joined the marriage procession from Kailāś. Pārvatī's mother Menā was anxious to see the bridegroom. She saw many handsome gods and asked whether anyone of them was Śiva. Nārada told that Śiva is more handsome as they were all Śiva's servants. The Lord was surrounded by ghosts and gaṇās and Śiva himself rode on a bull, dressed in tiger skin. At the sight of Śiva Menā fell unconscious. When she recovered Mena insisted that she would give poison to Pārvatī, than marrying her to Śiva. Pārvatī also resolved that she would not marry anyone except Śiva. At the request of Nārada Śiva showed his original form, which was glittering and Mena begged his pardon. The marriage went off and Pārvatī came to Kailaś.

Skanda: Śiva and Pārvatī's son was Skanda. The baby once got lost in the reeds and was found by six Kṛttikās so he came to be known as Kārtikeya. Kārtikeya was appointed as the chief of god's army and a terrible war broke out between Tārakāsura and the gods. The war lasted for ten days and Kārtikeya killed Tārakāsura.

Tripura

The three sons of Tārakāsura did long and difficult penance. Brahmā was pleased and granted the boon to create three forts, first one made out of gold, the second one out of silver and the third one out of iron, which would become one after thousand years and only that person could kill them, who can blow the three forts with one arrow. The three forts were in heaven, sky and earth respectively. As they were not unrighteous, Viṣṇu out of his power created a man and instructed him to teach the three sons a religion that was against Vedas. The three brothers adopted the new religion and stopped worship etc. Now the gods approached Śiva to destroy them. Śiva mounted the specially made chariot and went towards Tripura. By this time the three forts had become a single one and Śiva mounted a divine weapon in *Pāśupata*, which burnt the Tripura.

Ketaki and Champaka Flower

These two flowers should not be offered to Lord Śiva. The reason: When Rāma along with Lakṣhamaṇ and Sītā was living on the banks of river Fālgu, neẉs reached about the demise of Daśaratha. Lakṣhamaṇ was sent to fetch some material for performing obsequious ceremony but Lakṣhamaṇ did not return and Rāma went himself. When

Rāma also did not return Sītā was worried as the śrāddha had to be done before the sunset. Sīta took bath in the river, cooked some rice and offered. At that time two hands were stretched out and a voice said "Sītā I have accepted your offering and I am pleased. I am Daśartha." Sitā in turn said that Rāma and Lakṣmaṇ would not believe it. Then the voice said "there are four witnesses, the cow, the river, the ketaki bush and the fire". When the brothers returned Sītā narrated what had happened, but as expected both of them did not believe it. The four witnesses also refused to corroborate the statement, so Sītā again cooked some rice and it was offered by Rāma. Then the voice said "why are you calling me again? I have already accepted the *piṇḍa* offered by Sītā. Ask the Sun god". The sun god confirmed it. Then Sītā cursed all the four. The river Fālgu would flow only under ground, the cow's mouth would become impure as it told lie through mouth, Ketaki flower would not be offered to Śiva and fire will consume everything indiscriminately.

Nārada once happened to visit a Śiva temple in Gokarṇa. On the way, he admired a champaka tree with full of flowers. A brāhmaṇa came to pluck flowers but seeing Nārada he did not. When asked by Nārada where was he going, the Brāhmaṇa lied telling that he was going for alms. While returning from the temple Nārada again met the Brāhmaṇa with basket full of flowers and asked him 'where are you going"? He again lied that he did not get any alms and going back. He asked the tree whether somebody plucked flowers and the tree said 'no'. Nārada went back to the temple and found the champaka flowers offered on the Liñgam. There was another devotee in the temple and asked him whether he knew who brought those flowers. The devotee said "yes. He is an evil Brāhmaṇa, who daily worships with Chamapka flowers.

He is close to the king, so robs the king and also oppresses others". Nārada asked Śiva why was he encouraging such things and Lord said that he was helpless if somebody worshipped him. Just then a brāhmaṇa lady came running. She said that they got a cow from the king but the brāhmaṇa wants half of it. Nārada then cursed the Champaka tree that henceforth Śiva would not accept Chamapaka flowers and he cursed the Brāhmaṇa to become a demon.

Gaṇeś

In order to prevent the entry of someone at odd times Gaṇeś was created by Pārvatī from clay. She dressed him in nice clothes, instructed him to stand near the gate and that no one should be allowed to enter the place. Soon Lord Śiva turned up but was stopped. Śiva ignored him and tried to enter, but Gaṇeś started beating him. Nandi and Bhṛṅgī tried to retaliate but they were beaten very badly. Then Brahmā was asked to pacify the boy, but Brahmā's beard was pulled out. Viṣṇu suggested killing him by some trickery. Viṣṇu and Gaṇeś started fighting and when this was going on, Śiva stealthily cut off Gaṇeś's head. When Pārvatī came to know about it she decided to destroy the universe. Everyone was alarmed and Nārada was sent as an emissary. Pārvatī agreed on two conditions. Gaṇeś should be brought back to life and he should enjoy all divine rights. These conditions were agreed to but Gaṇeś's head could not be found. Śiva sent his '*gaṇas*' with the instructions that they should bring the head of the first living being, they saw. It happened to be an elephant and that head was brought and stuck on the torso of Gaṇeś. Brahmā, Viṣṇu and Śiva combined their powers to bring back Gaṇeś to life. He was made chief of all the '*gaṇas*', known as 'Gaṇapati.

Quarrel between Gaṇeś and Kārtikeya

Both the sons of Śiva and Pārvatī wanted to get married, but were not able to decide who should get married first. They were told that whosoever went around the world and came first would be married first. Kārtikeya started on his peacock, his vehicle, but Gaṇeś found an innovative method. He made his both the parents to sit down, circumambulated them seven times and bowed down to them. He said that he had gone around the world seven times. The puzzled parents asked how that was, and Gaṇeś said that Vedas say that circumambulating the parents is equal to circling around the world and the Vedas could not be questioned. Śiva and Pārvatī had to agree and Gaṇeś was married to Siddhi and Riddhi. After traveling around the world Kārtikeya returned only to find that he lost the game and felt that he had been cheated. He started living in the mount Krouñca and he was also known as 'Kumarā'.

Jyotirliṅgas

A liṅga is a symbol of Lord Śiva for worshipping. Though there are many liṅgas, there are twelve important ones which are known as **Jyotirliṅgas** and they are: Somnath, Mallikārjuna, Mahākāla, Omkāra, Kedāra, Bhīmaśankara, Viśvanāth, Trayambaka, Vaidyanāth, Nāgeś, Rameśvar and Ghuṣṇeśa.

Candra and Somanāth

Candra married twenty seven daughters of Dakṣa but he loved one daughter named Rohiṇī and the other daughters complained to Dakṣa about this. In spite of the warning from Dakṣa, Candra continued to behave like that. Dakṣa cursed Candra that he would gradually fade away. He did penance to seek the blessings of Śiva, where he made a liṅga on the banks of Sarasvatī. Śiva appeared and when Candra told him about the curse, the Lord said that, though the curse could not be nullified, Candra will wane for a fortnight and wax for a fortnight. This Liṅga is Somnath and Śiva is always present there.

Mallikārjuna

Kārtikeya left his parents and started living at mount Krouñca. In spite of repeated requests from the parents he would not return and hence Śiva and Pārvatī started living closer to their son and that place is known as Mallikārjuna, the second Jyotirliṅga.

Mahākāla

There were four religious Brāhmaṇa brothers, who were very devoted to Śiva, but a demon could not stand the righteousness and attacked the city. But these brothers were not perturbed and continued to worship the Lord. When the demon came to attack them, a big roar was heard and a big pit appeared in front of the Liṅga. Śiva came out and destroyed the demon and his followers. At the request of the brothers, Śiva agreed to be present there always. The place is Avanti, near the banks of the river Kṣhiprā. This is known as Mahākāla.

Omkāra

Nārada once visited mount *Vindhya*. *Vindhya* worshipped the sage and said that *Vindhya* Mountain has got everything. Nārada said that Sumeru was superior as gods live there. *Vindhya* performed *tapasya* and when Śiva appeared he requested the Lord to be present always there, which was agreed to. This place is called Omkāra, the fourth Jyotirliṅga.

Kedār

One of the incarnations of Viṣṇu was Nara and Nārāyaṇa and they did a long *tapasyā* of Śiva. The Lord appeared and said that they were to be worshipped and having done the penance, the Lord agreed to be always present in the peak of Kedār, in the form of a Liṅga, which is the fifth Jyotirliṅga.

Bhīmaśaṅkara

Bhīma was the son of Kumbhakarṇa and he wanted to take revenge on Viṣṇu for having killed his father. He did very hard penance and got a boon from Brahmā to be invincible. Then he conquered the king of Kāmarūpa because he was a devotee of Śiva. The king continued his prayer even in the prison and Bhīma came to annihilate him, so he wanted to cut off his head. Śiva appeared, repelled all his weapons and also killed Bhīma. On the request of gods Śiva is always present there in the Liṅga.

Visvanāth at Vārāṇāsī

The famous Viśvanāth at Vāraṇasī is the seventh Jyotirlinga. Brahmā himself had performed *tapasyā* here. It was so difficult a penance that Viṣṇu himself shook his head in disbelief and a jewel called *Maṇi* fell from his ears in Vārāṇasi. This place is known as *maṇikarṇika tīrtha*. While destruction rages at all other places, Śiva lifts Vārāṇasī with his trident and protects it. Once Śiva and Pārvatī visited Brahmā and Brahmā sung his praise with all his five mouths, but one mouth made mistake, which was cut off by Śiva. Having committed a crime against a Brāhmaṇa, the head got stuck to Śiva's back and it would not come off. But when Śiva visited Vārāṇasī, the head fell off and the sacredness of the place was realized. Śiva decided to be present there always.

Tryambaka

In the south, there was a mountain named Brahmāparvata and sage Gautama did penance here along with his wife Ahalyā. At that time there was a severe drought and the sage prayed to Varuṇa and asked for rains but Varuṇa said that it was beyond his powers, but granted a pond which would be always full of water. The other sages also started using the pond. Normally sage Gautama used to send his disciples to fetch water but as the wives of sages started teasing the disciples, Ahalyā herself had to go to fetch water. Gradually the other sages, to please their wives wanted to get rid of Gautama and hatched a plot. They prayed to Gaṇeś to grant a boon to get rid of Gautama and Ahalyā. Though the Lord knew this to be unreasonable, still he agreed so that those sages could be taught a lesson. So Gaṇeś adopted the form of a lean cow and started grazing in Gautama's fields. To drive away the cow, the sage used a stick and the cow fell dead. It was a sin to kill a cow. Sage Gautama was banished from that place and he circumambulated the Brahmāparvata hundred times and did severe penance. Śiva appeared and granted him a boon that river Gańgā would always be present in their hermitage, along with Śiva and Pārvatī. Thus Trayambaka was established.

Vaidyanātha

Once Rāvaṇa did a difficult penance to please Śiva at different places, but Śiva would not appear and finally, one by one, he severed his heads. When he had severed his ninth head Śiva appeared. Rāvaṇa asked for a boon that he should be very strong. The boon was granted and the place, where he worshipped is known as Vaidyanātha, the ninth Jyothirlinga.

Nāgeśha

Dāruka was a demon, who along with his wife was causing misery, because of the boon; they had received from Pārvatī that wherever they go the forest will go along with them. Righteous people went to a sage named Aurva and requested him to save them.The sage cursed that if the demons committed any violence they would die. Now because of the curse the gods attacked the demon and the demon fled to the ocean along with the forest, but they were troubling the people who traveled by boat. Once they caught hold of a Vaiśya and imprisoned him. The Vaiśya made a Śiva liṅga and started worshipping. Hearing this, the demons wanted to kill the Vaiśya, but Śiva gave the Vaiśya his Pāśupata – a weapon and the Vaiśya killed the demons. The Liṅga worshipped by the Vaiśya iṣ known as Nāgeśha, the tenth Jyotirlinga.

Rameśvar

While Rāma was thinking how to cross the ocean to go to Laṅka, he felt thirsty and asked the monkeys to fetch some water, but when the water was brought, he remembered that he should not take water before prayer and he made a liṅga with his own hands and worshipped and that is Rameśvar, the eleventh Jyotirlinga.

Ghuṣneśa

In the south, there is a mountain named Deva, where a Brahmin named Sudharma lived with his wife, Sudeha. Both were very religious but they had no son and Sudeha made her husband to marry her niece Ghuṣṇā. Guṣṇā used to make one hundred and one liṅgas daily out of clay and worship. After the prayers she used to immerse them in the pond. When one lakh liṅgas had been worshipped Ghuṣṇā gave birth to a boy. Sudeha felt jealous and one night cut the child and threw it into the pond, where liṅgas had been immersed. In the morning, seeing the blood, every body was alarmed but Ghuṣṇā was not distracted as she was busy in her prayers. Śiva was so impressed with her devotion that he restored the child back to life. The Lord wished to kill Sudeha but Ghuṣṇā prayed for pardon. The Lord was pleased and agreed to her wish that the Lord should always be present there. This is the twelfth Jyotirliṅga.

Nandikeśvara Tīrtha

A widow mother, who brought up her sons, had a longing to visit Vārāṇasī and she requested her sons to at least immerse the ashes at Vārāṇasī and she died. The eldest son, Suvādi set out to Vārāṇasī and it was a long journey so he stayed at a brāhmaṇa's house for the night. In the front of that house a cow was tied and the brāhmaṇa tried to milk the cow, but the calf would not allow. The brāhmaṇa beat the calf. Suvādi heard the cow talking to the calf expressing sorrow for the beating and that it would gore the brāhmaṇa's son to death, the next morning. Next morning the brāhmaṇa's son was done to death and as it was killing of a brāhmaṇa the cow's body had become completely black. The cow then started walking straight and Suvādi followed the cow. The cow went straight to the river Narmadā and bathed in the river. The blackness had gone and it became white, indicating that the sin had been washed off. Suvādi was wonderstruck and he started for Vārāṇasī, when he met a beautiful woman, who told him that he could immerse the ashes in Narmadā itself. When Suvādi asked about her identification, the woman said she was Gaṅgā and vanished. Suvādi immersed the ashes in Narmadā and his mother's voice was heard that she was gratified. Such is the power of the *tirtha.*

Atrīśvara Tīrtha

The sage Atri and his wife Anasuyā did penance to bring rain and it was difficult to say whose *tapasyā* was difficult. They did penance for fifty four years and Atri was thirsty and asked for some water. When Anasuyā went to fetch some water, Gaṅgā appeared and said that she was pleased with her penance and told her to ask for a boon. Anasuyā asked for a pond filled with the water from Gaṅgā. Sage Atri found the water very sweet and Anasuyā told the incident. Both of them went to the pond. Gaṅgā agreed to stay there provided Anasuyā gave her the merits of one year, she had earned in her penance and it was agreed. Lord Śiva also agreed to stay there on the request of Anasuyā and that place is Atrīśvara tīrtha.

Arjuna and Śiva

The Pāṇḍavas, having been deprived of their kingdom, were sent to forest. Vedavyāsa advised Arjuna to meditate on Śiva at Mount Indrakila, on the banks of Bhāgīrathī. Arjuna performed a difficult penance. One day he saw a boar and flung an arrow. Śiva wanted to test Arjuna, so he came there, disguised as a hunter and flung an arrow at the boar. The boar died, pierced by the arrow of Śiva in hind quarters and Arjuana's arrow in the mouth. Both began to fight as to who killed the boar. After some time Śiva appeared in his form and Arjuna begged pardon. Śiva granted him his *Pāśupata* weapon.

Sudarśan Cakra

Once the demons oppressed the gods and the gods approached Viṣṇu. In order to obtain a powerful weapon, Viṣṇu did *tapasyā* in Kailāś. To test Viṣṇu, Śiva stole one of the flowers, kept for his worship and finding that one flower was missing, Viṣṇu took out one of his eyes and put it in its place. Śiva was pleased with this and offered him *Sudarśan cakra*.

Śivarātri Vrata

The observance of the rites on Śivarātri day is glorified here. A hunter named Rurudruha happened to hunt on a Śivarātri day and when evening set in, he climbed over a *vilva* tree under which a Śiva liṅga was there. Unknowingly shaking the tree, vilva leaves fell on the liṅga. This resulted in Śiva blessing him by removing all evil thoughts from his mind. He appeared before him and named him as Guha.

Vedanidhi

This is another glory of Śivarātri. A brāhmaṇa named Vedanidhi stole the bangle, given to his father by the king. He gave the bangle to a dancing girl, so he was sent out of the house. On a Śivarātri day he found people carrying offerings to the Lord and he followed them to steal some food. He waited till the night, but people around him suspected him and killed him. Because staying the night near Śivaliṅga washed off all his sins.

Candraśekhara

This is the story told by Śiva to Pārvatī as why the Lord is wearing the moon. When Sati gave up her body, Śiva was performing severe meditation and wherever he went the trees and plants started burning. Gods went and informed

Brahmā. Brahmā along with gods took two pots, one containing amṛta with moon, and another one containing poison. Brahmā offered them to Śiva. As soon as the Lord opened the pot with amṛta, the moon got stuck to his head and so he is called Candraśekhara. From the pot containing poison, he touched the poison with his middle finger and touched his throat and it became blue, so he is called Nilākaṇṭha.

The Ashes

Once Parvati asked Śiva the reason for his applying ashes on his body. This story was told by Śiva. Once a brāhmaṇa did great *tapasyā*, by living only on greens and it so happened one day, he cut his finger and instead of blood, sap like thing was oozing. The brāhmaṇa was very delighted considering this to be because of his *tapasyā.* Śiva wanted to teach him a lesson. In the form of a brāhmaṇa he went and asked him why he was so elated. The brāhmaṇa explained to him. Śiva said that it was not a great achievement, as in his body blood has become ashes and showed to the brāhmaṇa by cutting his finger. Then Śiva showed his own form and since then ashes have been always on the body of Śiva.

Nandi

Śilāda, a sage, having come to know that his ancestors were suffering because he had no sons, performed arduous *tapasyā* and got a boon from Śiva that he would have a virtuous son. One day while ploughing the land, he found a boy and named him Nandi and taught him everything. Once two sages Mitra and Varuṇa came to his hermitage and blessed the boy with fame. When Śilāda asked the sages why they had not blessed for long life, he was told that the boy did not have more than eight years.

Seeing his father upset, Nandi performed meditation, by entering the river Bhuvana. Pleased with his devotion Śiva granted him that he and his father would stay always near Śiva and made him Gaṇapatī, chief of gaṇas.

Upamanyu

Upamanyu, son of sage Vyaghrapāda could not get milk and his mother felt sorry for their poverty. Upamanyu performed a difficult penance. Śiva appeared before him and taught him all sacred knowledge. When Śri Kṛṣṇa happened to visit the hermitage of the sage, Upamanyu taught Kṛṣṇa, what was taught by Maheśvara.

Andhakāsura

Once when Śiva was sitting, Pārvatī came from behind and closed Śiva's eyes and a drop of sweat fell from her body. A gigantic creature appeared and started roaring. Because Śiva's eyes were closed the asura was blind and was named as Andhakāsura. When Hiraṇyanetra [in other puranas Hiranyākṣa} had no sons and wanted a son. Śiva said he could have Andhakāsura as his son, and he agreed to it. When he was crowned, Prahlāda and his brothers told him that being blind he could not be a good king and Andhakāsura left for the forest. He did such a severe penance that he offered every drop of blood and flesh as offering and Brahmā was pleased. He got back his vision and also a boon that unless he wanted to marry someone like his mother, he could not be killed. Armed with this boon, he got back his kingdom, drove away the gods and ruled over all the three worlds. Once while exploring in the mount Mandāra along with his generals, they saw a cave and inside saw a sage meditating. On his side a beautiful woman was sitting, who was none other than Lord Śiva and Pārvatī. Andhakāsura wanted to marry Pārvatī and a fierce fight ensued lasting for years in which Andhakāsura was finally killed by Lord Śiva, because he wanted to marry Pārvatī, who is the Mother of the universe.

Ruru

There was another demon named Ruru who wanted to marry Pārvatī. He did such an unimaginable *tapasya* that everything started burning. Even Śiva and Pārvatī had to run. Pārvatī told Śiva to do something; Śiva replied that only she had to find a way out. She saw a lion fighting an elephant. She killed the lion and put on its skin as clothing, smeared with its blood and her appearance was terrible. Then she went to Ruru and asked him to stop meditating as he was doing it for her only. Ruru did not believe it and struck her with a mace. Terrible fight ensued. Śaktis started eating up the demons. Ruru fled but Pārvatī pursued him wherever he fled, caught hold of him and tore his head with her nails. Thus he got killed.

False Pārvatī

When Śiva visited a place called Śonitapara Pārvatī was not with him so he sent Nandi to fetch Pārvatī. The *apasaras,* who were there, disguised themselves as Pārvatī and it was so perfect, that the difference between true and false Pārvatī could not be made out. Another time when Pārvatī went to do *tapasyā,* she instructed Nandi not to allow any false Pārvatī during that time. An asura named Ādi, who had the boon from Brhamā that he would be strong, happened to come there and asked Nandi, what was he doing there. Nandi repeated Pārvatī's instructions. Ādi then disguised himself as Pārvatī, entered the gate in the form of a snake and met Śiva. Śiva without realizing that he was Ādi went to embrace and immediately Ādi adopted his original form. He tried to kill Śiva, but he was killed. Before dying he told Śiva that he had a brother who would come in the form of Pārvatī and kill him. So when the real Pārvatī returned Śiva mistook her to be the demon's brother and tried to kill her by creating many gaṇas and Pārvatī also created many Saktis. At last Śiva realized that this was real Pārvatī.

Yama

The sage Sanatkumāra, Brahmā's son once went to Yama the king of death and while they were discussing an aerial chariot came with a man and Yama offered his respects and sent him to Brahmāloka. Same thing happened to the next aerial vehicle. Sanatkumāra became curious and asked yama who they were? Yama narrated the following. Once Nandi was cursed by Pārvatī to become a jackal for allowing a false Pārvatī to enter into the Śiva's place. Nandi in the form of a jackal made a liṅga and worshipped for twelve years and came back. A king named Dhārapāla observed the jackal praying and dying. So he built a temple there and made arrangements to recite Purāṇas. That was the first man, who attained Brahmāloka because of his noble deeds. Another man, though was evil, happened to hear Purāṇas and was changed completely. He arranged many recitals of Purāṇa due to which he also attained Brahmā loka because of the *puṇya.*

Śatānīka and Sahasrānīka

A king named Śatānīka was very religious and donated a lot of alms to Brāhmaṇas. When his son Sahasrānīka took over the reigns, he did in a smaller way and the Brāhmaṇas complained that they were not getting as much as they used to. Sahasrānīka agreed and asked them to find out where his father was? The Brāhmaṇas approached the sage Bhārgava to help them and after much persuasion found out that the Śatānīka is suffering in the hell as he was donating the money by taxing his citizens. Knowing about this, his son started doing labor and gave away alms from that.

CHAPTER V

Section I

The View Points

Brahmā Purāṇa

[246 chapters]

1. Glorification of about 200 pilgrimage places had revealed the mystery of number 5.

- Mother Pārvati's child is of 5 heads
- Brahmā had 5 heads.
- Great subtle elements – 5.
- Lord Śiva too has 5 heads.
- Traditionally the five gods, namely Gaṇeś, Śakti, Śiva, Viṣṇu, and Sūrya are worshipped. But these deities are worshipped in the form of Lińgas also and they are:
- Bāṇa lingam obtained from Narmadā is the representation of Śiva.
- Śālagrama obtained from Gandhaki is the representation of Viṣṇu.
- Sphatika lingam represents Sūrya devatā.
- Metallic *Yantras* like *Śrīcakra* is the representation of Śakti.
- Four cornered, red color flat gem is the representation of Gaṇeś
- These are the five liñgas and it is known to very few.

- Lord Śiva's five heads are *Sadyojāta, Vāma deva, Tatpuruṣa, Aghora* and *Īśāna.*
- Five Kāśīs are Vāraṇāsī, Gupta Kāśī, Uttar Kāśī, Dakṣiṇ Kāśī and Śiva Kāśī.
- Five protectors are those who gave body, food, knowledge, holy thread and culture.

2. Faces of Gaṅga: In the north it is Bhāgīratī [Vindhya] and in south it is Gautamī. King Bhagīrath brought out Gaṅga, whereas another stream split from Śiva's head came to the hermitage of Gautama. *Ch – 30 - 50*

3. The holy rivers Gomatī and Godāvarī are the means of atonement. *[Prāyaścitta]*, since, those who take refuge in them by taking bath with faith and reverence, the sins committed by them are absolved. *Ch.70 - 175.*

4. Until and unless one has become free from most of impurities, one may not develop devotion and love to the lotus feet of Lord Kṛṣṇa. *Ch. 180 - 212.*

Brahmāṇḍa Purāṇa *[109 chapters]*

This Purāṇa is seen in Indonesia with all its glories. It is a geographical account of the universe and some of the contents belong to far and near. This shows that this Purāṇa has its wings outside of India. It refreshes the memory of the characters and accounts of Paraśurāma, Sagara, Bhagīrath, Gaṅga, etc. [already described]. *Ch. 27 and 58 - 60.*

Satya Yuga

- People were happy and lived longer life.
- People were righteous by nature.

- People lived in mountains and on the shores of ocean.
- There were no seasons.
- Nature was bountiful to provide juices.
- All had desirable traits, truthfulness and contentment. So there was no reason to lay down the norms of *dharma.*

Tretā Yuga

In the beginning of this era, thick clouds gathered in the sky and rain poured down.

- From this rain were born trees and shrubs.
- Hatred and jealousy appeared.
- Some *Kalpavṛkṣhas* helped to meet the need of the people.
- Heat and cold made people to go in for shelter. Towards the end of this *Yuga Kalpavṛkṣhas* disappeared. Hunger and thirst, seasons and seasonal roots and fruits appeared.
- Notion of property rights on rivers, trees and mountains raised the head.
- Four *Varṇas* came into being for livelihood and occupations.

Human beings approached Brahmā and begged for subsistence and earth was provided with milk, fruits and food grains. Here we may remember how Pṛthu milked the earth.

Dvāpara Yuga

The four classifications grew precisely and evils rose further and further in this *yuga.* Appropriation of the occupations of the four *Varṇas* started, as the duties have been prescribed in the scriptures. Along with *Varṇa dharma, āśrama dharma* too was prescribed. [Stages of life]. It was without any rigid compartmentalization but more or less it was *guṇa* that decided the divisions for overall benefits.

Kali Yuga

This *Yuga* is of about 5000 years old only. Evil reigns. Virtues and dharma suffer. It is the day of diseases, famine, drought and sufferings. People die early. People are liars, Brāhmins became evil and do not follow their *dharma. Śudras* became kings and rule over other classes. Thieves are kings and kings are all thieves.

Brahmāvaivarta Purāṇa *[276 chapters]*

Lord Kṛṣṇa is the initiator of the creation and from his body other gods have come into being such as Mahādeva, Durgā, Lakṣmī and Nārāyaṇa. The Sun god is the originator of *Āyur Veda* system of medicines and treatment, though contributed and developed by many others later, like Kāśirāj and Dhanvantari.

Some tips from *Ayur Veda* to keep fit are:

1. Washing the eyes with cold water.
2. Applying oil in the sole and heel and some exercises daily.
3. For healthy living, pudding of fresh cooked grain, clarified butter, curd etc are good.
4. Association with proper and young woman is recommended.
5. Use of curd during night meals is prohibited.

6. Food should be taken while feeling hungry, otherwise the system would be disturbed violently and to pacify the disturbed system crushed coriander seeds mixed with sweetened cold water is recommended.
7. Similarly in order to get relief from *pittam,* Bengal gram with ripe bilva fruit, sugarcane juice, ginger, green gram *dahl* and sesame seeds mixed solution are recommended.
8. Bathing immediately after food is not advised.

Goddess 'Svāhā' is the wife of *Agni* and 'Svadhā' is the wife of *Manes.* Sixteen names of Durgā is auspicious. The age of sixteen is the bench mark in the life of a woman and full development of faculties and beauty occurs at that age.

Worship of goddess with sixteen types of materials should be done [Ṣoḍaśopacāra]. Sri Gaṇeś is not to be worshipped with *tulsi* leaves [basil]. Charity of food is the best among all charities. *Brahmā khaṇḍa - Ch – 5 & 29.*

In the 23rd chapter Savitṛ *mantra* [Gāyatrī] is glorified as the destroyer of sins which are committed by one inadvertently, during the sojourn on this earth.

One incantation destroys the sins of the day.

Ten times repeated destroy the sins of the whole day i.e, day and night.

Hundred times repeated destroy the sins of the month.

Thousand times repeated destroy the sins of one year.

For repeating the incantations beads of either white lotus seeds or crystal are recommended.

Posture of the hand must be like hood of the snake, facing upward, half open and slightly tilted towards left. One should face east.

Mārkaṇḍeya Purāṇa *[137 chapters]*

In Sanskrit *Nara* means water and being the predominant abode of Lord, He is also known as **'Nārāyaṇa'.** He is with and without form [*saguṇa and nirguṇa*]. This Purāṇa glorifies Sītā, Maṇḍodarī, Draupadī, Tāra and Kuntī, as the most celebrated chaste women of the scripture. Though Draupadī had seemingly five husbands, actually the five Pāṇḍavas were part of Indra, apparently disintegrated energy and Draupadī was Sācī, Indra's wife. Sācī came out of sacrificial fire. Sincere atonement by Balrām relieved him from the sin of killing a *Brāhmaṇa.* The five sons of Draupadī, who got killed while sleeping by Asvatthāmā at the age of twenty and were unmarried, actually were the five *Vasus,* born to Draupadī because of a curse from sage Viśvāmitra for their sympathetic utterance in favor of Queen Saibyā, wife of Hariścandra, when Viśvāmitra struck her on the back with a stick. A mother can make or mar her child as she is responsible for molding the child as she wishes. Examples are Madālsā, mother of Rāvaṇa, Aditi and Diti. Creation has come out of Sūrya Devatā is the contention of Mārkaṇḍeya Purāṇa. ***Durgā Saptaśati*** is the feminine aspect of the universe. Number thirteen is considered to be auspicious in Veda. [Connected with Lord Śiva].

Ch. 1 -9 & 41 -92.

Vāmana Purāṇa *[95 chapters]*

Here the teacher is the sage Pulastya and the student happens to be our ***Devarṣi Nārada.*** It is in two parts but only one is available. This Purāṇa gives the account of Lord Viṣṇu in his incarnation as dwarf [*Vāmana],* so that he could gain the confidence of Mahābali to grant three paces of land to be measured by His own steps. Duryodhana entered Brahmā sarovar – a lake, after losing all people in Mahābhārata war, to cool down his body, which was burning from the heat of hatred, jealousy, agony and anger. Finally, he was pulled out by the challenge thrown by Bhīma to fight only to get killed [from the crushed thighs]. It was that thigh, on which Draupadī was abused to sit, in the full glare of the court room. It was an unforgettable insult towards the jewel among the women of the world. Lord Śiva gives protection to Mother Satī, so that rain water does not touch her on a request for a house as a shelter during rain. *Ch. – 23 & 89 - 95.*

Bhaviṣya Purāṇa *[212 chapters]*

Out of 50,000 verses of this Purāṇa only 28,000 are available at present. This text forecasts the future events to take place. This Purāṇa elaborately discusses the index of a marriageable woman.

- Red [rosy], soft feet, evenly placed pace is the sign of good luck in life.
- Dry, rough, cracked feet and uneven pace on the ground are indications of hardship in life.
- Fingers of the leg, close to each other, straight, round and fine nails indicate a life of royal family.
- Short fingers give longevity but short and staggered ones destroy the wealth of the house.
- If one has three wrinkle marks on the throat, within the distance of four fingers, she will be a very lively one

and will benefit the family of her both father and husband.

- Possessing a black mole on the left side of the neck, hand, above ear may have a first child as a male.

If a snake bite results into the state of sleep of the organs, no bleeding from the cut and hair plucking ceases to be painful, indicate that person concerned is on the death bed. There is a composition of ingredient to be administered through the eyes to bring back to life and there is also a *mantra* to be chanted.

Hereunder mentioned the benefits [merits] of planting trees:

- Ashoka tree, when matched with the name of the individual is capable of eliminating grief.
- Palas tree may give a good wife.
- Vilva tree [bilva] will grant long life.
- Berry tree will bring prosperity.
- Pomegranate tree would add pleasure [woman].
- Mango tree brings in fulfillment of desires.
- Tamarind tree would lead to losses.
- Jack fruit tree may lead to the destruction of the race.
- Banyan tree would lead to liberation.
- Kadamba tree would bring good luck.

The description of sacrificial fire place[*vedi*, *Homa kunda*]:

The shapes are square, round, lotus shape, half moon, *yoni,* moon shape, pentagon, seven cornered, octagonal and nine cornered one. While performing sacrifice, the *Pūrṇa āhuti* should be offered standing and never in the sitting posture. *Ch.124 -126.*

Viṣṇu Purāṇa *[126 chapters]*

Composed by the sage Parāśara, this Purāṇa has its body, consisting of six divisions. It is a model Purāṇa with respect to the regular and common features; some call this the '*lakṣaṇa*'. The sports of Lord Kṛṣṇa mark the objectives of the *avatāra Puruṣa*. Description of India [*Bhārata Varṣa*], the land where one can make or mar the future and also can settle the account of previous accumulated merits and demerits, prominently known as '*karma bhumi*' is given elaborately. Here only, one can go to the extent of coming out of the cycle of birth and death that is liberation, through the science of the knowledge which is the opportune opportunity. The time principle, which is otherwise known as destruction or state of unmanifestation is the distinct mark of the Purāṇa.

Ch. 24 -126.

"When nescience that is the cause of distinction become totally eradicated, who can create difference – which [really] does not exist – between the self and Brahmān?

6.7.96.

Bhāgavata Purāṇa *[335 chapters]*

Sri Bhāgavata Purāṇa and the episodes of Mahārājā Parīkṣit are the view points of arrival and departure of the era. It is the confluence of *Dvāpara Yuga and Kali yuga,* of the old and new generation [Dhṛtarāṣṭra leaving for the forest and new rulers of Hastināpur], culmination of hatred and jealousy, the doings of Aśvatthāmā and his deprivations of the jewel from his head, Kṛṣṇa returning to Dvārkā and glorification of the sports of Lord Kṛṣṇa by Śuka on the banks of the river, while Parīkṣit was preparing for his own death – through the bite of the snake Taksha. The most wonderful prayers to Lord Kṛṣṇa are by Bhīṣma Pitāmah, while leaving the body. Kuntī's payer was "Oh! The teacher of all teachers let our lives meet with miseries at every walk, so as to enable us to think of You, constantly". *Ch.8*

Those who desire pregnancy should meditate on *Prajāpati,* for wealth on *Vasus*, for rulership on *Viśvedevā,* for long life on *Aśvini kumāras* for beauty on *gandharvas* and for beautiful wife on *Urvaśī.*

Improper time of union – Diti gave birth to the *daityas Hiraṇyakaśipu and Hiraṇyāksha.* Lord Viṣṇu incarnates as sage Kapila and teaches his own mother, Devāhūtī the Sāmkhya philosophy. Jada Bharata was born as a deer for his attachment to the deer at the time of leaving the body.

Ch. 8, 10 and 14.

Nārada Purāṇa *[207 chapters]*

This Purāṇa consists of two divisions. The important topics are efficacious religious rites like *Makara sańkrānti, Śukla dvādasi,* and subject matters of Veda on *Samhitā, Brāhmaṇa, Āraṇyaka and Vedānta* etc. To study the Vedas the branches of its sciences are to be studied like *Śikṣa, Niruktam, Kalpa, Jyotiṣam, and Chandas* etc. Holy syllables are in all the three genders like the one that ends with 'hā' like 'Svāhā' is feminine gender. The ending of 'hum' and 'phar' are masculine and 'namah' is neuter gender. The left or right nostril, whichever is breathing at the time of getting up, the same foot should be put on the earth while leaving the bed, which is auspicious and lucky as the remover of the obstacles of the day. A number of *mantras* are given on Lord Viṣṇu to appease, though not mentioned here, but it is essential that these are initiated by proper teacher, if the potency and efficacy are to be achieved. *Sāma Veda* singing is a pleasure to the gods, sages, gandharvas, *manes* and all beings.

Garuda Purāṇa *[256 chapters]*

A *Brāhmaṇa* known by the name Kaśyap was on his way to nullify the poison of the snake bite of Taksha on the king Parikṣīt – grandson of the Pāṇḍavas – and proved his capacity to Takṣa himself, but returned back without completing the mission of saving the life of the emperor Pariksit. He was

- A deluded Brahmin.
- Disgrace to the purpose of *mantra.*
- Disgrace to the teacher, who taught him the life saving *mantra,* to the unfit one.
- The person, with the knowledge of this *mantra* on snake bite must respond, whenever he comes to know of anybody in need of it, is the glory of the *mantra.*

Padma Purāṇa *[641 chapters]*

Through five main and many sub divisions this Purāṇa makes many points to ponder over. The divisions are chapters and being addressed as *khaṇḍa* and they are *Sṛṣṭi khaṇḍa, Bhūmi khaṇḍa, Svaraga khaṇḍa, pātāla khaṇḍa and Uttara khaṇḍa.* The *Sṛṣṭi khaṇḍa* is further divided into five *Parvas* – sections.

Highlights: Performing annual rites to departed parentage is systematically and meticulously explained. The Purāṇa cautions that even if one is rich the commandments should not be expanded such as 'feeding one *Brāhmaṇa* means only one'. The woman desirous of pregnancy may eat the middle *piṇḍa* meant for *pitāmaha.*

Āditya Śayanam is a rite, which is very efficacious and should be performed under conjunction of Sunday, seventh lunar day and star *Hasta* or on *Samkrānti* day. During the performance of this rite, salt is prohibited. Similarly the ***Candra Śayana*** should be on a Monday, constellation of star *Rohiṇī* and full moon day. The glory of *Rudrāksha* is based on the number of faces the beads have.The crown *[meru]* should not be crossed over while counting the beads. Gooseberry in the water bath on *Ekādaśi* day is very important and is equal to the bath in the Gańga, but use of the same is prohibited on Sunday or the Sunday combined with seventh lunar day.

Bhūmi khaṇḍa is devoted to the glory of devotion to one's father. *Svarga khaṇḍa* describes about the places of pilgrimage on the banks of *Narmadā* River. It brings out *Viśva rūpa* of *Virāt Puruṣa* – Lord Viṣṇu is imagined through super imposition of eighteen Purāṇas as His limbs such as *Brahmā Purāṇa* is his head etc, but the functional part of the limbs, so compared are not striking one. *Pātāla Khaṇḍa* states that worship of Lord Viṣṇu through symbol of *Śāligrāma* should be in even number like 2, 4, 6, etc and not in odd number like 1, 3, etc. *Uttara khaṇḍa* makes reference to the importance of the holy pilgrimage to *Hardvār* and various accounts of *Ekādaśi vrata,* the eleventh day of waxing moon.

Varāha Purāṇa *[218 chapters]*

Penance [austerity] may grant one heaven, fame, longer life, pleasures, intellect, knowledge, beauty, and good luck. Non violence grants beauty, *dīkṣa* grants birth in a noble family, service to the teacher grants self knowledge and performing the annual *Śrāddha* to the ancestors, grants children. Self knowledge alone can break the cycle of birth and death. The misery of the world is due to the identification with the body and body related connections, that keeps the Ā*tmā* bound, though *Ātmā* is not the doer, but suffers for the actions done through the body. Therefore non identification with the body results in disowning of the action done by the body, thus liberation. This self knowledge, of course cannot be obtained through independent study, but only through the teacher and the scripture. Here Lord Viṣṇu is glorified in the Varāha incarnation. A great idol of Varāha is worshipped in Madhya Pradesh in Vidhya giri. The description is impressive one – worth visiting.

Vāyu Purāṇa *[112 chapters]*

This Purāṇa was composed at Kurukṣetra, where the wind *[Vāyu]* is more predominantly experienced. Lord Śiva is all bliss and He is the cause of the universe. Banks of Narmadā River is glorious and the water of the river is the embodiment of Brahmā, Viṣṇu and Śiva – the creator, sustainer and resolver. These are the functional designations of the same Lord. Ten *Prjāpatis* worship Lord Śiva, who is the cause of manifestation and these Prajāpatis were for propagating the species. This is the idea of ***Śvetāśvatra Upaniṣad*** "Since Rudra – who rules these worlds through His divine powers, who resides within every being, who after projecting the world and becoming the protector, withdraws them during desolution – is One, therefore they did not wait in anticipation for a second".

Lińga Purāṇa

[163 chapters]

Son inherits the characteristics from the *Jīvātma* of the father, thus the son is called Ātamja. At the death point of the body, the seed stored may be able to bring progeny. The Purāṇa cites an example of Pṛthu coming out from Vena, his father. The action born out of the body covers the soul that remains even after the body is destroyed to produce the fruits of action, to be exhausted through transmigration. When the creator wished to multiply himself into many, the first came into being was the ego and that gave birth to five great subtle elements, the material for creation of the universe – space, air, fire, water and earth. *Lińga* is a symbol of Lord Śiva; similarly beings have *lińga śarīra* which is known as causal body. There is no doubt that all actions of a man of knowledge get dissipated. Through playing with the various kinds of unrighteous acts, he does not become tainted.*L.P. E. 118.*

Skanda Purāṇa

[1671 chapters]

This Purāṇa has six *Samhitās* known as *Sanat kumāra, Sūta, Śańkara, Vaiṣṇava, Brāhma and Saura samhitās*. In the temple of Lord Śiva, one should not circumambulate going in between the *Lińga and Nandi.* Water is the bed of Lord Viṣṇu, who is the creator in the first phase and sustainer. Woman too is the substance of the beings, as they too have lotus, downward, below the *Nābhi,* as Viṣṇu has. Five women and the five elements delude the creation, as they come from water. The woman and man are engaged in the functions of Lord Viṣṇu only – the creation and sustenance. Charity has two purposes, six abodes, six organs, two results, four forms, three divisions and three means of destruction. Charity can be big or small in quantity, which is not important, but the significance is devotion, and capacity to part with. The quantity is that part which one can spare without undergoing suffering of self and dependents. The six abodes are *Dharma, Arta, Kāma, Lajja, Harṣa, and Bhaya.* The six organs are the occasion, the type of giver, the receiver, purity of mind of the giver, rightfully earned object in both the cases, place where the charity is given and conjunction of the stars and other criteria. The results pertain to this world or the life after. The four forms are the types such as social service [common good], given to the guest, with an eye on the result and on the occasion of scriptural rites. Under the division of charity house, land, cow, gold, knowledge and life are the highest in merits. Food, cloth, horse, transport etc are the medium type of merit. Shoes, umbrella, utensils and lamp fall under the third category of merit. The actions that destroy the merits of charity are the regret after giving, giving without honor and rebuking the receiver while giving.

The five types of fire in the body are the digestive, appearance of the face as the light or attractiveness, that which directs the intellect and mind, the juice of the food which gets converted into blood and that through which eyes can see and that which keeps the skin alive.

Agni Purāṇa *[383 chapters]*

The Mahābhārata was composed by sage Vyāsa and has about one lakh verses. It is known that what has not been described in Mahābhārata is not described anywhere else. The Bhagavad-Gīta [700 verses] is part of Mahābhārata. The invocation we find is separate and recent addition by Sri Madhusūdhana Sarasvatī. The war of Kurukshetra is the war between two opposing intent and content of just and unjust and continuing in every nook and corner in relative relation, behavior, thoughts and action. The action may be of an individual, groups and nations. When this war ceases one becomes a free bird – liberated. The concept of the God with form is a means to know the God without form, both being one and the same, the difference is on the understanding but not in reality. One can not be understood without the other. *Agni* stands for the fire [heat] principle, one of the basic constituent of the universe with various forms, names and functions, like sacrificial fire, digestive fire, lightning etc.

Agni devatā is perceptible, not the subtle divinity behind but the grossified one connected with rituals and sacrifices from birth to death. *Agni* is also a symbol of priesthood and foremost god in scriptures. Naturally, through the medium of *Agni Purāṇa* many rites, rituals and sacrifices are dealt with. The offering of oblations of various materials, meant for different gods [fire as a messenger] and also to fire god himself, are offered in the sacrificial fire. *Agni* has been repeatedly used for the rituals of the *karma kāṇḍa* of the Veda – an exemplary life of *gṛhasta* [householder] for fine tuning of the character that involves charity and that begins at home. In large scale *rājasuya yajna, aśvamedha,* and *āvahanti* etc and in small scale *Jāta karma, nāmakaraṇa, vivāha, upanayanam* and *antyeṣti* [final rites] are performed through *Agni.* This Purāṇa gives the details of the method, materials, and means, including the *mantra* to be used.

Matsya Purāṇa *[291 chapters]*

Lord Viṣṇu takes the incarnation of the fish [*matsya*] and saves the humanity during deluge. He advises *Manu* and sages. King Yayāti returned the youth to his last son Puru, which he borrowed to enjoy the comfort and pleasures of the world. He told his son that he had enjoyed the pleasures, which he understood that these were not satiable like the clarified butter, poured in the fire. It is to be understood that all the gold, wealth and women of this world is not sufficient for even a single man. Therefore one should keep calm and not get agitated with the lust.

Kūrma Purāṇa *[104 chapters]*

This Purāṇa is the teaching that came from Lord Viṣṇu, when He incarnated as a tortoise, to king Indradyumna and that was related by Romaharṣaṇa [Sūta] as *pāriphlava,* in a sacrifice spread over a span of 12 years to an assembly of eighty eight thousand sages. The four *āśramas – Brahmācarya, gṛhsta, vānaprasta* and *sanyāsa* have two divisions. A *Brahmācārya* after studying the scriptures enters into *gṛhastāśrama* is known as *Upakuvanik* and the one who continues to stay with the teacher and study is known as *Naiṣṭhika Brahmācāri.* The *gṛhasata* who looks after his family alone is called a *Sādhak* and he who performs his duty towards gods, sages and forefathers [manes] is known as *udasin.* That *Vānaprasta,* who observes austerity and performs sacrifices in the forest, is called *tapas* and the one who makes strenuous penance and does not care about the body is called *Samyasik.* Similarly one who goes through *yoga* and control the senses and desirous of liberation is a *Parameṣṭhik* and one who sees no difference between himself and the Lord is a *Yogi.* The eight *Rudras* are *Bhava, Sarva, Īśāna, Paśupati, Bhīma, Ugra, Aghora and Mahādeva* and the ninth is *Rudra.* When one dies in Kāśī, his subtle and causal body also die along with the gross body, through the grace of Lord Śiva and Mother Kālī, thus attains liberation. Īśvar Gīta is the dialogue between Lord Śiva and sages. The Lord said "All ignorant beings are *Paśu* and their master is known as '*paśupati*' and 'I am that'.

Wife should not belong to the *gotra* of either the mother or the father. Association with wife is forbidden on the following lunar days: 6, 8, 12, 14, and full moon and new moon day. Even when one sees either the rainbow or funeral pyre, others should not be invited to see. Rising and setting sun and moon should be avoided. While dining and in the residence also the guest should not be left to himself. One should not eat with the wife and she should not be seen while eating or sneezing. In the night eatables with sesame seeds and curd is not allowed. Recitation of Vedas in the night, when the wind is blowing with a whistling sound, in the day when there is storm dust is blowing or lightning and thunder or where there is a dead body in the village, in the water and on the lunar day of eighth, fourteenth and full moon day must not be done.

Section II

Points of View

Variance in Events

In this study, it is proposed to discuss certain concepts, which are seen as ambiguous, at random but to know that those ideas confirm to *Upaniṣadic* teachings, which is glorification of the Purāṇas. When a point is discussed with open mind it gives the readers an opportunity to analyze the points themselves, the views presented for and against, which lead to an asset of doubt free knowledge. At times some doubt is intentionally introduced to enable the readers to have free thinking before accepting it and that acceptance will be a lasting and fruit bearing one.

Some modern authors, in glorifying the Puranas go to the extent of giving the dates of Purāṇas, as of the Vedas or say that, it is earlier to Vedas. In validating the statement the quote of scripture is given where Purāṇas are equated as the fifth Veda, the other four Vedas being *Ṛg, Yajur, Sāma, and Atharvaṇa*. Even the four *Vedas* have not come at one stretch. *Ṛg* verses are borrowed and adopted by *Yajur and Sāma Vedas* to their peculiar characteristics. *Atharvaṇa veda* is of later origin. In fact in earlier scriptures, only three *Vedas* are talked about frequently. Srimad Bhagvad Gīta also has been given the honor of fifth Veda. The foundation of Gīta is *Upaniṣadic* verses. Many of them have been virtually lifted from *Upaniṣads* and put on the lap of Gīta. Lord Kṛṣṇa makes a reference to this in verse 8.11 that "this is not my own philosophy, but of Yore". Similarly Purāṇas have come later, is evident even from the age. Specific reference is available. In Bhāgavata Purāṇa, in the dialogue between Vyāsa and Nārada [1.5.9], Vyāsa makes remarks that he was not satisfied with the work of *Vedas and Upaniṣads* and had been requested to dwell more on Lord Kṛṣṇa's glory by Nārada. Thus he started with the sports of Lord Kṛṣṇa at Mathurā and Bṛndāvan. Further we may find many more topics of *Sṛuti* in Purāṇas rather we must say that it is *Sṛuti,* simplified and given another popular and comprehensible name 'The Purāṇa'. Some times, the culminating references, in the form of stories such as, coming together of the teacher and student or logic to undertake some sort of spiritual preparation and practice are termed as 'Purāṇas' in *Vedas* and *Upaniṣads*, an incident of the past. And in course of time that part had been plucked out separately and changed into a story to reflect some specific moral or ethical values as an example, to be taken for value based living.

Creation

Almost all Purāṇas deal with creation as a topic. The creation of the universe – sentient and insentient objects, five great elements, both subtle and gross is dealt with. *Hiraṇyagarbha,* is the total of subtle instruments of action and knowledge and *Virāt Puruṣa,* is the *Lokas,* [Seven up and seven below], with all the great elements, i.e, water, air, fire, earth and space and its modifications in micro and macrocosm. The *Upaniṣads* too see in the same way. "From that Brahmān indeed, which is this Self, was produced space, from space emerged air, from air was born fire, from fire water was created and from water was created earth. From earth was born herbs, which is food and from food was born man. That man, as such is surely a product of the essence of food. Of him, this indeed is the head, this is the southern side [right], this is the northern side [left], this is the Self, this is the stabilizing tail". *[Tai - II.1.1].*

"Thus He created these worlds, *Ambhās, Marīci, Maram, and Āpah.* That *Ambhās* is above the heavens supported by it. *Marīci* is the middle region. This earth is the *Maram.* The region of Waters below the earth is *the Āpah.* He, the Atman thought: These indeed the worlds [I have created]. Let me now create the guardians of these worlds. He then raised the *Puruṣa* from the waters [i.e., the five elements] and fashioned him. *The Ātman* brooded on the *Puruṣa*, and when he was thus brooded over there burst forth the mouth as an egg does. From the mouth proceeded the speech and from speech fire. The two nostrils burst forth; and from the nostrils proceeded the power of smell and from the power of smell air. Eyes burst forth: from the eyes proceeded sight; and from sight the sun. Ears burst forth; from the ears proceeded hearing and from hearing the quarters. Skin burst forth; from the skin proceeded hairs and from hairs, herbs and trees. The heart burst forth; from the heart proceeded mind and from the mind moon. The navel burst forth; from the navel proceeded the down breathing and from down breathing death. The generative organs burst forth; from the generating organ, seed and from seed water. *[Ai ch. 1, section 1].*

Points of Observation

The creation details and nature are the same and similar, but the objectives behind the narration are different projections. In the world of the Purāṇas, it is the duality that exists and each item is separate in nature, though creation is one and the same. The entities also maintain their own distance from the creator as well as between the entities themselves. The creation indicates the time scale of coming into existence and disappearance [return back to the source]. The cyclic order of appearance and disappearance of matters, beings and *guṇas,* that constitute the universe, is the world of diversities and the relation is that of the creator and the created – the master and the servants – the protector and the protected and so on. The *upaniṣadic* point of view is the cause and effect, production and produced. The effect or the product inherits the virtues of the cause that is the material cause. The creator is the material and intelligent cause present through and through in all creations. The effects are different as per the names and forms are concerned but essentially of the same nature as the creator. In fact the very idea behind the description is to establish the identity in diversities. The differences which are seen are unreal and those who see such differences are ignorant. Another point to be noted is that the creation is not a real creation but only a projection as in the dream. In dream the dreamer and the objects of dream are one and the same. The waker is the dreamer and the dreamer is the waker. Every *Upaniṣad* contains the topic of creation as the Purāṇas, since both have their own objectives behind the same content with difference. The word *Ātma* used too has different perception, one is on the *saguṇa* plane and the other is the *nirguṇa*, the absolute that is the *Īśvara* and *Brahmān.* In Purāṇas the Consciousness is the property of the matter, the *Upaniṣads* say that all matters exist in Consciousness and it is question of manifestation only. My teacher repeatedly used to tell that the current is throughout the length of the wire but the bulb lights where there is manifestation of the current.

Variations of Events

There are some variations in readings of Purāṇas. These variations are either between Purāṇas or the variations of the readings have been with reference to other authentic scriptures. Now the question is how these variations affect the understanding of the Purāṇas? Do they disturb the basic structure that is the essence, the effectiveness and the status or is it a cyclone in a cup? Here the variations observed are first highlighted and later the impact or impression is talked about.

- Śiva Purāṇa talks about Hiraṇyakaśipu fighting with lion, which strayed into his kingdom and got killed, by the lion man, without any torture to Prahlāda as given in other Purāṇas.
- Viṣṇu Purāṇa mentioned at one place that Kamsa set free Vasudeva and Devakī, when he realized that 'his would be killer' had been somewhere, whereas in other place it was Kṛṣṇa, who set them free along with Ugrasena after killing Kamsa.
- Nārada Purāṇa differs from Rāmāyaṇa and Matsya Purāṇa as Bhagīratha first prayed to Brahmā, who in turn asked him to pray to Lord Śiva. Nārada Purāṇa states that he prayed to Viṣṇu, who asked him to pray to Śiva.
- Mahābhārata states that Sagara prayed to Lord Śiva for a son and Lord Śiva granted the boon. Śiva Purāṇa speaks that he prayed to Aurva. Again it was Sumatī, who had one son and Keśni had sixty thousand sons. Śiva Purāṇa differs and claims that Keśnī had one son and Sumatī sixty thousand sons.
- Dakṣa performed Bṛhaspati Yajña and he invited all the devatas duly, but not his own daughter Sati and son-in-law Śiva. Sati heard the praise of the sacrifice

from the *gandharvas* and decided to attend in spite of Lord Śiva's objection. When she came to attend the sacrifice none came to receive her, except that her mother and sister took note of her presence. More drastic was that, there was no oblations to her Lord Śiva, thus she could not bear the humiliation to her husband by her own father. In anger she decided to forsake the body obtained through her father and jumped into the sacrificial fire. This is one version. And the other one is that with her yogic power she burnt herself.

How to reconcile this variance for the benefit of the readers and the validity of the incidents in the Purāṇas? Purāṇas have come down from the teacher – disciple tradition like the *Vedas or Upaniṣads,* but the bond between the teacher and the taught had not been as strong as in the *Upanisadic or Vedic* teachings. It was a casual assembly of learned and learners and that too not for full term but a piece meal teaching, unlike the *guru Kula* pattern. Naturally there could be gaps in time or continuity. Another point which comes into play is the singularity of the teacher. One part might have been learned from one teacher and the completion of the series might have taken place by another teacher. These two teachers might have come from different traditions and thinking. To see the effect of the inconsistency in the legends of the Purāṇas, we separate the terms, the accounts and events. The account is the feature of the legends that have been reorganized by usage in Purāṇas from time immemorial or say from the point of compilation under different titles of mythology. It is also a sum total of the elements of narration. Now we give the name of events for a free flow of discussion. Account is the primary and events are the secondary facts of the narration. From the examples, given above, we also see that the context and sequence have not undergone any variation and are intact, since they convey the subject matter or the subject – object, for which they have been brought into the fold of Purāṇas. But the events had undergone changes from the popular concept and they differ from each other between different Purāṇas. It is noticed only when one happens to read these two Purāṇas and remember the text in full, otherwise no contradiction and so one can happily accept, what is given by anyone. When we compare the variation in between the events as submitted, we find something is lacking in one or both statements and are not effective equally. What is missing is the impact. This impact is born out of the climax of the situation. For example Hiraṇyakaśipu is simply killed, being the highlight of the cruelty towards Prahlāda, his son. *Narasimha avatār* had no opportunity to show that Lord had come down to protect his devotee and faith in the Lord's help of protection when in distress is missing and also the thrill. Sati burning herself from her *yogamāya* is a lesser event of suspense than jumping into the sacrificial fire, where the oblation of matter to be offered is not a chaste wife or the daughter. Kamsa setting free his sister Devaki and his brother-in-law Vasudeva is different than Lord Kṛṣṇa himself setting them free. One thing is a grant of liberation and another, son doing his duty to the parents. However these variations in the events do not invalidate the facts for which these have been brought in. It loses its multipurpose objective for which the accounts of Purāṇas have to serve for its varying targets, which is general and not specific like the study of *Upaniṣad,* which takes granted that the students have attained certain degree of maturity before they approach the teacher of *Brahmā Vidya.*

The Hells *[Bhāgavata Purāṇa]*

- A thief goes to *Tamisaka naraka* and made to suffer from hunger and thirst.
- A violent one is sent to *rourava naraka,* to be harassed by snakes like beings. [Ruru].
- One who harms a *brāhmaṇa* is sent to *Kālasūtra* and burnt there.
- An opposer of *Vedas* is whipped at *asipatra vana* [with blade and sword like thing].

Purāṇa mentions about 28 types of hells, where individual sinner is subjected to burning, cutting, boiling in oil / water and many such types of torture which can be imagined by embodied ones only. We have heard similar nature of injury and humiliations inflicted by our custodians of law – police and in prisons, in spite of international safe guard [U.N.O] against such practices. We also come across the information about perverted ones in our society for cruelty. But all these abuses are subjected on the body of flesh and blood and effective so far as it gives pain and pleasure to the matter – the body. The departed soul, which is supposed to have no body, is the matter for thought provocating enquiry. Then there emerges three possible propositions.

One is given body, after death, purely to enjoy heaven or suffer the torture of the specific order, depending upon merits and demerits.

Or

It is the mental perception [experience] along with the reflected Consciousness.

[causal body]

Or

It is only a notion, all the rewards and punishments lie in this relative world, through various types and grades of body that one acquires, is the means of successive reward and punishment – cyclic order of transmigration.

Moral Lessons – The Punitive Way

Reference:

Yama's abode	-	Nārada Purāṇa.
Hells	-	Bhāgavata Purāṇa.
Hells	-	Śiva Purāṇa.
Yama	-	Viṣṇu Purāṇa.
Vikuṇḍala	-	Padma Purāṇa.
Mahāmati and Sumati	-	Mārkaṇḍeya Purāṇa, etc.

Naraka is also a scheduled topic of the Purāṇas under different titles and with some values. There are two ways of looking at the same expression – the positive and the negative stroke. Positive attitude says "do these, to get that". That is an encouragement for positive thinking and performance of the deeds that may yield the desired results. *Vedas* call this attitude as '*kāmya karma'.* As one progresses through the activities – *karma pradhāna – a rajo guṇa – a pravṛti mārga,* one chooses those activities which satisfy his basic needs first and the status and egoistic demands. Hardly one finds an end to the demand for pleasures just as the fire grows bigger and bigger, the fuel one adds to it. The wise are those who could win over the temptation and stop at reasonable point of time and progress. Our scriptures have made deep thinking and have come out with many suggestions and limitations, through austerity and sacrifices. They have also prescribed norms to lead a life, where one knows, where to stop, so that a proper attitude and character is developed, which will take care of the excesses.

But sad part of it is that, one becomes so addicted to it that one fails to heed to the call of *dharma* – a thin line of demarcation and over stepping on to the others' *dharma* becomes *adharma.* A one word definition of *adharma* is 'selfishness'. That is the transgression of others' freedom and right or fulfilling the self interest at the cost of others' interests. Normally this transgression was supposed to be checked by the ruler, through the institution of law, but in most of the cases, the human judgment and jurisdiction is not sensitive enough, also not amenable and not available. Here comes the divine institution, the *naraka* – the hell and its punishment, to deter the individual for fear of severity of the punishment. This stands as the sword of 'Damocles' keeps reminding the beings to behave and to be disciplined to avoid the sufferings of the punishment. In Purāṇas even the nature and types of offences and the punishments are described and it is the negative stroke approach to teach moral values. To illustrate from Bhāgavata Purāṇa "*Naraka*, the house of punishment, far away, in the underworld has a terrible path to travel, for deviating from the divine rules, which is a sin [crime] and the respective punishments, that are prescribed are to be undergone." It goes without saying that those who perform noble deeds, which are prescribed by the scriptures, are rewarded with the pleasures of heaven. The accounts of good and bad deeds are perfectly compiled and maintained. There is no chance of any mistake at all. *Yama* – the god of death is also called *Dharmarāja* as he is very true to his job and do not incur any merit or demerit for performance of unbiased duties. *Yama* is not an individual but a post, likely to be replaced at every *Kalpa* from other eligible ones, if any.

Atonement: Prāyaścitta

It is an instrument of self imposed punishment for individual commission and omission prescribed by the scriptures. The punishments are in the form of rituals, sacrifices, and religious austerities.

Scripture

Dualism does accept another body and loka such as *Vaikuṇtha* and *Kailāśa,* abodes of Nārāyaṇa and Śiva to be attained alongwith the pleasure instruments to enjoy such as dance and music and other objects. *Advaita*-non-dualism negates the existence of such thing and makes it as a notional concept. Physical body consists of matter that one manifests into, to reap the fruits of the actions of previous manifestations, so it is that manifestation / unmanifestation cycle till one goes to *atyantika pralaya*, which is the nature of the self, the merger into the total, the Infinite itself. *Advaita and Dvaita* both accept the beginning less of the cycle and immortality of the soul, whereas for the *Dvaitins* individual is also real. The sentence is not over from sufferings in the hells, as the residual of the offence has to be set off by rebirth in different types of bodies and sufferings. Thus the offences committed are discharged. This is the rebirth theory of the Purāṇas. The Bhagavad-Gīta 16th chapter says "Bewildered by many a fancy, enmeshed in the snare of delusion addicted to the gratification of lust, they fall into foul hell. Those cruel haters worst among men in the world, I hurl these evil doers for ever into the world of demons only." *G. 16 & 19.*

Simple Logic: [Reasoning]

When question is raised about the body to the soul for enjoyment of heaven and suffering in the hell, there can be two types of bodies that of *sura* and *asura* as these are *bhogha yonīs* unlike human beings which are *karma yoni.* The double punishment of first in the hell and then in the rebirth is perhaps an after thought by the Purāṇas to consolidate the ground of sufferings as the hell being an entity not available for perception. The statement of Gītā shows that for the hell one is to be born in an inferior womb, which is depriving of the knowledge and is of sinful nature.

Inference

We see how some in their handicapped and diseased body, the unfortunate souls such as beggars, *caṇḍālas,* worms and insects etc suffer. Further some get into trouble at some stage of life and have to undergo the torture by kidnappers, police and enemies. Also mauled by animals, meeting with an accident and become incapacitated, some suffer. Born as a dog, but even among dogs, one is the pet of a film artist, dogs too have different privileges. Among cows too, the cow of Śaṅkarācārya's *gośālā* has an enhanced status. Animals in captivity or the domestic animals have their own advantage altogether. Thus we see that there is gradation, even in inferior birth. It is presumed that hell is also on the earth, in our relative existence. In the plan of creation, care has been taken, for the merits and demerits, to be rewarded or punished, honored or dishonored and that is what the Lord's plans, when manifestation has to be projected. We often hear people talking that the life has become hell, though they do not know, what they mean. What we are concluding here that hell and heaven is not far away and one has not to travel for the scripture project, such a way to infuse a discipline, righteousness and balanced living in the span of life. Coming to this conclusion Gītā's verses also testify. We take the Gītā's teaching as practical and appropriate training manual for ideal life. The verses can also be taken as the valid proof, without questioning the propriety of it.

Instrument of Curse

The king Saudāsa, who was in a hunting spree in the forest saw two tigers there and killed one of them, but before dying, the tiger adopted the form of a forceful *rākṣasa,* while the other one said 'I will revenge' and lost into the forest. Thereafter the king performed a *yajña* with the help of sage Vasiṣṭha. Sage Vasiṣṭha finished the rituals and left. In his place the *rākṣasa* sat down in the form of Vasiṣṭha and asked the king some rice and meat at the end of the ceremony to eat. He said that he would be back in short while. Then the *rākṣasa* took the form of the cook of the palace and cooked human meat. With this preparation the king waited for the sage to return. When Vasiṣṭha arrived, the king served that preparation in a golden plate without knowing anything. The sage realized, about the preparation and cursed the king that he would become a *rākṣasa.* When Vasiṣṭha came to know what had actually happened, he reduced the curse to twelve years. The king Saudāsa felt that the curse was unfair. So he took water in his hand to curse the sage, but the queen Madayāntī intervened and said that it was wrong to curse the *guru.* The king checked himself from pronouncing the curse, but the water had been taken in the hand to curse and if the water was thrown on the earth or above, the grain or cloud would get destroyed.

So Saudāsa poured the water on his legs, resulting in the legs becoming deceased and black and he came to be known as *kalmāṣapāda.*

At Piṇḍaraka Yādava youths dressed up Sāmbha as a pregnant woman and brought him before the sages Kaṇva, Viśvāmitra and Nārada and asked the sages whether that woman would have a boy or girl baby. The sages saw through the mischief and were enraged at the insult and said "This person would give birth to a club and that club would destroy your clan". When the club came into existence, king Ugrasena pulverized the club into dust and scattered the dust in the ocean, but these dusts became sharp reeds and eventually at Prabhāsa, the Yādavas destroyed each other with this. Lord Kṛṣṇa too found a way to leave the mortal body, through a piece of the club, which was eaten by a fish and subsequently was made an arrow of a hunter, to hit him at the feet, which the hunter took it as a bird.

In quest of divine weapons, Arjuna, the hero of the Mahābhāratha war was learning dance under Citra Gupta, where Urvaśī was also present. Urvaśī was hurt because Arjuna refused to marry her and thus, she cursed Arjuna that he would become a eunuch.

The above are the examples of the curse on our legendary world to mind and maintain the momentum of the discussion. The other side of the coin of the curse, we have the blessings or boons. These two are the two wheels of the bi-cycle. Two wheels are the boon and curse, the rider is the accounts of the Purāṇas, handle bar is the understanding its import, peddle is its practice and the goal is the attaining of purity of mind for fitness of knowledge. Or one can say the rim and the hub of a wheel, on which the legendary rests and perpetuate their meaningful end. The boon and curses together are the causes of the following factors in our mythological accounts, especially, the Purāṇas.

- Cohesion and continuity
- Logical ends – the reasons.
- To tie the lose ends.
- Inspiration and aspirations.
- Leads to moral order.

Our Purāṇas take up the responsibility of the talk, which is smooth and inter connected with the beginning and end. The topic has not to be terminated abruptly without any significance or the bench mark to which it took course in the beginning with specific view point. The narration should move without any jerk that could cause damage to the authority and reliability. It must not go hay wire. The idea is to explain that there must be proper link between the character, incident, time, place and action such as the 'sleeping individual must come out of the dream' before he starts his work in the relative world of waking – the gross world – sense perception. In the first example given above, a lapse on the part of the king should have occurred to enrage the priest, as in this case Vasiṣṭha to pronounce a curse. Whereas in pursuance of the scriptural rites, sage Vasiṣṭha was there as priest and he was supposed to bless the king Saudāsa for wealth of this and other world, according to the injunction of the scriptures, provided for the specific propitiation. Purāṇa wants to emphasis that offering human meat, that too to a sage is a crime and crime attracts punishment, even if it was done unknowingly and unconsciously. So, one has to be very careful, against illogical sequence such as the priest asking for meat to eat, after performance of scriptural rites, as seen in the example. Here the instrument of justice for the offence was met out through the curse to become a *rākṣasa,* a man eater for the reason of offering human meat. While going through the stories of Purāṇas, one will find some times as though there was no cause for the events, which have been described without the interference of the boons granted by some sage or gods or cursed. For example Draupadī is said to be the wife of five Pāṇḍavas and at the same time glorified among the five glorious women of the world, as *a pativratā woman* is supposed have only one husband. Here due to four sins / curses on Indra, his energy was broken into four and was the resultant birth of the five Pāṇḍavas.

In the present example as above, the water was put down on his own legs by the king Saudāsa instead of its real target, the sage Vasiṣṭha, caused harm to his own legs. Likewise in Rāmāyaṇa, in the *svaymvara* of Sītā, the arrow put on the bow, given by Paraśuram to test the validity of the incarnation, had to be aimed to annihilate the ego of Paraśuram, as desired by him as an alternative option given to him as the arrow drawn could not be taken back. Some times, they were mere words, which had the divinity in potency to hit the target. In all the cases, where immediate and to the point, effect had to be there, one had to be an *upāsaka* of some deities like *Agni, Varuṇa, Indra* or some other gods and blessed with *satya kāma and saṅkalpa*. Even in *Kali Yuga* the curse works, but it is a double edged sword, especially when born of hatred, selfish motive and jealousy. It was a defensive weapon in the past for the helpless and for persons of disciplined living. It is to be remembered that misuse of the curse is self abuse as happened in the curse of Durvāsā to King Ambarīṣa.

Voice of the Fertile Mind

- Does the curse, change the course of the life determined already by cosmic law?
- Are the offences and the punishments through curse rationale?

Moral and Ethical Code

People talk about *Vedānta,* a topic too complicated to comprehend. The reasons given are the misplacement of *Ātma* and *anātma*, lack of concentration of mind and the *Vedic* usage of the words therein. [a technical term]. On the similar footings our Purāṇas grossify the substances and the import [real meaning], sometimes not clear [covered], thus we land in sacrilege. We have three main sources that tell us, what to do, what is prohibited and when to keep silence. The *Śruti* is the fountain head, from where have sprung *Smṛti [Itihāsa - Purāṇas]* and *Śṛṣṭhācāra. Śṛṣṭācāra* is the following of the path that had been treaded by our noble and great forefathers and sages, who lived an ideal life within the varying situations, during our sojourn on this earth.

One thing must be clearly noted here is that we are not supposed to go against the maxims laid down by the *Śruti.* When two things are interwoven and one of it is against the scriptural sanction, that part we must not take or even attempt. In this discussion may I submit herewith three examples for kind reference to the readers, in understanding the intention of the Purāṇas.

1. From the narration of Paraśurāma's character, we find that he had cut his mother's head as commanded by

his father, which is the primary meaning. When we analyse, we find that obedience of the father's command is the scriptural truth whereas the cutting of the head of a woman, who happened to be his own mother is a sacrilege and sin. *Śruti* never advises such action. The cutting of the head is the measure of the severity and weight of the command that is to be taken and as such the act concerned is not the ideal taught here at all, though often we mistake it in our slumber.

2. Kuntī asked her five sons to share among themselves, where the object happened to be Draupadī [noble lady]. *Śruti* can not even think such immorality [five husbands to a woman]. So we must remove from our thought the primary meaning, as the mother's command was that all five brothers must live together at normal as well as abnormal situations, they are likely to meet in their lives and nothing more is to be read in between the lines.

3. Ekalavya offered his right thumb to the teacher Droṇācārya as *dakṣiṇā.* This part is fine, as one has to offer *guru dakṣiṇā* but when it comes to asking for it – it is not according to the truth. Droṇācārya can not ask his *dakṣiṇā.* Here this part has to be ignored.

Sṛṣṭācāra is the path given by our celebrities, to be followed by us. Here too the condition is that its extent should not be against the scriptural truth. When the act crosses the limit, then that has to be ignored, where the model may be even Rāma or Kṛṣṇa [Lord in the human form]. One may ask 'why?' The answer is that it was their own intention as the God Supreme to keep *Śruti* above all, as the only guiding truth as our code of conduct. In the maxim there is provision that certain circumstances, where one can violate, but caution has to be exercised carefully and not according to whims and fancies.

B. G. 3 - 21.

Controversy with Respect to Verses

Authors unfailingly give the account of number of verses in Purāṇas, as it carries some weight and authority while talking about various Purāṇas and their subject matter. Unfortunately we have not made headway to come to a single point as it gives some confidence, especially to the readers, who have not established in it.

Purāṇas	**Source A**	**Source B**	**Source C**
Brahmā	10,000	10,000	9,000
Brahmāṇda	20,000	12,000	18,000
Brahmāvaivarta	18,000	18,000	18,000
Mārkaṇḍeya	9,000	9,000	9,000
Vāmana	11,000	10,000	10,000
Bhaviṣya	14,500	14,500	14,000
Viṣṇu	23,000	23,000	23,000
Bhāgavata	18,000	18,000	18,000
Nārada	25,000	25,000	25,000
Garuda	19,000	18,000	19,000
Padma	50,000	55,000	55,000
Vārāha	24,000	24,000	24,000
Vāyu / Śiva	24,000	24,000	24,000
Linga	11,000	11,000	11,000
Skanda	81,000	81,000	81,000
Agni	15,400	16,000	15,500

Matsya	14,000	14,000	15,000
Kūrma	17,000	18,000	17,000

Source 'A' – Srimad Bhāgavatam – Sri Vyāsa press, Tirupati

Sourse 'B' – The Purāṇas by Ramakrisna Math

Source 'C' – The Holy Purāṇas by B. R. Publishers

Appendix

Dvādaśādityas

The twelve sons born to Kaśyapa by his wife Aditi are called *Dvāśādityas* [twelve Ādityās]. The table shows the names of the twelve Ādityās and the sign of Zodiac over which each Āditya predominates and the colour of it.

	Dvādaśādityas	**Sign of Zodiac**	**Colour**
1.	Varuṇa	Meṣa [Aries]	Black
2.	Sūrya [Sun]	Ṛṣabha [Taurus]	Blood colour
3.	Sahasrāmśu	Mithuna [Gemini]	Slight red
4.	Dhātā.	Karkaṭaka [Cancer]	yellow
5.	Tapana	Simha [Leo]	White
6.	Savitā	Kanyā. [Virgo]	Pure white
7.	Gabhasti	Tula. [Libra]	Tawny colour
8.	Ravi	Vṛścika. [Scorpio]	Yellow
9.	Parjanya	Dhanu. [Sagittarius]	Parrot colour
10.	Tvaṣṭā	Makara. [Capricorn]	Snow white
11.	Mitra	Kumbha. [Aquarius]	Smoky hue
12.	Viṣṇu	Mīna. [Pisces]	Blue

The names given here are based on the Agni Purāṇa. The names may occur different in different Purāṇas

Devīpīṭha

The dead body Satīdevī crumbled into small pieces and fell at different places in Bhārata. Each place where a piece of the dead body fell, is known as Devīpīṭha. There is a reason why the body crumbled into pieces. Lord Śiva, who became furious, killed Dakṣa and carrying the body on his shoulder walked the length and breadth of Bhārata like a mad man. To rescue Śiva from this mental disposition, Mahāviṣṇu, unseen by others, followed Śiva with a bow and arrow. Whenever it was convenient Viṣṇu sent an arrow at the body of Satīdevī on the shoulder of Śiva. By the hitting of the arrows the body was crumbled into pieces and fell here and there.

	Devīpīṭha	Name
1.	Vārāṇasī	Viśālākshī
2.	Naimiṣāraṇya	Liṅgadhāriṇī
3.	Prayāga	Kumudā
4.	Gandhamādana	Kāmukī
5.	Dakshina Kailās	Kumudā
6.	Uttara Kailāsa	Kumudā
7.	Gomanta	Gautamī
8.	Mandara	Kāmacāriṇī
9.	Caitraratha	Madotkaṭā
10.	Hastināpura	Jayantī
11.	Kānyakubja	Gaurī
12.	Malayācala	Rambhā
13.	Ekāmrapīṭha	Kīrtimatī
14.	Viśva	Viśveśvarī
15.	Puṣkara	Puruhūtā
16.	Kedārapīṭha	Sanmārgadāyinī
17.	Himavatpṛṣṭha	Mandā
18.	Gokarṇa	Bhadrakarṇikā

	Devīpīṭha	Name
19.	Sthāṇvīśvara	Bhavānī
20.	Villvaka	Villvapatrikā
21.	Śri Śaila	Mādhavī
22.	Bhadreśvara	Bhadrā
23.	Varāhaśaila	Jayā
24.	Kamalālaya	Kamalā
25.	Rudrakotī	Rudrāṇī
26.	Kālañjara	Kālī
27.	Śālagrāma	Mahādevī
28.	Śivaliṅga	Jalapriyā
29.	Mahāliṅga	Kapilā
30.	Mākoṭā	Mukuteśvarī
31.	Māyāpurī	Kumārī
32.	Gayā	Maṅgalā
33.	Puruṣottama	Vimalā
34.	Sahasrākṣa	Utpalākṣī
35.	Hiraṇyākṣa	Mahotpalā
36.	Vipāśa	Amoghākṣī
37.	Puṇdravardhana	Pāṭalā
38.	Supārśva	Nārāyaṇī
39.	Trikūta	Rudrasundarī
40.	Vipula	Vipulā
41.	Malayācala	Kalyāṇī
42.	Sahyādri	Ekavīrā
43.	Hariścandra	Candrikā
44.	Rāmatīrtha	Ramaṇā
45.	Yamunātīrtha	Mṛgāvatī

	Devīpīṭha	Name
46.	Vikota tīrtha	Koṭī
47.	Mādhavavana	Sugandhā
48.	Godāvaritīrthā	Trisandhi
49.	Gaṅgādvāra	Ratipriyā
50.	Śivakuṇda	Śubhānandā
51.	Devīkātaṭa	Nandinī
52.	Dvāravatī	Rukmiṇī
53.	Santāna	Lalitāmbikā
54.	Vṛndāvana	Rādhā
55.	Madhurā	Devakī
56.	Pātāla	Parameśvarī
57.	Citrakūṭa	Sītā
58.	Vindhya	Vindhyādhivāsinī
59.	Karavīra	Mahālakṣmī
60.	Vināyaka	Umādevī
61.	Vaidhyanāthatīrtha	Ārogyā
62.	Mahākāla	Maheśvarī
63.	Uṣṇatīrtha	Abhayā
64.	Vindhya	Nitambā
65.	Māṇḍavya	Māṇḍavī
66.	Maheśvaripur	Svāhā
67.	Chagalāṇḍa	Pracaṇḍā
68.	Amarakaṇṭak	Caṇḍikā
69.	Someśvara	Varārohā
70.	Prabhāsa	Puṣkarāvatī
71.	Sarasvatī	Devamātā
72.	Mahālaya	Mahābhāgā

	Devīpīṭha	Name
73.	Payoṣṇī	Piṅgaleśvarī
74.	Kṛtaśauca	Simhikā
75.	Kārttika	Atiśaṅkarī
76.	Varttaka	Utpalā
77.	Soṇasaṅgam	Subhadrā
78.	Siddhavana	Mātā [Lakṣmī]
79.	Bharatāśram	Anaṅgā
80.	Jalandhara	Viśvamukhī
81.	Kiṣkindha	Tārā
82.	Devadāruvana	Puṣṭī
83.	Himādrī	Bhīmā
84.	Kapālamocan	Śuddhi
85.	Kāyāvarohan	Mātā
86.	Śaṅkodhara	Dharā
87.	Piṇḍāraka	Dhṛti
88.	Candrabhāga	Kalā
89.	Acchoda	Śivadhāriṇī
90.	Veṇā	Amṛtā
91.	Badaryāśram	Urvaśī
92.	Uttarakuru	Auṣadhi
93.	Kuśadvīpa	Kuśodakā
94.	Hemakūṭa	Manmatha
95.	Kumuda	Satyavādinī
96.	Aśvatta	Vandanīyā
97.	Vaiśravaṇālay	Nidhi
98.	Vedapatana	Gāyatrī
99.	Śivasannidhi	Pārvatī
100.	Devaloka	Indrāṇī
101.	Brahmāloka	Sarasvatī

	Devīpīṭha	Name
102.	Sūryabimba	Prabhā
103.	Mātṛloka	Vaiṣṇavī
104.	Kāṣmīra	Medhā
105.	Satītīrtha	Arundhatī
106.	Rāmatīrtha	Tilottamā
107.	Citta	Brahmākalā
108.	Jīvaśarī	Śakti

References

	Title	Publishers
1.	Purāṇic Encycopaedia	Motilāl Banārsidās
2.	The Purāṇas	Ramakrishna Math.
3.	Srīmad Bhāgavatam	Sri Vyāsa press, Tirupati
4.	The holy Purāṇas	B. R. Publishers

List of Abbreviations

Bh	:	Bhāgavatam
BG	:	Bhagavad Gīta
Bṛ	:	Bṛhadāraṇyaka
Brh	:	Brahmāṇḍa Purāṇa
De. Bh	:	Devī Bhāgavatam
Kai	:	Kaivalyopaniṣad
Kath	:	Kathopaniṣad
MB. AD	:	Mahābhārata Ādi Parva
MB. Aś	:	Mahābhārata Aśvamedh Parva
MB. Mau	:	Mahābhārata Mausala Parva
MB. Sab	:	Mahābhārata Sabhā Parva
MB. Sh	:	Mahābhārata Śānti Parva
MB. Vp	:	Mahābhārata Vana Parva
Ma	:	Māṇḍukyopaniṣad
Mat	:	Matsya Purāṇa
Mu	:	Muṇḍakopaniṣad
Pad	:	Padma Purāṇa
Pad. Uk	:	Padma Purāṇa – Uttara Khāṇḍa
Tai	:	Taittiriya
Ta	:	Taṇḍya Mahābrāhmaṇa
Va	:	Vāmana Purāṇa
Vis	:	Viṣṇu Purāṇa

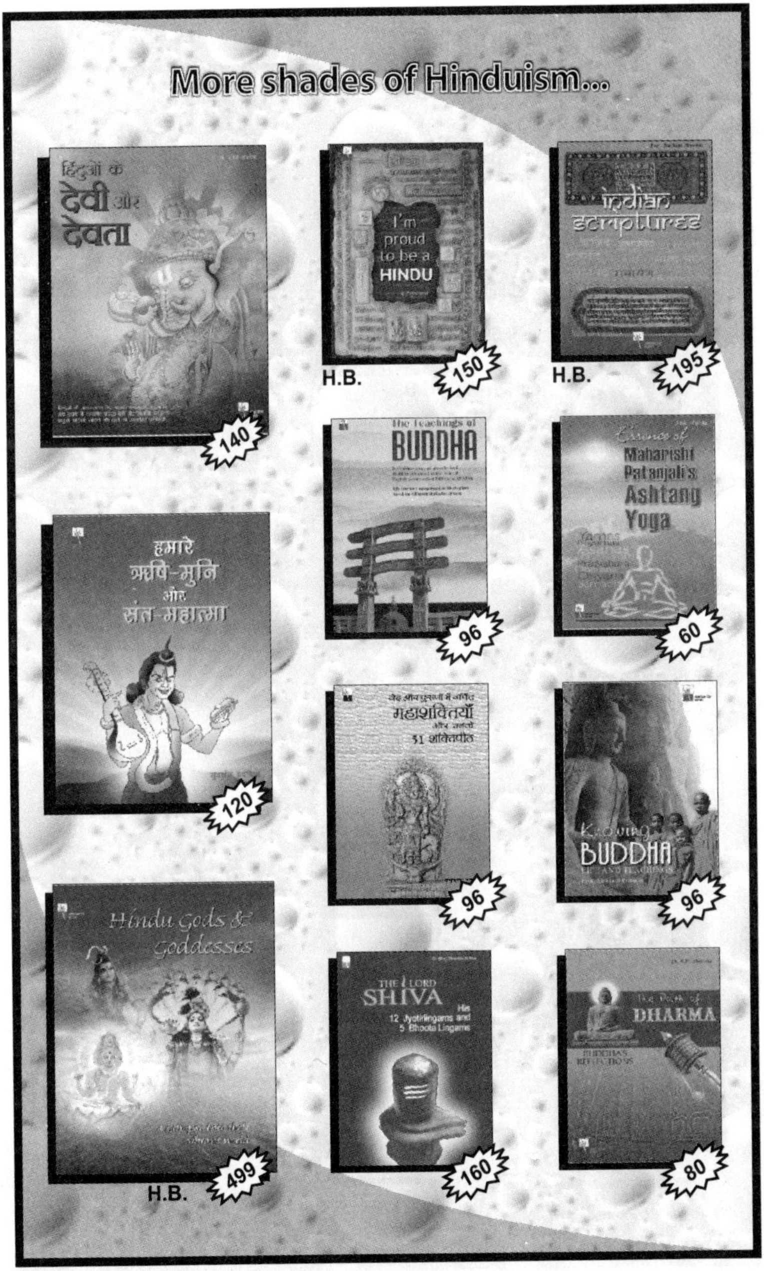
More shades of Hinduism...
हिंदुओं के देवी और देवता
140
I'm proud to be a HINDU
H.B.
150
Indian Scriptures
H.B.
195
The Teachings of BUDDHA
96
Maharishi Patanjali's Ashtang Yoga
60
हमारे ऋषि-मुनि और संत-महात्मा
120
महाशक्तियाँ
51 शक्तिपीठ
96
Knowing BUDDHA
96
Hindu Gods & Goddesses
H.B.
499
THE LORD SHIVA
His 12 Jyotirlingams and 5 Bhoota Lingams
160
DHARMA
80

More shades of Hinduism...
हमारे तीर्थ-स्थल
150
Ancient Indian Wisdom
H.B.
295
Krishna
The God Who Lived as Man
H.B.
350
HINDU Pilgrimage
... The Teerthas
H.B.
499
Krishna
H.B.
195
16 Hindu Samskārs
195
हिन्दुओं के
रीति-रिवाज़
मान्यताएं
H.B.
160
Bhrigu Samhita
H.B.
295
Panch Mahabhuta Tatwa & SHARIRA
195
Know the Vedas
At a Glance
80
The LORD's Song
gita
160

Four Objectives of Human Life

DHARMA
ARTHA
KAMA
MOKSHA

J. M. Mehta

THE PHILOSOPHY OF HINDUISM

The book basically deals with philosophy of Hinduism which consists of four main objectives that can be achieved only in this life on earth, and none other.

On the basis of the study of ancient spiritual thoughts, the author has made an honest endeavour to briefly explain the contents of these objectives and how to achieve them.

Human life is a priceless gift of God and has a divine purpose. It should not be wasted in mundane pursuits.

This is a must-read for all sensible persons who are striving to know the true purpose of their existence on earth.

Demy Size • Pages: 80
Price: Rs. 80/- • Postage: Rs. 15/-

Veda
A Way of Life
Ramanuj Prasad

A treasury of Vedantic teachings

The Veda (Sruti) is the most comprehensive doctrine on religion ever revealed to mankind that answers all man's queries on the here and now and the hereafter. Human objectives can be broadly grouped under four categories: Desire (*kama*), material gain (*artha*), religious merits (*dharma*) and liberation (*moksha*). The Veda holds the key to fulfil all these aspirations. But the Veda simply reveals the Truth, never pressurising anyone to follow a particular path to self-discovery. Each person is free to choose his own path to discover the Self or God. The Veda acts as a means to the ultimate knowledge that is possible through direct perception.

VEDA: A Way of Life seeks to increase awareness amongst readers about this wonderful treasury of ancient wisdom. Study of this enlightening text will increase values of brotherhood, love and compassion, which are the need of the hour in our troubled times. The Vedic or spiritual way of life promoted by the Veda was later advocated by Lord Krishna through the *Bhagavad Gita*. This book presents basic tenets of the Veda so that mankind functions according to just eternal laws to ensure universal peace and brotherhood.

Demy Size • Pages: 144
Price: Rs. 96/- • Postage: Rs. 15/-

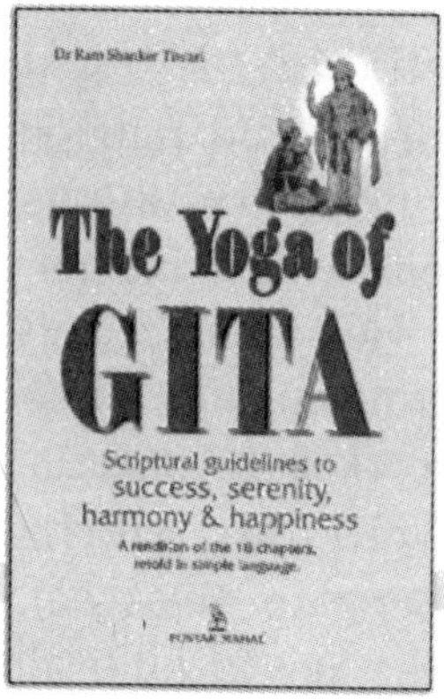

The Yoga of
GITA

Dr. Ram Shankar Tiwari

Scriptural guidelines to success, serenity, harmony & happiness

A rendition of the 18 chapters, retold in simple language.

The *Bhagavad Gita* is replete with universal wisdom and the techniques to attain this. *The Yoga of Gita* contains the essence of this wisdom, the philosophy of creation and the Ultimate Reality, as revealed by Sri Krishna to Arjuna. The book outlines the various paths for realisation. For the layman, the emphasis is on the Yoga of Action – acting without worrying about the rewards for our actions.

The book is a rendition of the 18 chapters, retold in simple language, with a brief account on Yoga and Meditation, which will ensure success, serenity, harmony and happiness for readers who follow these principles, finally leading to Salvation.

Demy Size • Pages: 156
Price: Rs. 80/- • Postage: Rs. 15/-

Know the

UPNISHADS

Plus verses from the Vedas & the Bhawad Gita

Ramanuj Prasad

A treasure-trove of wisdom, the ancient texts are elaborated upon in simple words

Like the proverbial fish that has heard a lot about the Great Ocean and spends an entire lifetime searching for it, not realising it has always been an inseparable part of the ocean, man spends his lifetime searching all around for God. All man has to do, in fact, is simply turn his gaze inwards to realise that God or the Self has always been an inseparable part of him.

The *Upanishad* tells man that he is not a mere mortal, but a part of the Immortal One. *Know the Upanishads* shows you just how to go about uncovering the layers of ignorance and illusion to realise your true nature – the Self. This is the path to *moksha* or *nirvana* (liberation), which every seeker wishes to tread upon in order to break the cycle of birth and death.

With pearls of wisdom from the *Upanishads*, the *Vedas* and the *Bhagavad Gita*, this book could transform your way of life forever, teaching you the true meaning of existence.

Demy Size • Pages: 120
Price: Rs. 80/- • Postage: Rs. 15/-